The Little Emperor

The Little Emperor

Governor Simpson of the Hudson's Bay Company

JOHN S. GALBRAITH

Macmillan of Canada   Toronto

ISBN 0-7705-1389-1

Printed in Canada for
The Macmillan Company of Canada
70 Bond Street, Toronto M5B 1X3

TO LAURA

THE JOURNEYS OF SIR GEORGE SIMPSON, 1820-1860

FROM—TO	APPROXIMATE ROUTES	YEARS TRAVELLED (Years underlined mean the return journey was made the same year)
New York—Lachine	–x–x–	1820, 1826, 1839, 1847
Boston—Lachine	ooooooo	1841, 1844, 1845, 1847
Lachine—Lake Winnipeg, en route to either Red River or Norway House (via Toronto and Detroit in 1848 and 1857)	——	1820, 1826, 1827, 1828, 1829, 1830, 1833, 1834, 1835, 1836, 1837, 1839, 1841, 1843, 1844, 1845, 1846, 1847, 1848, 1849, 1850, 1852 to Sault Ste. Marie only, 1853, 1854, 1855, 1856, 1857, 1858, 1859
Red River—Norway House	+++++	1820, 1822, 1824, 1826, 1828, 1829, 1830, 1831, 1832, 1834, 1836, 1837, 1846, 1847, 1848, 1849, 1850, 1853, 1854, 1855, 1856, 1858, 1859
Norway House—York Factory	–··–··–	1821, 1822, 1823, 1824, 1825, 1826, 1827, 1828, 1830, 1831, 1832, 1834, 1846
Norway House—Athabasca and Great Slave Lake	–o–o–	1820, 1821, 1822, 1823
Norway House or Red River—Columbia	········	1824, 1825, 1828, 1829, 1841
Moose Factory—Lachine, Red River Route	x═x═x	1827, 1829, 1834, 1836, 1837, 1839, 1843, 1844, 1851
Lachine—Lake St. John	+++++	1839
Ft. Vancouver—Sitka	–··–··–	1841
Lachine—St. Paul	x·x·x·x·	1860
Red River—Detroit, via St. Paul	x·x·x·x·	1858

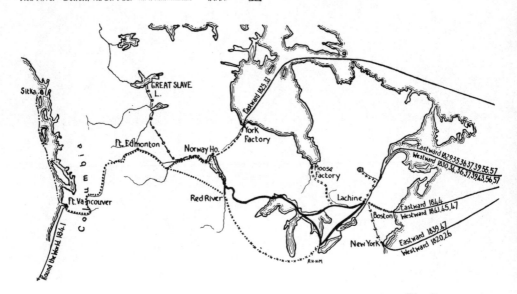

courtesy *The Beaver*

CONTENTS

PREFACE

Over thirty years ago Arthur S. Morton well described the problems in writing a biography of George Simpson. His extant business correspondence, most of it preserved in the Archives of the Hudson's Bay Company, is enormous. In contrast, letters bearing on the personal side of his life are few. And information on his life before he joined the Hudson's Bay Company is almost nonexistent. We know that he was the illegitimate son of George Simpson, but who was his mother? When was he born? Where did he go to school? What influences helped to mold his childhood life? When did he go to London? These are all questions without answers.

Morton in the preface to his "pen picture" of Simpson referred to the decision of the Hudson's Bay Company to publish documents from its Archives, and expressed the hope that "when these are published in their plenitude, the time will have come for a comprehensive life of Simpson." That hope will not be realized by this account of Simpson's life. The publications of the Hudson's Bay Record Society and other works since Morton's biography have added substantially to our understanding of Simpson the governor, but the information on his private life remains sparse. In the absence of such evidence the biographer is tempted to engage in surmises. I have tried not to fly too high beyond the evidence.

The reader will note that I am by no means an unqualified admirer of George Simpson. His abilities as a businessman were impressive. Unquestionably he was one of the great business leaders of the nineteenth century, and his influence was felt not only in the affairs of his Company but also in the larger history of British North America. Some of his attributes as a man were not so admirable. In his ascent to power he was ruthless against those who stood in his way. When he had achieved power, he was influenced by his vanity in decisions about officers under his jurisdiction. His attitudes toward the mixed-blood women with whom he associated were not enlightened, even by the standards of his age. These aspects of his character I find repugnant. But I hope that I have not dwelt upon the negative to the point of obscuring his virtues. He was flawed—as we all are—but he was one of the giants of his day.

I acknowledge the courtesy of the Governor and Committee for permitting me access to the Hudson's Bay Archives. For permission to use the illustrations which appear in this book I am indebted to the following: Mrs. Helen Burgess, Editor of the *Beaver*; Mrs. M. Porritt of Bury St. Edmunds, England; and the Trustees of McGill University. I also wish to thank Mrs. Elaine Mitchell for allowing me to read the Cameron Papers which are in her possession. Miss A. M. Johnson, long-time Archivist of the Hudson's Bay Company, Lewis G. Thomas, Professor of History, University of Alberta, Mrs. Shirlee A. Smith, Archivist of the Hudson's Bay Company, and Laura H. Galbraith who read the manuscript and gave me valuable assistance. It is perhaps unnecessary to add that the judgments on Simpson and his contemporaries in this sketch are mine, and do not necessarily represent their views.

JOHN S. GALBRAITH

CHAPTER I

The Unknown Years

Sir George Simpson cherished fame but guarded his private life. He wanted to be remembered only for his business achievements, and he succeeded. During his forty years with the Hudson's Bay Company he wrote prodigiously, but the correspondence that has survived is almost entirely devoted to business. Of the first thirty years or so of his life we know almost nothing, and what little is known contributes to further mystery. This was as Simpson desired it. He rejected all efforts to elicit personal information about himself. After he was knighted, he submitted a "biography" to *Dodd's Peerage, Baronetage, and Knightage* which must be among the shortest ever recorded:

> SIMPSON. Knt. Bachel. Creat. 1841. Sir George Simpson, Governor of the Hudson's Bay Company settlements. Residence—New Grove House, Bromley.

The editor, accustomed to lengthy accounts of family antecedents, pressed Simpson to provide additional details, but his plea went unanswered.

Faced with a paucity of evidence, Simpson's biographers have resorted to speculation about his early life. One fact is beyond doubt. He was the illegitimate son of George Simpson, born of an unknown mother somewhere in the parish of Loch Broom in Ross-shire, Scotland. But beyond that, imagination must fill the void. Writers, with varying degrees of assurance, have assigned dates for his birth ranging from 1786 to 1796.[1] The bases for these assertions are rarely indicated. No birth records for the parish of

Loch Broom during this period have survived. Almost as if fate had granted Simpson his wish, there is a hiatus.

Having decided upon the year of Simpson's birth, each biographer has proceeded to describe his early years in terms of "how they must have been". Arthur S. Morton, on whom subsequent authors have generally relied, states that Simpson was born in 1787 in "wild and for the most part desolate Ross-shire . . . in the secluded parish of Loch Broom where the arm of the sea bearing that name opens out into the broad Atlantic". His father, the eldest son of the Reverend Thomas Simpson, minister of the parish of Avoch, was unable to care for the child, and "at some stage of his infancy or boyhood" young George was taken across "the wild mountains of Ross-shire" to his grandfather's manse in the quiet little village of Avoch, which was situated on the Moray Firth across from Inverness. There he grew up as a member of his grandfather's family.[2]

For information on his life after he left the manse, writers have depended on Alexander Simpson, brother of Thomas, the explorer, and cousin of George. Alexander was the son of Mary, a daughter of the Reverend Thomas Simpson, who was the second wife of Alexander Simpson, a schoolmaster at Dingwall, a village at the western end of the Firth of Cromarty, near Inverness. By the younger Alexander's account, George Simpson owed his success largely to his aunt Mary. She was responsible for his early education, and prevailed upon her brother Geddes, who had moved to London and established himself in the West Indian trade, to take George into his firm. In this position George came into contact with men who had the power to advance his fortunes.[3]

These accounts of Simpson's early years contain some facts, some errors, and much conjecture. It is true that his father was the son of the Reverend Thomas Simpson, but he was not the eldest. The grandfather, who was born in 1718, had entered the clergy relatively late in life. When he was about thirty-seven, he was presented to the parish of Cromarty but the call was rejected by the assembly, and in 1756 he was installed as the minister of Avoch, where he remained for the rest of his life. In the year that he took up his pastorate at Avoch, Thomas married Isobel Mackenzie, daughter of a minister in Inverness, and the next year they had a son, William, who became a minister. Thomas's first wife died at William's birth, and in January 1759 Thomas married again, to another Isobel Mackenzie, granddaughter of the celebrated Duncan Forbes, Lord President of the Court of Session. George Simpson's father was born in October of that year. There were nine children by this second marriage, which lasted for twenty-seven years.[4]

The story of George's early life at the manse, "youngest of a family of eight, happy and lively",[5] is a charming one, but unfortunately untrue. Thomas Simpson died in September 1786, and the family scattered.[6] But the assumption that the family became the surrogate for the father in taking care of George is correct. It was common practice in eighteenth-century Scotland for the unwed father not only to acknowledge but to care for the child, and if he were for some reason unable to do so, for the family to accept the responsibility. George's great-grandfather Duncan Forbes of Culloden, who sired an illegitimate daughter, concealed the identity of the mother and gave the daughter the same care he would have provided for a legal heir. Aemilius, a son of Alexander Simpson by his first wife, was the father of a natural son, Horatio Nelson Simpson, and likewise assumed full responsibility. George's father, however, appears to have been a feckless, ineffective person. He lived out his life in the village of Ullapool on Loch Broom. The community had been established by the British Fisheries Society in the last years of the eighteenth century when the herring trade was at its height. Its promoters hoped to make it a model town, but the catch in herring slumped, and the village became a pocket of poverty with a population of between seven and eight hundred. The life of the elder George is almost as shadowy as that of his son during the early years. Even his occupation is unknown. Simpson's relationship with him remained friendly. When Governor Simpson in 1826 desired to employ a piper to accompany him on his canoe voyages, he secured the help of his father in selecting one.[7]

Simpson's relationship with his father was never intimate. The family that he knew best was that of his aunt Mary and her husband, and he was also close to his uncle Duncan. A passage in a letter to Simpson in 1851 at first gives the reader a start. Hugh Munro, writing of the deaths of so many of their mutual friends and relations, referred to the pleasant fortnight he had spent many years ago with Simpson's "respected father and mother in Dingwall".[8] The "parents" to whom Munro referred were undoubtedly Alexander and Mary Simpson.

Simpson's education almost certainly was under the auspices of Mary. She married Alexander in 1807, and whatever year is assigned to Simpson's birth, he probably had completed his education prior to that time. The most likely date of his birth is 1786 or 1787,[9] but even if the latest date, 1796, were to be accepted, he would have almost finished school by the time of Mary's marriage. By the evidence of his correspondence, Simpson's formal education did not go beyond the parish school, where he had instruction in reading, English grammar, arithmetic, and geography. He may have learned some elementary Latin and Greek, but there is no indication of it in his later correspondence. In the late eighteenth century the vaunted Scottish educational system was not yet a vehicle of mass literacy. There were many parishes in the Highlands without schools or schoolmasters, but Simpson with the support of his family received the basic skills necessary for his subsequent advancement.

The Simpson family circle also imbued George with an outlook that might be described as essentially Whiggish. Memories of "the '45" were still fresh during his youth. The field of Culloden was not far away. Most of the common people of the Dingwall area were Gaelic speaking, and among many of them was a continuing nostalgia for that lost cause. Such sentiments were not found among the Simpsons. The downfall of the clans evoked no

sense of sorrow. On the contrary, like their forebear Duncan
Forbes they were strong supporters of the established government and believed that Scotland must go forward as part of the
Union rather than look back upon a dead era. In the 1780s and
1790s the passion for "improvement" that had gripped the Low-
lands spread to the Highlands. In 1784 the Highland and Agricultural Society had been formed to promote greater efficiency in
agriculture and in cattle-raising. The "improvers" recognized
that their objectives were likely to dispossess many small tenants,
but they believed that these people would be absorbed in non-
agricultural employment in the new villages which would be built
to support industrial development. Ullapool, where George's
father resided, was one of these, as was Beauly, not far from
Dingwall.[10]

The Simpsons believed in the virtue of hard work and in the
reward of that virtue. But the Dingwall area, as indeed the western Highlands generally, was a poor place for the attainment of
material success. Most of the model villages were failures, and
though there was some improvement in agriculture, the area
remained generally depressed. Dingwall sat in a beautiful environment of hills and valleys clothed in forests, but the village
provided few visible means of support for its inhabitants. It was a
sleepy little community with no manufacturing establishments
and with one main street half a mile long. The population in 1800
was just over fourteen hundred, of whom almost sixty per cent
were female. Young men went elsewhere to make their living.
Among them were George Simpson's two uncles, who took the
well-travelled road to London where their education and ability
might produce more lucrative returns than could be had in Scotland.

Duncan, born in 1771, and Geddes, the youngest of Thomas
Simpson's children, born four years later, both became successful businessmen.[11] The details of Duncan's life in London are
unknown, but he was able to retire at a relatively young age to an
estate at Bellevue, on the Beauly Firth, not far from Inverness.

George's relationship with Duncan was very close, and during his years as governor of the Hudson's Bay Company he stayed at Bellevue whenever he visited Scotland.

Geddes Mackenzie Simpson became a partner in the firm of Graham and Simpson, in the city of London, which was engaged in the sugar brokerage business with the West Indies. Some time between 1809 and 1812, the name of Wedderburn was added to the partnership with consequences of great moment to the future of George Simpson, who by this time had become an employee. When George arrived in London is unknown. Most writers propose the year 1809, but this date is highly unlikely. Simpson would then have been from seventeen to twenty-three years old, depending on which birth date is correct. He must have left school in Dingwall by the time he was thirteen or fourteen. There was no scope for his abilities in Dingwall, and unless he found employment in some other city before setting out for London, he probably came to London in 1800 or shortly thereafter. His cousin Alexander maintains that George was employed as a result of Mary's "assiduous entreaty".[12] This may well have been true, though George's subsequent relationships with his uncles Duncan and Geddes and the closeness of the family circle suggest that no strong urging was necessary. Whatever Geddes's receptivity may have been, it must soon have become apparent that his nephew had exceptional qualifications for the work assigned him in the counting-house. George Simpson was in every sense a man of business. Indeed, business was his life. Many years later when infirmities and self-doubts had ravaged his constitution and the thought of retirement had come to his mind, he thrust the idea aside. To retire, he concluded, was to die.[13] A zestful and voracious appetite for work characterized his entire life, and his mastery of business methods won him the favourable attention of the partners in his firm, including Andrew Wedderburn.

Wedderburn was four years the junior of Geddes Mackenzie Simpson. In the rebellion of 1745 his family had been on the other side from that of the Simpsons. His grandfather had been prominent enough in the cause of Prince Charles that he had been executed, and his son, the father of Andrew, had been exiled to Jamaica, where he had become involved in the sugar business and had founded the firm of Wedderburn and Company. Andrew Wedderburn took over the family business, and his amalgamation with the firm of Graham and Simpson represented a logical step in the expansion of his trade. At the time he fused his interests with Simpson's, Wedderburn's vistas were broadening still further. His sister had married Lord Selkirk, and through Selkirk's involvement with the Hudson's Bay Company, Wedderburn's interest was aroused. He became a shareholder in 1808 and two years later was elected to the governing committee. Through his family connections and his own business ability, Wedderburn (who changed his name to Colvile in 1814) soon became one of the most influential members of the board. He saw in Simpson the same qualities that he prided in himself. Colvile revelled in "counting house conversation". His world was that of balance sheets, of the contest of business brains which determined success or failure. Colvile had a first-class mind for analysis of the prospects and he was rarely wrong. Those who negotiated with him and later found that they had made a bad agreement evoked no sympathy from him. He maintained that "no man has a right to complain of hardship when he gets a bargain of his own making."[14] Colvile did not allow considerations of personality to intrude into his business affairs. The clerk in his sugar brokerage office was affable. That was not necessarily a liability, and indeed could be an asset if it were used for the advancement of sound business. George Simpson, Colvile concluded as he observed him over the years, was a man who had the attributes to become a leader in commercial undertakings.

Simpson may have suffered from his illegitimacy but Providence made ample amends to him. The experience in the sugar firm was maturing him at the time the affairs of the Hudson's Bay Company were moving toward a point where the needs of the Company would converge with his developing abilities.

Simpson's training and talents were largely alien to the characteristics of the fur trade in the early years of the nineteenth century. During the first two decades, the conflict between the Hudson's Bay and the North West companies had increased in intensity until it had become a war to the death, and the methods used on both sides were any deemed appropriate to secure furs and to deny them to the opposition, including on occasion the use of violence. Restrictions imposed by the United States after the Jay Treaty of 1794 and made more stringent after the War of 1812 deprived the North West Company of valuable fur territories to the south and directed their activities north of the border, where the North Westers collided with the Hudson's Bay Company. The North West Company after its absorption of the rival XY Company in 1803 was a remarkable combination of business ability, energy, and daring. The principal officers on the field, the "wintering partners", received a share of the profits, a great incentive to activity and efficiency, and their agents were able businessmen. The names associated with the North West Company are among the legends of the North—the McGillivrays and Mactavishes, John McLoughlin, Peter Skene Ogden. They were "the lords of the lakes and the forests", and they held their ponderous London-based rivals in contempt. But they underestimated their opponents. The chartered Company lacked the glamor of its Canadian rival, but it had great assets at its disposal, particularly after Lord Selkirk became the dominant shareholder. After 1810, when Selkirk, Wedderburn, and another brother-in-law of Wedderburn, John Halkett, joined the governing committee, the Hudson's Bay Company became much more militant. The North Westers soon came to realize that far from being assured of success, their enterprise was in mortal danger.

The two main theaters of conflict were the country around Lake Athabaska and the Athabaska River, and the lands at the junction of the Red and Assiniboine rivers. The Athabaska country had been the most lucrative source of revenue for the North West Company which had considered it virtually their preserve, for the few forays by the Hudson's Bay Company had been completely ineffectual. Until Wedderburn became a member of the committee, the governing board had been inclined to concede the North Westers their monopoly in the Athabaska in the hope that they would not intrude into the chartered territories. Some of the Hudson's Bay Company's more active traders in the field chafed under the restrictions of this weak, defensive policy. They—most notably Colin Robertson—advocated all-out war in the Athabaska to destroy their rivals by capturing the seat of their power. Wedderburn was opposed to both extremes. The Hudson's Bay Company as then constituted, he was convinced, could not mount a successful campaign in the Athabaska. Its finances were depleted and its business practices were slovenly. The Company must institute a regimen of rigorous economy and efficient accounting. Its posts must be manned by active traders who were strongly loyal to the Company. By these measures the Company could build a powerful base, and then, but only then, should it challenge its rival in its home territory. Wedderburn (Colvile) soon became the dominant member of the committee, and his policy eventually became the means of bringing the North West Company to its knees. But before the struggle erupted in Athabaska the two companies collided in the Red River area.

The Earl of Selkirk for many years had been much involved with the plight of Scottish Highlanders who had been deprived of their homes and livelihood when their chiefs had herded them out to make room for sheep and a more efficient agriculture. Thousands of these clansmen migrated overseas as the only alternative to a life of destitution, and Selkirk had assisted many of them to resettle in British North America. He had founded a settlement of eight hundred in Prince Edward Island and another in Ontario, and he now conceived a plan to establish still another community in the territories of the Hudson's Bay Company. The area he selected was predominantly in present-day Manitoba as well as some territory now in Minnesota and North Dakota. The Company granted him 116,000 square miles, including the lands at the junction of the Assiniboine and Red rivers. Selkirk's motives were not entirely philanthropic. The area was known to be fertile and the climate was not too severe for agriculture, but there were other areas which could have fulfilled these specifications. One of the attractions to Selkirk of a settlement at Red River was that it would sit astride the north-south and east-west communications systems. If that junction were blocked, the North West Company's trade system would be disrupted. Selkirk probably did not intend to take such drastic action, at least at first. The North Westers were to be allowed to trade and to provide themselves with pemmican and other supplies. But Selkirk's control of the colony gave the Hudson's Bay Company a great competitive advantage and subjected the North Westers to the continuing threat of strangulation. The partners of the North West Company had no doubt that they would be ruined if Selkirk's plans were successful. They made strenuous efforts to discourage prospective colonists, with some effect, but Selkirk's agents managed to recruit sufficient numbers in Scotland and Ireland to establish the nucleus of a settlement. A party of 120 men accompanied by an unknown number of women and children arrived in October 1812, and others followed in 1813 and 1814. The beginnings of agriculture began to be apparent throughout the colony, which was named Assiniboia. Given the conviction of the North West partners that the colony was intended to be their nemesis, little provocation was required to ignite an explosion. Selkirk's governor, Miles Macdonell, unfortunately contributed not just a spark but a flame. Macdonell, to assure an adequate supply of food for the settlement, issued a proclamation prohibiting the export of pemmican and other supplies. Also in 1813 and 1814 he issued notices to the North West Company to abandon the posts which they occupied in Assiniboia.[15] These actions were taken at the same time that American victories on the Great Lakes had cut off the North West Company from their supply points to the south. The North Westers decided that the colony must be destroyed. In 1815 by a combination of cajolery and threats they seemed to have succeeded. Many settlers, disillusioned with life in the wilderness, were induced to migrate to Canada, and the North Westers and their Métis allies drove the others out by threats and then set fire to their dwellings. When the colony was restored by Colin Robertson in 1816, the North Westers resorted to more violent measures culminating in a massacre in which the settlement's governor and nineteen other men were killed. The slaughter of 1816 began a period of disorders which did not end until the amalgamation of the two companies five years later.[16]

One of the facts that convinced the North West partners to take summary measures against the settlement was that the Hudson's Bay Company was manifesting a new aggressiveness in the Athabaska country. Colvile's policy of retrenchment and consolidation had given the chartered Company new vitality, and by 1816 he and his associates had concluded that the time to take the offensive had arrived. The fight for Athabaska did not involve further armed encounters, but short of bloodshed there was little restraint on either side. In addition to high prices and plentiful liquor, the rival companies resorted to attempts at intimidation of their opponents and of the Indians. The party that had a predominance of power at a particular time used strong-arm methods against its adversary. Selkirk, with a contingent of ex-soldiers, captured the North West post at Fort William and arrested several North West traders on the authority of his warrant as a Canadian justice of the peace. He also stopped North West canoes and confiscated their cargoes of furs and other goods. The North Westers, on their part, arrested Hudson's Bay men, sometimes on the strength of warrants and sometimes without any such pretence. There were seizures of goods on both sides, and on occasion Indians were forcibly prevented from trading with the opposition. Sometimes the techniques were less physical, though no more ethical. Each company spread reports among the Indians calculated to turn them against its competitor. North West traders told the Indians that the Hudson's Bay men meant to exterminate them and that the tobacco they offered was mixed with poison.[17] This was an extreme form of the practice by both companies of maligning the opposition.

The all-out struggle between 1815 and 1820 required a certain type of leadership. Courage and resolution were essential, and considerations of economy had to be subordinated to the main concern—the ruination of the opposition. Simpson was not lacking in courage. Indeed he could display the pugnacity of a bantam cock as he—at most five feet seven inches tall—faced up to the massive bullies of the North West Company. His sturdy constitution enabled him to endure hardships and privations. But Simpson's great strengths were not suitable for the kind of economic warfare that was being waged in the Athabaska district before 1820. During these years he was developing his talent for efficient economical administration, which would be necessary in the postwar era. And since he was not involved in the bitter conflict between the two companies until its last stages, he was relatively unmarked by the enmities of the past and was able to apply his genius for managing men to the reconciliation of old enemies and the creation of a new spirit of loyalty to the amalgamated company.

Simpson's life in London during these years is almost as obscure as that of his early youth. Clearly he had risen to a position in the firm much more responsible than that of a mere bookkeeper, for he had attracted the attention of Andrew Colvile as being a man of sound business judgment. In 1820 Colvile wrote that "I have long known him and have perfect confidence in his honour and discretion in case you should find it necessary to have any confidential communications with him, he is active and intelligent with sufficient promptness and determination." Selkirk at the same time described him as "intelligent and active in business".[18] These comments describe a person with some responsibility. But precisely what his functions were remains a matter of speculation. Allusions in his correspondence suggest that he may have been sent by his employers to the West Indies on at least one occasion, and in one of the few letters of his to have survived from the period is a suggestion that his work involved not only responsibility but some hazard. In 1815 he referred to "all the dangers &c to which you know I am Daily and Nightly so much exposed".[19] As to what these "dangers" may have been he gives no clues, and he may have been merely engaging in light-hearted banter about the hazards of life in London.

Simpson off-duty was capable of levity. It was one of the attractions which drew others to him that he could laugh not only at others but also at himself. In his later years when he was recognized as a person of importance he still displayed toward his associates a warm and outgoing disposition. Even those who were alienated from him admitted that he had charm, though they contended that his exterior masked a cold, vindictive nature. His cousin Alexander Simpson, who despised him in later years, nevertheless admitted that he "was clever, active, plausible, and full of animal spirits."[20] John McLean, who hated him as a tyrant whose "cold and callous heart was incapable of sympathizing with the woes and pains of their fellow men", conceded that most people were deluded by Simpson's "prepossessing manners" and superficial warmth.[21]

During his years in London, before the exuberance of his youth was cooled by the exercise of power, Simpson must have been a vivacious personality. His letters to the Pooler family, with whom he had become a close friend, reveal an engaging young man. The Poolers lived in Reigate—presumably they had moved there from London—and they had two children of Simpson's generation, Helen and "my old friend Dick". He enjoyed visiting with them "to have a gossip for an hour or two" during which he could "coil out a few tough yarns"[22] before he had to return to London and the business on Tower Street.

This relatively relaxed life came to an abrupt end in 1820 when Andrew Colvile called on him to undertake an important mission for the Hudson's Bay Company. The superior resources of the Hudson's Bay Company and the intensity of the Athabaska campaign had told heavily upon the North West Company, which was showing signs of disintegration. Despite the vigor of its key personnel, the North West Company was vulnerable to sustained attack by its powerful rival. Its land route to the west was more expensive than the route through Hudson Bay. In addition the structure that gave the North West Company its vitality was also a source of weakness. Shares in the enterprise were held by capitalists and by officers in the field, the "wintering partners". Each year the profits were divided with no provision for reserves to meet any crisis. The invasion of fur-rich Athabaska by the Hudson's Bay Company was a major crisis with which the Canadian company could not cope for long, and in 1820 both the "wintering partners" and their agents in Canada realized that they were in desperate straits. The plight of its rivals was known to the London board even before the North Westers sued for peace.

But the Hudson's Bay Company had problems of its own. The general of the campaign in Athabaska had been Colin Robertson, who had been a strong advocate of resolute resistance in the chartered territory and of aggressive competition in the Athabaska. The North West Company paid tribute to his effectiveness by singling him out as the principal culprit. In 1819 they captured him by a ruse and sent him off to Canada. Robertson suspected that they meant him to suffer a fatal "accident" en route, and he made his escape after being nearly drowned. Robertson fled to England to escape trial and charges of attempted murder, which had been initiated by the North Westers. In 1820 he returned to the fur territories but his influence with the London board had been undermined. Colvile regarded him as an incompetent administrator. Furthermore he was a fugitive and he became a bankrupt.

As the principal officer in North America, the London board had selected William Williams, "who was apparently chosen for his courage rather than for his business acumen or for his good judgment." Williams's previous career reportedly had been that of a ship captain in the East India Company, an experience seemingly alien to that of a fur-trade governor. In the crisis of 1818 he gave the committee what it desired, a courageous defence of the Company's interest. One member of the committee, Nicholas Garry, described him as "a gallant manly Character who had so bravely defended the Rights of the Company at every personal Inconvenience and Hazard of his Life".[23] Williams elated the activists in the Company by capturing the North West Athabaska brigade at Grand Rapids and arresting several of the officers. Williams's courage was not matched by his legal techniques. He had used Rupert's Land[24] warrants for offences in Athabaska, outside the chartered territory, and Canadian warrants for murder at Red River, within the chartered territory. The London board disapproved of his impetuosity, particularly since it exposed him to the risk of arrest. With Robertson discredited and Williams in danger of being committed for trial, the board sought a person on whom they could rely to take charge of the Athabaska district. Their choice was George Simpson.

CHAPTER II

Trial by Ordeal

Some men rise to prominence through a series of gradations, others are catapulted by circumstances which neither they nor anyone else could have foreseen. In the New Year of 1820 George Simpson had no anticipation of the great events in which he was about to become involved. In February he had a pleasant visit with his old friends the Poolers and returned to London expecting to go on with his work in the sugar business. The tenor of his life had changed somewhat. He was no longer a junior clerk; his talents had earned him greater responsibilities. And there had been a shake-up in the top management. Andrew Colvile took over complete control of the firm, which was now renamed Colvile, Wedderburn and Company, and Simpson's uncle Geddes established himself with another company.[1] George Simpson's career was linked thereafter to Andrew Colvile, but his days in the sugar business were over; his destiny was to be in the fur trade.

In 1820 the Hudson's Bay Company was in an excellent strategic position against its North West competitors. The inherent weaknesses of the North West organization coupled with the new energy infused into the chartered Company by Colvile in London and Robertson in Athabaska had brought the Canadian company to the verge of disintegration, and before the Christmas holidays news arrived in London which confirmed the board in the opinion that its opponents were in grievous difficulty. On Christmas Eve, Gale, Selkirk's lawyer in Canada, conveyed the news that influential wintering partners were dissatisfied with their agents in Montreal and wanted to make terms with the

Hudson's Bay Company.[2] This intelligence cast a new light on negotiations that had been going on between Edward Ellice and Colvile since autumn. Ellice was the London agent for the North West Company and a rising Whig politician. He had made a fortunate marriage in 1809 to Lady Hanna Althea Bettesworth, widow of a captain in the Royal Navy and the youngest sister of the second Earl Grey. Through this marriage Ellice joined a family circle which was dominant in the Whig party of the 1820s and early 1830s.[3] Ellice, born in 1783, was the son of Alexander Ellice, who had made his fortune in the American fur trade and later shifted his business to London, where he was the supplier of the North West Company. Young Edward learned the business from his father, and became its head on his father's death in 1805. Edward Ellice was a businessman of acumen comparable to Andrew Colvile's. He had not been nicknamed "Bear" because of any ursine qualities.[4] Thomas Carlyle, it is true, detected "a certain oiliness" in Ellice but this was related to Ellice's preference for negotiation rather than collision.

Ellice, aware of the deepening crisis of the North West Company, had approached Colvile with an offer to buy out the Hudson's Bay Company at its own valuation. The ailing Lord Selkirk—he died in April 1820—had refused to entertain such a proposal. It was "merely a question between money and principle," as Lady Selkirk wrote.[5] But Selkirk was in desperate financial trouble, and he had to contemplate the sale of his Hudson's Bay stock. And the issue of money and principle did not evoke the same answer from Colvile as it had from Lady Selkirk. Colvile evaluated Ellice's offer in terms of business interest. He correctly surmised that the proposal reflected the crisis in the North West Company, and this opinion was reinforced by the intelligence regarding the wintering partners.

The Hudson's Bay Company had its own vulnerability. Colvile was aware that the ruination of the North West Company would require heavy expenditures; an accommodation on favorable terms might be preferable. An additional factor of increasing importance was the attitude of government. Violence in the fur-trade territories had attracted the notice of the Colonial Office, which became increasingly importunate in its demands that these disorders end.

This was the state of affairs when Colvile selected Simpson for an important mission. The Company's men in the field who had been involved in the conflict all had disabilities for leading its operations at this critical phase. Colin Robertson's expenditures in the Athabaska campaign Colvile considered profligate, and Robertson's personal bankruptcy was convincing evidence that he was no businessman. William Williams had plunged into the fray with the North Westers with great energy. His coup in capturing several of the wintering partners at the Grand Rapids in 1819 was a lethal blow to the North West Company, but it was also illegal, and legality had become important since the government had involved itself. The North Westers contended that he had been contemptuous of the Prince Regent's Proclamation ordering mutual restitution of all seized goods and an end to violence. He had replied, they said, that he cared "not a curse for the Prince Regent's Proclamation" and that "Lord Bathurst [the Colonial Secretary] and Sir John Sherbrooke [Governor of Lower Canada] by whom it was framed are d——d rascals."[6] The language may have been apocryphal, but the sentiments were not. His exploit at the Grand Rapids made him a marked man. The North Westers obtained warrants for his arrest, and the Hudson's Bay Company's legal advisers indicated that he should come to England for trial.[7] His availability for service was consequently highly doubtful.

Colvile turned to Simpson "to take care of our affairs in case Governor Williams should be dragged away." His observations of the young man had convinced him that he had the requisite qualities of business judgment, discretion, and courage to undertake the responsibility.

Colvile's selection, quickly approved by the Governor and Committee, caught Simpson totally by surprise. He wrote the Poolers on February 23 that "unexpected circumstances" had

arisen which compelled him to leave for North America and that
he would be unable to pay them a visit because he had only five
days to get ready.[8] During that brief time he was required not only
to put his own affairs in order but to receive briefings from the
board on the problems he would encounter and the policy he
should follow. The mission outlined to him was essentially that of
providing insurance against a mishap to Williams or to the governor of the Red River Settlement, Alexander Macdonell. He expected to spend several months in the Athabaska country and at
Great Slave Lake, and perhaps even at the remote Coppermine
River. He hoped to return by one of the Company's ships in
November, or, if he were too late, to winter in the north and come
back to England the next year.[9]

When Simpson was selected to go to North America, he knew
little of the continent and next to nothing about the environment
of the fur-trade territories. There is evidence that, through his
association with Colvile, Simpson had been involved in some
business activity for the Hudson's Bay Company as early as
1818.[10] How intimately he was acquainted with confidential matters cannot be determined, but he had probably developed some
understanding of the fur-trade business from the perspective of
London before he left for North America. His knowledge of
Rupert's Land, however, was certainly not intimate. His assumption that ships would be available to take him back to England in
November was a reflection of his general naïveté with regard to
the conditions he would meet.

His letters prior to his departure and after his arrival in Canada
manifested his mounting excitement at the prospect of facing the
bullies of the North West Company and his determination to show
his courage. During his voyage on the *James Monroe* from Liverpool to New York he seemed to be rehearsing the role he was
going to play in Rupert's Land. His adversaries in this case had
nothing to do with the fur trade. John George McTavish, one of
the wintering partners of the North West Company, was on
board, but he and Simpson established an amicable relationship,
the beginning of a close friendship that was to last for the rest of

their lives. Simpson's animus was directed at those fellow passengers who incited the prejudices he had developed over the years, in particular his abhorrence of "radicals". Simpson's hatred of revolutionaries and antipathy for Americans undoubtedly derived in large part from the family environment in which he had been nurtured. George Simpson, descendant of that Duncan Forbes of Culloden who had been the bulwark in Scotland of the Hanoverians, was deeply imprinted with these views, and his detestation of revolution applied not only to Scotland but to societies everywhere.

Among the passengers on board the *James Monroe* were the Spanish ambassador to the United States and his suite and several other "respectable" people, but there were also two "vile radicals" from Spain and the wives of some others. These despicable people tried to argue their case, Simpson wrote, but Simpson and some other passengers silenced them by a combination of threats and "actual hard lumps". Simpson's contempt extended to the women. Even though he had had little or no contact with them, he was prepared to believe the worst:

> Of the ladies we fortunately saw little, they were of the same cast, going to join their husbands who by their treasonable proceedings had found it necessary to take refuge in the states, an assylum for the outcasts and malcontents of all Nations; these precious nymphs were confined to their cabins the greater part of the Voyage, and if the Steward's be true, solaced themselves with copious brandy draughts to the downfall of the House of Bourbon.[11]

With the insulation of these malcontents, the principal subject of conversation on the voyage was the weather. The North Atlantic was boisterous and as the ship approached the Banks of Newfoundland the weather became very cold. The spray immediately congealed, the decks were covered with ice as much as a foot thick, and the sails were frozen rigid. After a voyage of thirty-one days it was with a sense of relief that Simpson set foot in New York, even though he was prepared to dislike it. His observations were more characteristic of a military intelligence officer than of a civilian visiting the United States for the first time. He acknowledged that there were some handsome streets and a few elegant public buildings, but his attention was principally directed to the state of the city's defences, and he noted that several men-of-war were being built at the Dock Yard on Long Island, which he toured with some American naval officers. The officers baited him with remarks about the way the Americans had mauled the British vessels on the Great Lakes in the recent war, and he responded by "calling their attention" to the destruction of Washington. Having launched himself so propitiously, he proceeded to castigate Americans generally; he expressed "contempt for their weakness, vanity and arrogance and assured them that John Bull merely wanted the opportunity to chastise them for their presumption & insolence."[12] Simpson did not record the response of his American companions, but his outburst represented courage to the point of rashness. By boasting of his combativeness to his friend Pooler, he may well have been convincing himself that he was ready to face down the North Westers. But his antipathy for things American was already evident. Though he was in the United States only a short time and talked with few Americans, he concluded that "the Americans generally speaking have a rooted and insuperable hatred towards the English." This hatred, he conceded, was reciprocal, and another war between the two countries was not unlikely.[13] Simpson's first impressions of the United States softened somewhat in his later years, but he never lost his distaste for American democracy and his conviction that this rising power was a threat to Britain.

After a few days in New York during which he apparently had no further battles of words, Simpson took a steamboat up the Hudson to Albany, "a neat pretty town", and then proceeded in an open cart toward Montreal. He had no opportunity for sightseeing; the roads which had been covered with snow were now a quagmire from the spring thaw. After seven days of travelling and "about 50 spills" in which he "had numberless bruises and contusions", he finally arrived in Montreal. On this horse-drawn journey he first displayed the characteristic that was to mark his governorship—his penchant for speed and for pushing ahead despite all obstacles. Instead of adapting himself to inclement conditions, he defied them, and he drove himself and his horse and driver nineteen hours a day to meet his schedule. Finally, on the seventh day he arrived at the St. Lawrence and was able to boast that he had been the first to cross the river that season, braving the floating ice which menaced his boat.[14]

Throughout his career with the Hudson's Bay Company, Simpson was constantly proving to himself his capacity for feats of endurance beyond those of ordinary men. His entry into Canada was the first such demonstration.

Montreal at first did not impress Simpson; this scrubby little town of less than thirty thousand inhabitants, "a filthy irregular place", had little visually to recommend it, and its dreariness was unrelieved even by scenic attractions in the neighborhood. He readily admitted that the St. Lawrence was a magnificent river, but he maintained that the town had been established by its founders in the wrong place. This judgment was made not on aesthetic but on business grounds. He had noticed that vessels of any size could not dock because of the shoals and that the currents were so strong that other craft had difficulty in making their way upstream; thus he maintained the city should have been built several miles downriver.[15]

Despite Simpson's strictures on the city's appearance, it was the commercial capital of Lower Canada, and its sustenance had been drawn in large part from the fur trade of the North West Company and its predecessors. Under the circumstances he might have expected to encounter some hostility, for the agents of the North West Company were leading members of Montreal society. But in 1820 the North West agents were intent on peace, not war. The ebullient optimism of the earlier years had long since vanished. The Beaver Club of the North West partners, which had become notorious for its boisterous, drunken, and expensive entertainment, still met, but its vitality was draining away. Its motto, "Fortitude in distress", seemed in 1820 to have special meaning.[16]

Simpson as the representative of Selkirk and the Hudson's Bay Company consequently was treated with all the warm hospitality that Montreal society could provide. It was his first taste of the wine of social status, and he savored it. He wrote Pooler that his time was "pleasantly divided between business & amusements; Dinner parties, Tea squalls, Cards, Balls, Theatres, & Masquerades occupy my evenings, and I assure you the representative of the Hudson's Bay Coy & Lord Selkirk is looked upon as no inconsiderable personage in this part of the World."[17]

Simpson, however, was not in Montreal to socialize. He devoted his days to learning all he could about the condition of the North West Company. One important informant was George Moffatt, who had close associations with the North West Company and had become an intermediary between the disaffected wintering partners and the Hudson's Bay Company. And he also conferred with Samuel Gale, Selkirk's attorney, who had been performing a similar role. Before leaving London, Simpson had been provided with a dispatch from Lord Bathurst commanding both companies to desist from any further violence. He learned from his contacts in Montreal that the North West agents had enjoined their personnel to avoid collisions. This intelligence did not preclude further violence, but the prospects of it had declined. In his letter to Pooler, however, Simpson sounded like a soldier on the eve of his first combat, reassuring himself that his courage would not fail. "I suspect I shall have some hard blows," he wrote. "I am not however paid for fighting and will therefore keep my bones whole if possible." But, he went on:

> Yet, I must show my Governors that I am not wanting in courage if necessity puts it to the test. There is a possibility that I may be obstructed in the route as the North West Company, a band of unprincipled, lawless marauders, stick at nothing, however desperate to gain their ends. I am, however, armed to the teeth, will sell my life if in danger as dear as possible, and never allow a North Wester [to] come within reach of my rifle if flint, steel and bullets can keep him off.[18]

This is not the language of a veteran but of a new recruit convincing himself that he will measure up in the crisis. The former London clerk had to demonstrate to his employers—and to himself—that they had made a wise choice in selecting him for a position of responsibility in the wilds of North America where he would be subjected to danger and privation. He was anxious to prove not only his courage but his toughness. He told Pooler that his journey to the interior would be in a canoe "pulled by 10 stout fellows", that his cloak would be a bed, and the canoe turned bottom up a chamber so that "there is no danger of my getting enervated by ease and luxury." He set himself a schedule of forty days to reach Rock House on the Hayes River, where he was to rendezvous with Governor Williams.[19] These were themes which would continue to infuse his activity—defiance of hardships and record-breaking travel in the service of his employers.

Simpson proceeded inland to Fort Williams to deliver Bathurst's dispatch to the North West wintering partners, who had assembled to debate the line they were going to take with regard to the renewal of the partnership and the policy they would pursue in response to the chartered Company and in particular, William Williams and Colin Robertson. The sentiment was that the aggressive actions of Williams must be met by a strong response, and Simpson learned that a few days before his arrival on May 28 a party had been dispatched to the Grand Rapids to capture Hudson's Bay officers in retaliation for Williams's coup. This party a month later captured Colin Robertson.[20] Simpson's impressions of the North Westers and their impressions of him at this first encounter were not recorded. Probably they saw little to inspire fear in this little blue-eyed "pork-eater".[21] At their next meeting they would acquire more respect for his powers.

Simpson arrived some time in July at Rock House on the Hayes River, the new depot for the Athabaska campaign, where he received the news from Governor Williams that Colin Robertson had been captured. The loss of Robertson, the leader of the Athabaska campaign, required Williams to find a replacement.

Instead of being a substitute for Williams, Simpson replaced Robertson in charge of Athabaska. His temporary sojourn in the fur trade would now become permanent.

Williams recognized that a man so new to the life of a fur-trade officer would need experienced assistance. He assigned an intelligent clerk, Robert Miles, to accompany Simpson. Miles had worked with Robertson and was able to give Simpson useful information and advice, and he also kept Simpson's Athabaska journal. Any reader of that journal is struck by the grasp it evidences of the problems of the trade and of the techniques of managing men in this remote environment, and the question naturally arises whether the author of these ideas was Simpson or Miles or Robertson through Miles. The answer almost certainly is that Simpson drew heavily upon those who had experience and whose judgment he respected and that the policies he pursued owed much to Robertson as transmitted through Miles. To say this is in no way to demean Simpson. It denotes a good leader that he can appropriate the best ideas of his subordinates and make them his own and that he has the capacity to differentiate between good and bad advice and advisers. Simpson had these qualities, and the fact that he adopted others' ideas as his own does not make him unique.

Whatever his debt may have been to Miles and Robertson, Simpson had to depend on his own resources in one essential area—the art of managing men. No amount of experience in a London office could have prepared him for the problems he encountered in the Athabaska country. Even before he took up his station, he began to discover practices that reflected serious defects in the Company's organization. During his canoe voyage he noticed that many of the Canadian voyageurs had become so addicted to rum that they even bartered their shirts and blankets for it. Their suppliers were English employees of the Company. This "disgraceful traffic" on one occasion incapacitated Simpson's canoemen for a whole day after a drunken spree and he ordered a stop put to it. The barter of liquor was one element of a private trade by employees in violation of the Company's monopoly. English servants received less money than did the Canadians but were able to buy goods at only seventy-five per cent above cost, whereas Canadians were charged exorbitant prices—three hundred per cent of cost. This practice by the Company, which encouraged the Canadians to buy from the English employees, was extortionate, a fact that Simpson chose not to notice.[22]

As the agent of the Company, Simpson considered his highest rule of conduct to be the promotion of its interests. When he spoke of exorbitant wages his words were formed in that context. High wages, by which he meant those above the level a monopoly could impose, spoiled the men. Even employees who were good material became slothful and insolent, but a high proportion of the Company's servants in Athabaska were "the very dross and outcast of the human species".[23]

From the time that Governor Williams had assigned him to Athabaska, Simpson's mind was occupied with thoughts of promoting an active, efficient, and cheap work force. The first entry in his diary after his meeting with Williams deals with his intention to reduce wages. He was confident that, if contracts for officers and men were renewed during the winter when they were isolated and could not take advantage of a competitive market, wages could be cut substantially and morale improved simultaneously.[24] Implicit in his point of view was the belief that opportunities for alternative employment not only made higher wages necessary but stimulated discontent. Men remote from civilization with no temptations from competitors would happily accept their lot. Those who did not could be dealt with by removal to more remote districts or by summary disciplinary action, including beatings.

His first observation of the North West competition led to depressing comparisons. He encountered several North West Company brigades which he was relieved to find did not threaten violence. But he was struck by the quality of their equipment and the efficiency with which they used it. The North West canoes were new and well built, the baggage was stowed in an expert manner, and the crews acted with precision. In his party, in contrast, the canoes were "old, crazy, and patched up, built originally of bad materials without symmetry and neither adopted [*sic*] for storage nor expedition, manned chiefly by old infirm creatures or Porkeaters unfit for the arduous duty they have to perform."[25]

The weakness and ineptitude of the Company's lower-level personnel Simpson saw as a reflection not only of competition but of laxity on the part of those officers who had hired such poor human material and who had failed to impose a sense of discipline. This impression became a conviction when he penetrated into the Athabaska district and observed the life-style of the district managers. Some of them seemed to consider themselves to be grand seigneurs entitled to the perquisites, comforts, and deference appropriate to a superior class. Rather than devoting themselves to the interests of the Company they fed their personal vanity. The man who came to epitomize in Simpson's mind the derelictions of fur-trade officers was John Clarke.

Clarke was an example of the kind of personality that comes to the fore in an environment where courage rather than judgment is at a premium. He had been recruited by Robertson after service with John Jacob Astor's Pacific Fur Company because he was "a dashing young man" who could stand up to the ruffians of the North West Company in the campaign Robertson was planning in Athabaska. Robertson soon became aware that Clarke was lacking in discretion and "can only act as a second, or associate with a person of a graver cast of mind."[26] Nevertheless Clarke was employed as head of the Athabaska brigade and Robertson's judgment was fully vindicated. Clarke proved both his courage and his rashness. In 1815 he led a party into the remote Peace River area with almost no food, hoping to live off trade with the Indians. When the North West Company removed the Indians from his path, Clarke and his men faced starvation. Sixteen died, but Clarke survived, resisting offers by the North West Company to provide him with food if he would turn over his trade goods.[27]

Clarke had his virtues, as he demonstrated the year after the tragedy at Peace River. In the Athabaska country he carried on a vigorous and successful campaign against the North Westers. By a combination of lavish prices and personal influence, he won over many Indians. Robertson said of him:

> The first brush or onset of Clarke is irresistible. No servant will attempt to disobey his orders, and few Indians can resist his entreaties. He cajoles, condoles, and seeks to command every string that can touch the heart of a Canadian.[28]

To this complimentary assessment, however, Robertson felt compelled to add,

> but his inordinate vanity is such that the management of John Clarke is as arduous a task as that of opposing the N. W. Co. All his movements must be watched and humoured with the utmost nicety and it is only by asking his advice, and as it were engrafting your own upon it, that you can hope to plant in his mind measures of prudence.[29]

The Clarke whom Simpson met in 1820 was as wayward as ever and as unaware of his limitations. His sense of self-importance had risen to vaingloriousness. He was now established at Ile-à-la-Crosse, a key post and provision depot on the route from Lake Winnipeg to Lake Athabaska, and he carried on the affairs of his district almost as an independent potentate. Even when Robertson had been in charge, Clarke had been accustomed to follow his own inclinations. Now Robertson was gone, Williams was new to his job, and Clarke was under no restraining authority.

Such a man was certain to collide with George Simpson. Clarke had not been bridled by men whom he respected, and he could certainly not be expected to listen to a greenhorn on a temporary sojourn in the fur territories. And Clarke embodied the excesses that lack of discipline and unrestrained competition had brought to the fur trade.

Ironically in view of his later tirades against Clarke's extravagance, Simpson's first impression of the man was his dedication to the cherished principle of economy. Clarke he observed, had a remarkable influence over the French Canadians and was able to engage their services for as much as one-fourth less than could any other officer in the service.[30] But this favorable judgment did not last long, for Clarke soon manifested his unwillingness to be harnessed. His refusal to obey orders directly challenged Simpson and threatened the success of his Athabaska operations.

Clarke and Simpson travelled together as far as Clarke's headquarters at Portage La Loche, and the true characteristics of Clarke began to appear. Clarke was travelling with his wife, who was a daughter of a fur trader and an Indian woman, and he removed two men and some cargo from one of the canoes to make the trip more comfortable for her and her servants. Simpson was indignant that an officer *"merely for the accommodation of an Indian Mistress"* should set aside the needs of the service, and his ire was intensified by Clarke's insistence that all the supplies he was carrying were required in his own district and that none would be available for the Athabaska.[31] These first instances of irresponsibility were soon followed by others. Simpson heard that Clarke had instructed his subordinates to provide no assistance to the Athabaska district but to keep their supplies for their own trade. Clarke was obviously concerned only about the returns of his own district. The more furs he could secure the better, even if it meant seducing Indians away from other Hudson's Bay districts. "Mr. Clarke's fame resounds over the country," Simpson wrote in his diary at Portage La Loche on September 13, 1820. He "has attracted Indians from all quarters; from him they expect unlimited supplies, without recompense, and calculate on passing an easy comfortable winter without the trouble of hunting." Simpson took leave of Clarke with a feeling that this anachronism must be removed as soon as possible—"this Gentleman . . . is certainly one of the Company's worst bargains."[32]

In the arrangements for 1820–21 Clarke was instructed by Governor Williams to send supplies of pemmican and other necessities to Portage La Loche where they would be available for the Athabaska district.[33] Months went by, autumn turned to winter, and provisions at Athabaska became short. Finally Simpson at the end of November wrote Clarke a letter which was a thinly veiled reprimand. He could not believe, he told Clarke, that the nonarrival of the supplies was due to any negligence on his part, particularly in view of "the warm interest you profess to take in the welfare of the Company's general affairs". Obviously there must be another explanation. Perhaps an accident had befallen the supply canoes. If this was not the case someone would have reason to regret his neglect of duty, and he assumed that "it would not require much ingenuity" for Clarke to "exculpate" himself. If the men assigned to bring the supplies were still at Ile-à-la-Crosse they had better be sent off "without the delay of one hour".[34] This was strong language, but Simpson was not yet in a position to go beyond language in dealing with Clarke, and the result was a continuing irritation during Simpson's first winter.

Before he arrived at the Athabaska headquarters at Fort Wedderburn, Simpson had thus already been exposed to the frustrations and vexations which befall a person whose authority has not been established. He now had to face the test of "standing up" to the doughty North Westers. Fort Wedderburn, on Lake Athabaska, had been built by Clarke in the winter of 1815–16 to overlook the North West post of Fort Chipewyan and draw Indians away from it. The North Westers were irritated by this intrusion, and a party under A. N. McLeod captured the fort in 1817 and arrested fifty men, who were set free on their oath not to return to the Athabaska for two years.[35] The post had been subsequently reoccupied by the Hudson's Bay Company but was in such a state of dilapidation that it was decided to rebuild it. The old fort was so close to Fort Chipewyan that one Hudson's Bay trader noted that "their buildings now flank us on both sides, and with the desperadoes they have, our lives are in greatest danger." Consequently the new fort was built a short distance away, but the North West Company built a watch-house immediately adjacent to it, and the new fort provided little improvement in comfort over the old one.[36]

Simpson's mind was not on comfort when he arrived at Fort Wedderburn on September 20, 1820, but on the ordeal for which he had steeled himself since he arrived in Canada—his confrontation with the North West "bullies". His first observation seemed to confirm his fear that there was imminent danger of violence —the North Westers had done their best to harass his men with threats that they intended to seize the fort, and there was a great deal of swaggering around the gates with an ostentatious display of swords and pistols. On the next day the North Westers sent Simpson a newspaper account of the death of Lord Selkirk, obviously with the intent of contributing to despondency.[37]

The North Westers at Fort Chipewyan were at the time under the command of George Keith, one of the wintering partners who had been actively involved in the vendetta between the two companies. But Keith was among those who saw the imminent ruin of the North West Company, and he was not disposed to initiate violence. He contented himself instead with permitting petty harassments that would test the mettle of the new arrival at Fort Wedderburn. He misjudged his man. Simpson, determined to prove his courage, was highly sensitive to any actions which reflected contempt of his authority, and within a month of his arrival an incident occurred where he seized the opportunity to show his mettle. One of Keith's subordinates was Simon McGillivray, Junior, son of the renowned North West partner but deprived of hereditary patrimony in intelligence and judgment. Young Simon had the qualities of the bull rather than the fox. On October 19 the North Westers began construction of a watch-house within a few yards of Fort Wedderburn. Simpson countered by ordering the erection of a stockade to mask the fort from the spying of their opponents, whereupon McGillivray and several other people, all armed, ordered the Hudson's Bay men to stop. This was the challenge for which Simpson had long prepared himself and he confronted McGillivray. The ensuing conversation, as Simpson reported it, was as follows:

> When standing close to McGillivray on the bank of the Trench I remarked, "My name is Simpson, I presume yours is McGillivray," he replied: "it is."—I then said, "I intend erecting these Stockades from the corner of the Bastion in a direct line to that stump" (pointing to the stump of a Tree, about five feet within another stump which is understood to be the boundary of the two establishments) "pray Sir, what are your objections"? He answered: "I understood from Mr. Oxley [Jonas Oxley, a Hudson's Bay Company employee] that he intended to run them beyond the boundary line which I shall not permit." I rejoined: "we have no intention to encroach on what is understood to be the line of demarkation, nor shall we tamely submit to any encroachment on our rights, we are inclined to be quiet orderly neighbours if permitted to be so, but are determined to maintain our privileges with firmness, and shall promptly resent any injury or insult that may be offered." He sullenly replied: "time will show." In the interim my Tarrier [sic] Dog Boxer (a very playful fellow) was amusing himself with a stick close to Soucisses feet [Joseph Soucisse of the North West Company], and while the Bully was regarding him with an ill natured look, as if about to give him a kick, I with a smile addressed the dog, "come here Boxer, you do not seem to be aware that you are committing a trespass." McGillivray with a good deal of asperity observed: "We have no intention to molest your dog Sir," to which I replied: "nor shall you his Master with impunity." Here ended the conversation; McGillivray and his bullies retired somewhat crest fallen, and in the course of two hours afterwards, the fence was completed and an annoyance removed which has been a source of great vexation to the inmates of Fort Wedderburn since it has been established.[38]

Whether or not Simpson adorned his report of the conversation, clearly he had successfully met his first test and was jubilant at his performance. He followed this display of resolution with a coup in which he showed that he was also crafty. Among his employees was Amable Grignon, a "clerk" who could neither read nor write. Grignon's virtues evidently related to combat rather than to correspondence and ledgers. Simpson learned that Grignon had the status of a Canadian constable and that he possessed a warrant for the arrest of McGillivray. Here was an opportunity to take the offensive in the guise of upholding the law. Grignon should arrest McGillivray on his authority as a constable; Simpson would accept no responsibility, but of course if a police officer called upon him for help he would be obliged to come to his assistance. Simpson rehearsed this "assistance". His men were all provided with weapons and stationed at strategic places to await Simpson's signal. He and several men, all well armed, proceeded to the area where construction was going on, where they met McGillivray. Simpson professed to want to talk about the boundary, but while he and McGillivray were in conversation, Grignon "collered" McGillivray and placed him under arrest. The North Westers were taken by surprise; some reached for their weapons, but decided not to fire when confronted with the guns of the Hudson's Bay party. McGillivray was hustled off to the fort, spewing out abuse at his captors. His ire was not cooled by Simpson's protestation that the officer had acted on his own responsibility and could alone be liable for the consequences. This was also the line which Simpson took when Keith asked by what authority he had seized McGillivray and demanded his immediate release.[39]

A few months earlier Simpson's action would probably have resulted in an outbreak of violence as the North Westers sought to release the prisoner. But he had cunningly placed himself on the side of the "law", and any attack by the North Westers would be in defiance of the Imperial government's strict instructions to keep the peace. He had made a shrewd calculation, and he won the gamble. The North Westers fumed and threatened but they did not attack. Simpson had established himself as a man who deserved respect; he now proceeded to build on that foundation.

Economy and discipline were two related problems he had to

deal with immediately. The more information he acquired from the various posts, the more he become convinced that there was no system or regularity in the Company's operations. There was insufficient attention to such basic considerations as conservation of food. The men went from feast to famine. Officers did not know what goods they had in stock because they did not make proper inventories, and there was no co-ordination of effort to ensure that posts did not compete with one another for the same furs. Clarke was a notorious example of such self-centeredness but he was not alone. The experience of his first few months in Athabaska made Simpson pessimistic about the Company's future unless there were drastic changes in the conduct of the fur trade. He wrote in March 1821:

> There never was perhaps a concern so completely ruined through neglect, the arrangement of Officers, men and Goods are not sufficiently attended to either at the Compys. establishments in the Lower Country or in Canada, and those who were in charge of the business inland have never studied it's interests so that it is a matter of surprise that we have not been under the necessity of abandoning it altogether, and I am of opinion that another such year as the last will prove fatal to the Compys. prospects in it: — for my own part I would not on any consideration undergo a repetition of the vexations, misery, and anxiety I have this year suffered, arising solely from the want of means to carry on the Business as it ought to be conducted, indeed every Gentleman and Servant in the concern who have an interest in it's welfare view the state of affairs with sentiments of heartfelt despondency."[40]

The outlines of the policies with which the mature Simpson would be identified first appeared during his winter in Athabaska. At first his judgments on matters peculiarly relating to the fur trade leaned heavily on the advice of other more knowledgeable people, but there were principles that he considered applicable to all businesses, and he attempted to impose them on Rupert's Land. He recognized that officers considered themselves to be important men, and toward them he applied whatever combination of sternness, exhortation, and flattery he considered would be most effective in each case. But the fundamental message was always the same—there must be greater attention to economy, efficiency, regularity, and co-ordination. During his years as governor, Simpson with some success sought to convince his officers that he had an intimate awareness of what they were doing and that nothing could escape his vigilance. This characteristic he was already developing in Athabaska. To Joseph Greill, in charge of Berens House, he communicated the report that Greill was "addicted to the Bottle". This rumor, he assured Greill, he would not believe until it was further substantiated.[41] But Greill understood the message. His treatment of ordinary employees was quite different. Despite Simpson's continuing complaint about extravagant wages, life for the lowest echelons of the fur trade was hard. In the remote regions they were subject to despotic discipline; there was no recourse to the courts; and whether they were harshly or kindly treated depended on the character of their officers. During the long Arctic winters they experienced privation and, sometimes, near-starvation. It was understandable that they should seek relief from this dreary existence by drunken orgies whenever they could acquire liquor, which was, however, infrequently. At Fort Wedderburn, Simpson had to deal with disaffection. Some men talked of desertion to Fort Chipewyan, some were insubordinate, and some merely grumbled about their lot. His view of punishment was that it must be "exemplary" and graded to the nature of the offence but also that it must be certain. Those who talked of desertion he threatened with handcuffs and short allowances; others were chastised by fines or reprimands, as appropriate. On occasion he resorted to blows. John McLoughlin, who himself was well known for his use of physical punishment, once saw Simpson knock a man down, and "I never saw a man get a neater blow."[42] But that was not the Simpson style; other, less violent measures he generally considered more effective. And Simpson also prided himself on being a judge of men, though in his first months in Athabaska this judgment had to be at least partially derived from more experienced people. Nine days after his arrival at Fort Wedderburn, he was already delivering opinions that could hardly have been based on experience. He delivered a lecture on the handling of men of different nationalities to Duncan Finlayson, in charge of the Peace River district, and an experienced fur trader:

> You will bear in mind that it is Canadians you have now to deal with, not cool phlegmatic Orkney men, if humoured in trifles anything may be done with them, but if treated with uniform harshness and severity, they will Mutiny to a certainty.[43]

Whatever his credentials were for describing Orkneymen, Simpson's first-hand knowledge of French Canadians had been limited to his canoe voyage west, scarcely an acquaintance sufficient to qualify him to make such a confident assessment of national traits. But the recognition that discipline was an art infused Simpson's policies, then as later.

Simpson by 1820 had developed another attribute which characterized his later life. He identified himself completely with his employers; his ambitions would be realized through them; their approval was the mark of his success. This preoccupation left no room for ethical considerations. Those actions were justified which advanced the Company's interests. Simpson's arrest of McGillivray involved duplicity. His treatment of another North West servant was a greater deviation from the Christian ethic. One of the clerks at Fort Chipewyan, Thomas O'Hara, had become disaffected toward his employers and sought to change allegiance. As a means of winning favor, he conveyed to Simpson information on the North Westers' plans. Simpson recognized the value of having a "spy in the Enemy's camp", and he led O'Hara to believe that he would appoint him as a clerk in the Hudson's Bay Company. As proof of his good faith he gave O'Hara a note to that effect addressed to a Hudson's Bay agent in Canada. But he had no intention of appointing O'Hara to any position. He had no sympathy with traitors; when they were no longer useful they must be discharged; and he countermanded the appointment while continuing to delude O'Hara.[44] Critics might describe such deception as immoral; Simpson considered it good business.

Men who concentrate their energies on the pursuit of material success often pay a price in shrivelled humanity. Dr. Faustus's compact with the devil has many counterparts in real life. The Simpson of Athabaska had already developed the characteristics that made him the "Emperor of the Plains". His future was dependent on the approval of powerful men in London, in particular Andrew Colvile, and he applied himself with complete dedication to justifying their confidence in him. Toward Colvile he expressed almost a filial devotion. Simpson manifested different qualities toward those who obstructed him or those he sought to manage. He was an expert dissimulator. On the surface he was usually warm and affable. He believed that men were usually managed better by persuasion or flattery than by threats or actual violence. This preference for the soft approach masked the hard, calculating character which lay beneath. One Hudson's Bay employee in 1821 described Simpson as "a gentlemanly man" who would "not create much alarm" and who was not "formidable as an Indian trader".[45] This assessment of Simpson's powers was soon proved greatly mistaken, but on his first appearance in the fur trade his ruthlessness was still concealed beneath the bland exterior. In his private communications in his journal and in his communications to the directors, however, he expressed himself as a man committed to efficiency to the exclusion of any other considerations. The foibles of employees or their personal tragedies were significant only in terms of their effect on the Company's operations. Throughout his forty years in the service Simpson subordinated any considerations of humanity to the welfare of the chartered Company.

After the arrest of McGillivray, Simpson was for some weeks apprehensive that the North Westers might attempt to rescue the prisoner by force. His concern was increased when he heard that Samuel Black had arrived at Ford Chipewyan. Black had two things in common with Simpson. He was an illegitimate child whose father's family had helped him to get his start in business, and he gave his complete loyalty to the firm that employed him. But there the similarity ends. Black was a great bear of a man who was not at all averse to the use of violence, and he had been in the thick of the encounters between the Hudson's Bay and North West companies. Among the actions which had made him a marked man were the capture of Ile-à-la-Crosse and Green Lake in 1817, the latter in company with Peter Skene Ogden, who by this and other exploits joined Black in the Hudson's Bay Company's select list of most wanted men. Black had also been the leader of the party that had captured Colin Robertson at Fort Wedderburn. Black's violent deeds caused even his superiors some unease, and at their suggestion he had crossed the Rocky Mountains to put himself out of reach of warrants for his arrest. But he returned to Fort Chipewyan on October 27, 1820, when it became evident that the Hudson's Bay Company was mounting a major campaign to drive the North Westers from the Athabaska.[46]

Black's reputation for violence was well known to Simpson and must have caused him some trepidation, but Black had no intention of breaching the peace. Like other "wintering partners" he saw the end of the North West Company as imminent, and he saw no advantage in acts of violence in a losing cause, particularly since he was already in danger of arrest for his previous exploits. He consequently confined himself to vigorous trading activity to prevent the Indians from selling their furs to the Hudson's Bay Company.[47]

Simpson in his letters to Colvile chose to interpret Black's failure to attack in terms of his fear of Simpson. Three years later he described a meeting with Black:

> Black could at first scarcely look me in the face, he recollected my Athabaska Campaign and never will forget the terrors in which he was kept that winter.[48]

This picture of the formidable Mr. Black being faced down by a little newcomer from London is ludicrously unrealistic. But the fact that Simpson believed it, or professed to believe it in his communications with his employers, speaks eloquently of Simpson's character. The Athabaska campaign, as he described it, had been won by his display of resolution and courage. In his report to the Governor and Committee at the end of the winter, he gave a version markedly similar to his reference to Black three years later:

> Our opponents have upon the whole been less troublesome this year than I had reason to expect, but their pacific behaviour arose more from a dread of the consequences of a different line of conduct, than from inclination, as their proceedings in the early part of the Fall indicated greater hostility than has been experienced for some years; indeed they were never so formidable in the Athabaska Department as this Season, and both Agents and Actors appear to have been carefully selected as fit engines for a renewal of their outrages and atrocities . . . but the decisive measures I found it necessary to adopt, prevented their attempting the excesses which Mr. Archd. Norman McLeod seems to have taken so much pains to recommend and inculcate. . . . miscreants were chosen to make the test, who were capable of the foulest crimes which they would have carried into effect had they found me so passive as they anticipated.[49]

Under the circumstances, the escape of Simon McGillivray on December 3, 1820, allegedly by bribing one of his guards, produced no perturbations. The North Westers at Fort Chipewyan restricted themselves to petty irritations.

Simpson's main concern during his season in Athabaska was not so much with the North Westers as with the perennial problem of survival. Supplies of pemmican at the various posts were never adequate at best, and as the winter drew on, more and more reliance had to be put on fisheries. When fish were not available, men had to go on short rations, which were sometimes supplemented by dog meat, an expensive commodity in view of the dependence on dogs for transport.[50] In part these shortages of food related to the failure of the distribution system, when officers, notably Clarke, kept supplies for themselves rather than following orders to send certain amounts to other districts.

Simpson's first impressions were that the defects of the Hudson's Bay Company's organization and personnel were so great that it would be in the Company's interests to come to an arrangement with some of the North West Company's wintering partners. But as the months went by the weaknesses of the North Westers became more and more apparent and he shifted his position to advocacy of all-out competition.

Simpson on his way out of the Athabaska country reached Lake Winnipeg in June 1821 where he met some North West traders. By his account he expected some hostile action from them, but instead they informed him of the coalition between the two companies. The ex-enemies were now allies. This intelligence he professed to find most unwelcome. He noted in his journal:

> The information seems to discount both Officers and Men, and I must confess my own disappointment that instead of a junction our Opponents have not been beaten out of the Field, which with one or two years of good management I am certain might have been effected.[51]

That these were Simpson's true sentiments may be doubted. His journal was intended for the eyes of his employers, and he was anxious to impress them with his zeal in their cause. Whether or not his sentiments were sincere, the fates had again been kind to George Simpson. The coalition produced a monopoly with great potentialities, which Simpson would be given the opportunity to realize. The virtuosity with which he did so made him one of the great business figures of the nineteenth century.

CHAPTER III

Simpson Attains the Pinnacle

When George Simpson left Liverpool in 1820 he had foreseen that his tenure in the "Indian country" would be short and violent. He expected to confront ruffians who would stop at nothing to gain their ends, men whose hands had been bloodied with the massacre of the Selkirk colonists, unprincipled scoundrels for whom no means was too foul. As the representative of the Hudson's Bay Company, which he naturally assumed to be the victimized party, he would be exposed to great danger—his life might be forfeit, he indicated to his friends, but he would sell it dearly. The hyperbole that infused his communications reflected both apprehension and a thrill of anticipation; it was certainly well calculated to elicit smiles of appreciation from the London board for the resolution of their agent. He had, so they read in his dispatches, cowed the North West bullies and had introduced a new era of economy to the fur trade. Whatever exaggeration he had used in accounts of his martial prowess, he had certainly employed his energies to counteract the wasteful, disorganized practices that had developed, and the Governor and Committee were convinced that here was a man who must be given substantial power in the reorganized Company.

Though the coalition had been effected without any advice from Simpson, the requirements of the new era were perfectly adapted to his talents. Years of conflict had severely strained the Hudson's Bay Company and brought its competitor to the verge of ruin. The decision of the great men of the two companies to coalesce involved the recognition that fusion of strengths would produce far greater returns than continuing strife, even if the competition ended in the defeat of one of the rivals. There had been an additional incentive to amalgamation. Turmoil in the fur territories had attracted the notice of the governments of Canada and Great Britain. In 1816 Governor General Sir John Sherbrooke had appointed a commission of inquiry to investigate the causes of the disturbances. In London the Colonial Office had taken note of the fact that British businessmen were acting in a most un-British way, and was determined to bring violence to a halt. The Colonial Office favored amalgamation and, as a prod to the chartered Company, was prepared to reopen the question of the validity of the charter. This was not a threat to be taken lightly. In 1749 the Company had survived a severe parliamentary attack on its rights, but there could be no assurance that it would again be successful, and it had no desire to attract public attention to the issue. Chartered monopolies were not in vogue in the nineteenth century. The other survivor of divine-right monarchy, the East India Company, had been badly mauled by the free traders, and the Hudson's Bay Company was concerned to avoid controversy. With the threat, the government also offered a substantial inducement to peace. It would grant a coalesced company exclusive trading privileges in British North America outside of Canada and Rupert's Land, and would not challenge the Company's rights in Rupert's Land itself. This was a tempting offer, for it meant governmental recognition of a monopoly stretching from the St. Lawrence Basin to the Pacific.

The Great Monopoly which came into being was a blend of the two rival organizations, and the benefits to both were great enough to allow both sides to claim a "victory". The capital for the amalgamated enterprise was to be supplied in equal amounts by the two parties. The profits would be divided into one hundred shares. Twenty were assigned to the Hudson's Bay Company shareholders and twenty to the North West Company proprietors. Forty were allocated to the officers in the fur trade, the successors to the wintering partners, five went to the Selkirk family, and five to Simon McGillivray and Edward Ellice for the loss of their London agency, and the remaining ten were kept in reserve. This distribution could be interpreted as giving the North West Company a predominant position, but in fact the control of the new Company remained firmly in the hands of the old London board of the chartered Company. The reorganization also provided for the appointment of two governors in North America. One would preside over the "Southern Department", which included the James Bay area and posts along the American border as well as some in Canada. The other would supervise the "Northern Department", which embraced most of the rest of British North America all the way to the Pacific coast and included the most lucrative fur territories. Each governor would be advised by a council of chief factors and chief traders that would meet annually to deal with the conduct of the fur trade in the various districts. George Simpson was appointed governor of the Northern Department and William Williams of the Southern, and it was provided that Williams would be the senior and would preside at any councils when both he and Simpson were present. Williams had been given his choice and had selected the Southern Department,[1] a choice which further documented his limitations as a leader in the fur trade.

Whatever the motives of the London board for such a division of responsibility, the effect of their decision was to ensure a clash between Simpson and Williams which Simpson was almost certain to win. Williams was assigned areas that competition and over-trapping had made unprofitable. Simpson was given control over the best fur territories and the opportunity to show his abilities not only by increasing the margin of profits in existing areas, but by leading the advance in new areas, notably the Pacific Coast. The old sea captain, whose greatest virtue was courage, was pitted against a youthful adversary far better qualified for the conditions of the new era of monopoly, ambitious for power and recognition, and utterly unscrupulous in eliminating any obstacles in his way.

Williams's fate was foreshadowed in the methods Simpson used to deal with manifestations of independence within his own department. Simpson had to contend with two interrelated problems in dealing with the officers of the new coalition—hostility between the two companies which years of strife had engendered, and expectations that the independence of the North West "wintering partners" would continue to be evident in the annual councils. Among the chief factors were some of the most prominent of the old antagonists, and all of these officers were accustomed to being treated as men of importance. His council included George Keith, his adversary at Chipewyan; James Leith, another of the most militant wintering partners; and John McLoughlin, whose imposing physical stature was matched by the force of his character—he would later be renowned as the "White Headed Eagle" who ruled the fur trade of the Pacific Coast. And there was Colin Robertson, who believed that he had been the principal architect of the policies Simpson was pursuing. To reconcile such powerful personalities required great powers of diplomacy; to dominate them required managerial virtuosity. Simpson succeeded to a remarkable degree in accomplishing both. He did so, not by the assertion of authority, but by persuasion, affability, and a considerable element of guile.

Simon McGillivray, Senior, after the coalition, had warned his old friends of the North West Company to be wary of Simpson, who was "a more dangerous man than the other [Williams] altho' not so violent and if they did not take care . . . [Simpson] should lead the Council by the nose." The remark was perspicacious, and when Simpson heard of it he considered it such a compliment that he reported it to his patron, Andrew Colvile.[2] Simpson had come to realize that power is best exercised when it is not exposed, and that men are better managed when they follow what they themselves have concluded is their self-interest. The officers of the fur trade soon realized that if they desired advancement and attractive stations they should follow the governor's wishes, for somehow those who did not do so seemed to be passed by. But

Simpson was not blatant; all outward signs showed him to be kindly, amiable, and unpretentious. The quintessential Simpson was in evidence at a banquet held at York Factory in 1822 to celebrate the amalgamation. Many years later John Tod still remembered that evening as one of his memorable experiences. As Tod recalled it, the atmosphere at the beginning was thick with tension. Old enemies glared at one another across the no-man's land between the clusters of ex-North Westers and Hudson's Bay men. When the bell summoned them to dinner the two groups marched into the mess hall in perfect silence and stood about, uncertain as to where they should seat themselves. Simpson appeared "all bows and smiles", and paid particular attention to the North Westers whose frozen countenances soon began to relax, and he proceeded with great dexterity to break down the barriers between the ex-adversaries to the point that most of them where able to engage at least in polite conversation, and they sat down together without the risk of imminent violence. There were some tense moments. The North Wester John McDonald of Garth, called "blind McDonald" or "one eye", was seated directly across from his most hated enemy, Alexander Kennedy. The two had fought each other in the fur trade not only with goods but with swords. One of them bore a scar on his face from their encounter, "the other, it was said, on some less conspicuous part of his body". When McDonald saw Kennedy, Tod recalled, his nostrils seemed to expand, he snorted, writhed in his chair, and spat between his legs. Tod thought it fortunate they were without weapons, but there were knives and forks. A collision, Tod wrote, was probably averted when Simon McGillivray, Senior, who had some of the same diplomatic quality as Simpson, took note of the situation and sent word to McDonald that he would be honored to take wine with him. McDonald, his glare fixed on Kennedy, at first ignored the invitation, but was finally prevailed on to join McGillivray at the head of the table.[3]

The animosities of the old era soon subsided as the officers of the amalgamated company realized that their economic interests were well served by the new arrangements. Their positions were assured, and the economy measures introduced by Simpson contributed to their profits, since his pruning was done largely at the expense of lower-grade personnel. Simpson's objectives, however, ran athwart the chief factors in another respect. He expected them to follow his policies, and some of them, notably Colin Robertson, expected the council to have at least an advisory role. Robertson was already marked for Simpson's antipathy before their encounter in the council. Robertson made no secret of his belief that he had been the planner of the Athabaska campaign, and that Simpson had merely been following his policies during the winter of 1820–21. This contradicted Simpson's line to the Governor and Committee that before he had arrived in Athabaska the trade had been in hopeless confusion, with no direction and no leadership. Obviously Robertson had to be discredited, and Simpson, while he was in Athabaska, was already making slighting references to his predecessor's lack of system and regularity.

Given Simpson's dedication to convincing his London superiors that he alone had rescued a tottering enterprise and infused it with a new vitality, Robertson's opposition to Simpson was certain to result in his own ruination. Robertson after the coalition was an anachronism. His talents had been appropriate to the era of intense competition, but he was not well fitted for the meticulous bookkeeping and rigorous economy which were introduced with the monopoly. It was easy for Simpson to magnify Robertson's managerial defects, particularly since the London board was already predisposed to believe him in view of Robertson's own bankruptcy. Furthermore, Robertson had made enemies during his campaign against the North Westers, and some of them sat on the council, which he sought to lead in the assertion of its prerogatives. By the terms of the amalgamation, the governor could be overruled only by a two-thirds majority of the council, and Robertson had no hope of gaining such support against a man who had not only far greater power, but far superior talents in the art of getting his way.

Robertson, then, was no menace to Simpson's ambitions, and the virulence with which the governor attacked him was an indication of Simpson's capacity for malevolence. At first he concealed his animus from Robertson. While he publicly radiated good will, he was privately attacking him. In September 1821, while Robertson was still under the impression that he was "a pleasant little man", Simpson wrote to Colvile that "Colin Robertson I suspect is a luke warm partizan, he has an eye to the Chief Factorship of the Uttawas River and would like to take up his quarters at Montreal, this is merely a hint for your private information; he is inclined to curry favour with the McGillivray party." Furthermore, he was "useless, speculative and extravagant, and if I am not mistaken he will soon find our councils too warm for him, he will not now be allowed to squander property away to maintain his own consequence."[4]

By these and other similarly derogatory comments, Simpson destroyed the last remnants of Robertson's reputation with the London board. And in 1823 he humiliated Robertson in the presence of his peers at the annual council. The issue was the Red River Settlement, which most fur-trade officers regarded as a liability and quite likely a menace. By the terms of the officers' contract with the amalgamated Company, assurance was given that no expenses related to the settlement could be charged to the fur trade. The board's payment of salaries to the governor of the settlement and to a clergyman seemed to the chief factors to be a violation of the agreement, and Simpson had to contend with manifestations of discontent. Officers met together in private sessions where they fed one another's irritations, and for a time Simpson was rebuffed in his efforts to placate them. There was never any danger, however, of actual rebellion. The issue was primarily symbolic, and the vested interests of the chief factors were served by co-operation with Simpson rather than by conflict. Consequently, when Simpson decided to make an example of Robertson, he did not have to contend with an eruption. Robertson indeed played into Simpson's hands by his indiscretions, and the governor was able to divert attention from the original issue to that of authority. Simpson proudly related to Colvile how he had asserted his mastery:

> Robertson was one of the leading malcontents, but his blustering folly knocked the whole on the head, and in order to make himself pass for a man of weight came out with all their secrets which gave me an opportunity of bringing them to their senses; in short I found it necessary to show my power and authority and in full Council gave them a lecture which had the desired effect, made them look on each other with suspicion and restored their confidence in myself. . . . McDonald (one eye) was likewise inclined to be violent about the expenses incurred on account of the Colony, and was to have given me a set down or prepared speech theron at the close of the sittings, but the lecture to Robertson had the desired effect, none seemed inclined to enter the Lists with me again, and on the whole we all separated on excellent terms and I believe they have now a greater respect for me than ever.[5]

Simpson avowedly made Robertson his target because he was extravagant, incompetent, and insubordinate. There was considerable justification for each adjective, but animus was strongly apparent in the zest with which Simpson proceeded to destroy him, and this antipathy was almost certainly fed by Robertson's insistence on taking credit for achievements which Simpson had advertised as his own. Simpson's final assessment of Robertson in his "Character Book" of 1832 went beyond clinical analysis:

> A frothy trifling conceited man, who would starve in any other Country and is perfectly useless here. . . . He was bred to his Father's trade, an operative Weaver in the Town of Perth, but was too lazy to live by his Loom; read novels, became sentimental and fancied himself the hero of every tale of Romance that passed through his hands. Ran away from his Master, found employment for a few months as a Grocer's shopman at New York, but had not sufficient steadiness to retain his situation. Pushed his way into Canada and was at the age of 25 Engaged an Apprentice Clerk by the N.W. Coy for whom he came into the interior but found so useless that he was dismissed the Service. His age about 55 and his person of which he is exceedingly vain, large, soft, loosely thrown together, inactive and helpless to infirmity, is full of silly boasting

and Egotism, rarely deals in plain matters of fact and his integrity is very questionable. To the Fur Trade he is quite a Burden, and a heavy burden too, being a compound of folly and extravagance, and deranging and throwing into confusion whatever he puts his hand to in the shape of business.[6]

In George Simpson's universe sentimentality was a weakness. The advancement of his Company and himself consumed his energies, and whatever sympathy for others he may have had dwindled as he pursued these ends. He may have had a genuine affection for Andrew Colvile, who was so important to his success, but this is impossible to determine since self-interest and friendship were entirely congruent in this case. The closest association he developed in the forty years in the fur trade was with John George McTavish, whose attributes perfectly fitted Simpson's needs. McTavish, though an ex-North Wester, had been assigned after the coalition to York Factory, the principal depot of the fur trade in the new era, and Simpson, after his Athabaska sojourn, spent several months with him and undoubtedly learned much from McTavish's knowledge of the fur trade and of the personalities of other North Westers. McTavish, however, unlike Robertson, saw that his own interests were best served by devoted support for Simpson. He became completely a governor's man; he could always be relied upon to back Simpson's position; and he shared Simpson's penchant for light-hearted camaraderie. He was an officer of considerable competence who had the capacity to inspire loyalty in his men. His niece, Letitia Hargrave, described their feeling for him as "a sort of hero-worship". In McTavish's last years, a fur trader who saw him among some other retired officers wrote to Letitia's husband, Chief Factor James Hargrave, "John George, good man . . . Oh! Hargrave what a contrast he shows to the other North Westers—but he is a gentleman in any country and in any society."[7] McTavish was knowledgeable, genial, and competent, and he posed no threat to Simpson, who considered him perfectly discreet.[8] This combination of virtues made McTavish Simpson's most trusted associate.

How much Simpson owed to McTavish and other experienced officers can never be determined. Simpson felt no need to acknowledge the sources of his ideas, but his communications with the London board from the beginning evidenced a grasp of the fur trade not to be expected in a tyro governor. In part this can be attributed to the fact that his greatest responsibility was in the area of his greatest experience. He was required to inaugurate a system of economy and fiscal regularity for which his background in business well qualified him, and he carried through this policy of retrenchment with a dedication that earned him the esteem of his superiors. At the time of the coalition there were 1983 employees of the Company. During the next four years this number was reduced to 827; wages of ordinary employees were slashed approximately fifty per cent.[9] These reductions were made in both the Northern and Southern Departments, but the greatest opportunities for economy were in Simpson's Northern Department, which was for the most part free from competition, and here was where the greatest economies were possible. These economy measures were initiated by the London committee; their North American governors were obligated to carry them out, but Simpson's zeal for retrenchment sometimes outran that of his superiors. He reduced the wages of employees as much as one-fourth below that prescribed by the board, and he was ruthless in the elimination of "old and useless men" and in the withdrawal of support for dependants.[10] In most of these actions he had the full support of his Council, for the reduction of expenses meant greater profits for the commissioned officers, but they were not so pleased with his attacks on perquisites. Officers had developed tastes for European commodities which were a drain on revenues, and many of them maintained "country wives" and their progeny. To ensure that the affairs of his Department were conducted with "system and regularity" he inaugurated the practice during his first year as governor of making rapid journeys to the various posts to see for himself how the trade was being conducted. His first tour on a journey of about fifteen hundred miles[11] gave him a chance to display his great endurance as well as to make officers concerned about the perennial imminence of his presence.

From the standpoint of his employers, Simpson seemed almost a paragon. He carried out their instructions with such vigor and efficiency that they had almost no complaint. If there was any cause for concern, it was his excess of zeal. With him the only consideration was the elimination of waste, regardless of human consequences. But the London board was somewhat affected by humanitarianism and much concerned not to offer any occasion for the anti-monopoly critics to attack the Company. One member of the board, Benjamin Harrison, was a prominent member of the Clapham Sect, which was concerned not only with souls but with bodies, and others on the committee were sensitive to the possibilities of powerful political opposition. John Halkett, who like Colvile had married a sister of Selkirk, reminded Simpson that monopolies were unpopular and "I trust those who were hostile to the principle of such monopoly will never have it in their power, should any inquiry ever be instituted on the state of the country, to charge the general body of the gentlemen employed in the Company's service, with contributing nothing towards the maintenance of their families on the spot."[12] But such humanitarian strictures did not weigh very much against considerations of profit.

The Hudson's Bay Company was not a philanthropic enterprise. It existed to make money from furs. This involved implications not only for the fur-bearing animals, but for those who divested them of their skins. The board expressed concern for the spiritual and material welfare of the Indian population, in particular for their conversion to Christianity and their protection from the scourge of alcohol. Simpson did not adorn his views on Indians in such comely garb. By the time he had spent a few months in North America, he had already developed rigid stereotypes about Indians, which remained substantially unmodified the rest of his life. Essentially these views were those prevailing among most of his fellow fur traders. They were not anthropologists analysing folkways and mores. Nor did they give much thought to the causes of the disease and drunkenness that they observed. The fur traders sought to maintain friendly relations with the Indians with whom they traded. It was good business for them to do so. Hudson's Bay officers maintained a high standard of honesty and fairness. Such practices, of course, were good for trade, and the Company's reputation was a great asset. But there was little intimacy on a human level. Indian women were a source of sexual gratification, but with some notable exceptions their white mates did not treat them as equals. The social barriers between whites and Indians inevitably produced stereotypes on both sides. To the fur traders, some tribes were "manly", others "cowardly"; some were "treacherous", others "honorable". But in every case they were seen as uncivilized, improvident people whose moral and intellectual development was retarded. They craved alcohol, which debauched them, and coveted trinkets, which contributed nothing to their welfare. When food was plentiful they gorged themselves, and they then faced starvation in the months of scarcity. Simpson, by the time he had spent a few months in the Athabaska country, was already expressing such judgments. The Indians with whom he first came into contact, the Chipewyans, were in his eyes devoid of any redeeming traits. Before the advent of the Europeans, he asserted, they had been indolent and simple. After traders had given them the taste for European goods they had become good hunters "from their insatiable rapacity", but they had grown fat and lazy from the bounty which competitors in the fur trade had brought them. Not only were they uninterested in work, but they were "Cunning, covetous to an extreme, false and cowardly", with "no particle of honor". Lest there be any doubt as to his opinion, Simpson added "the Chippewayan character is disgraceful to human nature."[13]

The Beaver Indians who resided in the Peace River area, on the other hand, impressed him favorably. They were "naturally of a bold, Manly character, quick in resenting injuries, but with none of that detestable treachery which characterises the Chippewyans, nor have they any of their selfish, covetous, and avaricious dispositions.'' They were strictly monogamous, and violations of marriage contracts were punishable by death. While they were kindly and hospitable to Europeans, they rejected intermarriage, and there were no Beaver Indian mixed-bloods.[14] The Beaver Indians in Simpson's stereotype were noble savages unadulterated by the vices of civilization, and their dedication to "racial purity" impressed him. Racial purity, however, was not of such moment when it conflicted with the interests of the fur trade. From information he had acquired about the Indians of the Pacific Coast, he concluded that a very different relationship was desirable with them: "Connubial alliances are the best security we can have of the goodwill of the Natives, I have therefore recommended the Gentlemen to form connections with the principal Families immediately on their arrival, which is no difficult matter as the offer of their Wives & Daughters is the first token of their Friendship & Hospitality."[15]

With the coalition, Simpson had the task of reconciling the Indians to a new order in which the tariffs for their furs were drastically reduced. In some districts, such as around Edmonton, the Indians indicated that they would do no more hunting unless the prices were raised, and some among the Cree and Slave tribes threatened war against the new monopoly.[16] Simpson was convinced that a strong policy was necessary to put down this discontent. After a journey around the posts in the spring of 1822, he wrote Colvile:

> I have made it my study to examine the nature and character of Indians, and however repugnant it may be to our feelings, I am convinced they must be ruled with a rod of Iron to bring and keep them in a proper state of subordination, and the most certain way to effect this, is by letting them feel their dependence upon us.[17]

Simpson knew his Indians as settlers in South Africa thought they knew their Africans. He prided himself on his understanding of the Indian psychology, and his ability to overawe them with his presence. In 1825, while on a tour of the Pacific coast, he wrote in his journal:

> Two Nez Percés Chiefs arrived to see me from a distance of between 2 & 300 miles; my fame has spread far and Wide and my speeches are handed from Camp to Camp throughout the Country; some of them have it that I am one of the "Master of Life's Sons" sent to see "if their hearts are good" and others that I am his "War Chief" with bad Medicine if their hearts are bad. On the whole I think my presence and lectures will to [*sic*] some good.[18]

Firmness and fairness, Simpson maintained, would in time convince the Indians that the Company served their best interests far better than the free traders, and they would become reconciled to the lower prices paid by the monopoly. Indeed, he professed to see lower prices as being beneficial to the Indians. The era of competition had surfeited them with European goods and they had lost the incentive to work. They had become lazy and shiftless. Now the whip of austerity would stimulate them to industriousness again. Reduction in the supply of spirits would redeem them from drunkenness.[19] Their characters would be restored in accordance with the Calvinist ethic.

Simpson's moral principles owed little to organized religion. There was no evidence in his life of the influence of his grandfather. He was a Sunday Christian, and even his Sabbath observances were quite irregular. Religion performed a useful function when it inculcated honesty and industry among the poor. But Simpson had no time for meddling churchmen, and in particular for those missionaries whose zeal for conversion seduced Indians from their way of life as fur-gatherers.

Simpson's attitude toward missionaries when communicated to Colvile was unadorned by cant or pseudo-piety. Those who helped to promote the interests of the fur trade were assets; those who worked against these interests should be given no help. The London board had the same standard, but their position was affected by a sense of responsibility for the moral and religious instruction of the inhabitants of Rupert's Land, Company employees and Indians, and the settlers of Red River. At their behest, officers were enjoined to conduct services on the Sabbath and to encourage Company personnel to give religious instruction to their wives and children.[20] These injunctions were carried out with varying degrees of enthusiasm at the different posts, but the commercial Company could hardly be expected to devote much energy and money to purposes unrelated to profit. The philanthropy of the board extended to permitting missionaries to reside near the posts and to providing some financial support for religion and education at Red River. They appointed the Reverend John West as chaplain in 1820. West was not an ideal selection for the colony. He was an Anglican in the midst of a population which was predominantly Roman Catholic and Presbyterian, and he did not develop a sympathetic rapport with the non-Anglicans. But his deficiencies in the eyes of Simpson had no relationship to this problem. West was a meddler. He objected to trading on Sunday, and he wanted to promote the education of Indians. Simpson's reaction was predictably hostile. He wrote to Colvile:

> Mr. West has some idea that through the interest and exertions of Mr. Harrison a fund may be raised or got from some of the Charities to open Schools for the instruction and maintenance of Native Indian Children; he takes a very sanguine view of these scheme which is to diffuse Xtian Knowledge among the natives from the shores of the Pacific to those of the Bay and will no doubt on paper draw a very fine representation of the advantages to be derived therefrom, which may attract the attention of Philanthropists, but in my humble opinion will be attended with little other good than filling the pockets and bellies of some hungry missionaries and schoolmasters and rearing the Indians in habits of indolence; they are already too much enlightened by the late opposition and more of it would in my opinion do harm instead of good to the Fur Trade. I have always remarked that an enlightened Indian is good for nothing; there are several of them about the Bay side and totally useless, even the half Breeds of the Country who have been educated in Canada are blackguards of the very worst description, they not only pick up the vices of the Whites upon which they improve

but retain those of the Indian in their utmost extent. The Indians of this Country are certainly quick of apprehension and have a thirst for knowledge; they would gladly be relieved of the burthen of maintaining their children, but I suspect the plan would not be productive of any real good. I give my ideas thus freely for your private information in case the subject should come before the Committee, if they were known by the very pious I might be looked upon as a true North Wester.[21]

West also ran afoul of Simpson as with other officers in the fur trade by his uncompromising stand on moral issues, particularly encouragement of drunkenness and sexual licence among the Indians. Simpson supported a policy of reducing the amount of liquor made available to the Indians but was not yet prepared to order an immediate cessation to the detriment of the fur trade. West's absolute rejection of country marriages was also a sore point with Simpson. West was, in short, an irritant which had to be removed and Simpson saw to it that his stay in Rupert's Land was a short one. West was discharged in 1824.[22]

In considering what was best for the Indians, neither Simpson nor the missionaries thought it necessary to consult the Indians. Given the assumptions of nineteenth-century Europeans with regard to non-European peoples they could hardly have been expected to do so.[23] Those Europeans who thought about the welfare of other peoples believed that Europeans were givers conferring a boon on the receivers. Simpson never allowed himself any doubt that the welfare of the Indians was best served by the paternalism of the Hudson's Bay Company, and he could cite abundant documentation for this opinion in the effects of free trade among the Indians south of the border. In the Hudson's Bay territories there was general tranquillity in contrast to the convulsions in the western United States. The Company's prices might be low, but the quality of its merchandise was reliable. Its traders were generally under discipline in relations with Indians, and the Company was generally trusted. Consequently it was able to carry on its trading operations in peace with a small number of personnel, while the Americans had to be constantly on the alert against hostile Indians. Good relations with the Indians were good business for the monopoly, and Simpson and his officers were highly successful in maintaining such rapport.

Collisions between Indians and Americans were frequently triggered by maltreatment of Indian women. This apparently contributed to the massacre of the Jedediah Smith party on the Umpqua River in 1828.[24]

Simpson's views on the proper treatment of Indian and mixed-blood women derived from the practices current in the fur trade when he arrived. The unavailability of white women inevitably resulted in liaisons with Indian women. Beyond the sexual satisfaction they provided, Indian partners were assets to the trader if the association was approved by the woman's people. The North West Company had recognized the benefits of such alliances in terms of promoting friendly relations with the Indians and helping the traders to communicate with Indian peoples. At first the Hudson's Bay Company had prohibited its servants from having any sexual contact with Indian women, but eventually it recognized that the policy was not only hopelessly unrealistic but unwise. Consequently it followed the North Westers' lead, and at the time of the coalition it was common for the officers of both companies to live with Indian and mixed-blood wives in a relationship known as marriage *à la façon du pays*. This union, derived from Indian custom, involved an agreement to live together for an unspecified time, not too different from common-law marriage. There was no law for the protection of the partner whose mate had deserted, but most fur traders abided by the code that they had undertaken much more than a casual obligation, and that they had assumed some responsibility both for the woman and for their progeny. If he left her, as when he retired from the service or took another wife, the man usually tried to make provision for his ex-mate by finding her another provider, and frequently the father provided assistance for the advancement in life of the children of such marriages. Some indeed married their partners in accordance with English law, a practice encouraged by the clergymen at Red River, but most adhered to the fashion of the country and accepted more or less seriously the responsibilities involved. These unwritten obligations were reinforced when the Company's board prevailed on the officers to accept a regulation that no employee would be permitted to live with a woman without providing for her and the children not only during his residence in the country but after his departure. This rule had an economic as well as a moral basis. The maintenance of the families of fur traders was a considerable drain on the Company's resources, and Simpson and the London committee sought to shift at least some of the burden to the fathers and husbands.

As governor, Simpson zealously carried out the board's policy of reducing the number of women and children who were dependent on Company largesse. At Ile-à-la-Crosse in November 1822 he noted that there were 102 women and children in the district and that there had been three births since his arrival a few days before. The white-fish diet of the district, he remarked, "seems to be favorable to procreation."[25] Simpson was himself a contributor to the increase in population, although he wrote to McTavish, "had I a good pimp in my suite I might have been inclined to deposit a little of my spawn, but have become so vastly tenacious of my reputation that no one can say to me black is the White of your Eye."[26]

The expression of fastidiousness with regard to interracial sex reflected both an increasing concern for his reputation as governor and a change in his attitude toward non-white women. But Simpson's resolution in these early years often gave way to temptation. Before he arrived in North America he already had had sexual experiences which in at least two instances had resulted in the birth of a child.[27] In both cases he accepted the responsibility of paternity. It could hardly have been expected that in the environment of Rupert's Land he would forswear sexual pleasures. There were many opportunities for easy sexual contact with Indian and mixed-blood women, and Simpson often responded to the opportunities. He wrote John George McTavish

George Simpson joined the Hudson's Bay Company in 1820 and was appointed Governor-in-Chief of Rupertsland in 1839. (Hudson's Bay Company)

Frances Simpson married her cousin George Simpson on February 24, 1830, when she was eighteen. This portrait of her as a young woman is from a miniature in the possession of Mrs. M. Porritt. (Mrs. M. Porritt and the Hudson's Bay Company)

Hudson's Bay House at Lachine was bought by the Hudson's Bay Company as a residence for Simpson in 1833. It was here he died in 1860. (Hudson's Bay Company)

Sir George and Lady Frances Simpson in their later years. (Mrs. M. Porritt and the Hudson's Bay Company)

Sir George Simpson in the 1850s. Originally a daguerreotype, this copy
was made by Notman in 1872. (Notman Photographic Archives,
McCord Museum)

in June 1822, "I suspect my name will become as notorious as the late Gov in regard to plurality of wives."[28] At the time he made this comment, Simpson was in the process of disengaging himself from a liaison which had again made him a father. During his first winter in the Athabaska country he had taken a sexual partner who became the mother of a daughter, baptized on February 10, 1822. The mother was Betsey Sinclair, daughter of the late Chief Factor William Sinclair and his Indian wife, Nahovay.[29] The child, named Maria, was baptized by the Reverend John West, and Simpson acknowledged responsibility for her, but his relationship with Betsey scarcely qualified as marriage *à la façon du pays*. Simpson wanted no burden of family responsibility at that time, and particularly not with Betsey. Whatever ardor he had felt for her had cooled. From the first she had been an object of gratification and little more, and he soon grew tired of her. His references to her as "my article" or "my Japan helpmate" reflected the contempt he undoubtedly felt. At first he thought of sending her to live with her brother-in-law Thomas Bunn, stationed at Rock Depot, but he soon decided that he would leave the problem in the hands of his friend and confidant, John George McTavish, and when Simpson departed from the Factory on his tour of the fur-trade posts, Betsey was left under the protection of McTavish. Simpson's instructions to McTavish leave no doubt about his feelings for Betsey:

> My Family concerns I leave entirely to your kind management, if you can dispose of the Lady it will be satisfactory as she is an unnecessary & expensive appendage. I see no fun in keeping a Woman, without enjoying her charms which my present rambling Life does not enable me to do; but if she is unmarketable I have no wish that she should be a general accommodation shop to all the young bucks at the Factory and in addition to her own chastity a padlock may be useful; Andrew is a neat handed Fellow & having been in China may perhaps know the pattern of those used in that part of the World.[30]

These comments reveal a lack of humanity in Simpson that cannot be explained simply in terms of the general attitudes of the fur trade. The woman was indeed an "article" that had lost its value to him, and though he did not want what had once been his possession to be passed around freely, he wanted to be rid of her as expeditiously as possible.

Simpson did not have to concern himself about Betsey Sinclair for long. Shortly after he left she became the country-wife of Robert Miles, who had been Simpson's clerk in the Athabaska country, and the union was an enduring one. She and Miles had at least eight children, and when he retired she accompanied him to Canada.

The contrast between Betsey's experience with Miles and Simpson does not in itself demonstrate an absence of feeling on Simpson's part, but his references to women of the Indian country were generally devoid of respect for their humanity, as his comments to McTavish made clear. He wrote McTavish about two washerwomen being sent to York Factory, "Let them be kept inside the Stockades & distant from the young bucks other-ways we shall have more ——ing than washing."[31] These "bits of brown", as he called them, were an expensive luxury. Not only were they an expense, but some of them exerted an undue influence over their mates. Simpson referred to such women as "petty coat politicians".[32]

Yet they did provide great pleasure, which Simpson had no desire to forgo. In the same letter in which he was directing McTavish to get rid of Betsey Sinclair, he was asking him to arrange a "private or separate entrance to my apartments".[33] It is probably not coincidental with such requests that in 1823 a son named James Keith Simpson was born to an unknown mother.

As Simpson became more and more immersed in his responsibilities as governor, he became increasingly concerned that his liaisons with women of the country might be detrimental to his interests, and in the winter of 1823–24 he first manifested the desire to return to Britain to marry, and he avowed that while at Fort Garry he had shunned the local women and lived as one of the most exemplary there.[34] This good resolution did not last; the

Company's interests prevented his early return to England, and he resumed, if he had ever stopped, his relationships with mixed-blood women. Given Simpson's record of philandering, his comments on Colin Robertson were particularly obnoxious. Robertson had married a mixed-blood woman to whom he remained devoted throughout her life. This constancy Simpson condemned as a liability to the fur trade, since Robertson's efficiency was affected by his concern for his wife. "I make a determined stand in respect of Non-intercourse in the Family way," Simpson wrote McTavish. When Robertson brought his wife to the Red River Settlement in 1831, Simpson chastised him for his impropriety.

> Robertson brought his bit of Brown with him to the Settlement this Spring in hopes that she would pick up a few English manners before visiting the civilised world, but it would not do —I told him distinctly the thing was impossible, which mortified him exceedingly.[35]

At the time he made these remarks Simpson had become a respectable married man, with a proper English wife.

Although the Simpson of the early 1820s was mean-spirited and deficient in humanity, on the credit side he was prodigiously energetic and dedicated to carrying out his instructions to introduce "system and regularity"[36] into the fur trade. The vast territories encompassed by the Northern Department presented him with a variety of problems. In the interior posts far from competition, his task, uncomplicated but difficult, was to reduce expenses by culling out unneeded personnel and lowering wage rates and by adjusting downward the amounts of European commodities paid the Indians for their furs. Along the borders with the United States, particularly around Rainy Lake and Rainy River, the Company faced competition from American rivals. There the principles of economy that could be introduced into areas of monopoly could not be applied. The policy laid down by the London board was to destroy competition by an active trade with the Indians with prices sufficient to acquire most of the furs, thus compelling opponents to absorb ruinous losses. The most active officers in the fur trade were stationed in competitive areas. After the coalition, the officer in charge of Rainy Lake was Chief Factor John McLoughlin, the ex-North Wester, who was destined to be shifted to the Columbia, where he would achieve renown.[37]

American fur-trade competition in the 1820s was vigorous but not violent, and, particularly after the arrival of American customs officials, both sides generally resisted the temptations to cross the borders, relying instead on attracting the Indians across the boundary line. Simpson even complimented his principal opponent, the American Fur Company, on its good trading manners.

The settlement at Red River presented quite another problem. From the beginning of its existence, fur traders generally had regarded it as a menace, but despite natural and man-made disasters, it had continued to grow. In 1821 the population was less than two thousand, but its numbers were being augmented by the arrival of retired servants and others thrown out of work by the coalition. Among the settlers were several fairly distinct groups. Increasingly predominant in numbers were the Métis, mixed-blood descendants of Indian women and French and British fur traders. There were also many Scots, some survivors of the Selkirk colonization and other ex-Company employees. Also in the early 1820s there were the De Meurons and the Swiss. The De Meurons were mercenary soldiers brought in by Selkirk to defend the colony, and the Swiss were settlers attracted by his agents with expectations of a prosperous life in agriculture. Both of these latter groups were disaffected, but instead of becoming a permanent source of trouble they removed themselves to the United States after a particularly devastating flood in 1826. In the early years of Simpson's governorship the settlers were not yet a serious direct threat to the Company, though the beginnings of a free-trade movement among them was already causing annoyance. Simpson nevertheless viewed the settlement with loathing. This "mass of renegades and malcontents of disruptions" were contemptuous of law and authority and could be kept in order only by a military and police force which would overawe them.[38] Such a force would be a great drain on the Company's resources, and the colony had little to offer the fur trade in return. The governor of the settlement, Andrew Bulger, appointed by the Company's board, was honest and competent; he was also prickly, particularly when inflamed with wine, and was consequently unpopular. Predictably he clashed with the self-important John Clarke, who was in charge of the fur trade of the area. Simpson could see no virtues in the colony or in anyone associated with it. He wrote to McTavish in 1822 that he was "sick & tired" of Red River. "All the black legs of Rupert's Land" seemed to have been drawn to it, and Bulger was "totally unfit for management".[39] There was little that Simpson could do, however, to change the state of affairs. The Governor and Committee did not share his opinion that the settlement was an unrelieved disaster and, even if they had, they did not possess the resources to eliminate the problem.

The other area of Simpson's superintendence, the Pacific Coast, presented a problem of a very different character. Almost simultaneously with the coalition, the region became an area of political significance, involving the rival claims of Russia, the United States, and Great Britain. So far as the Russians and the British were concerned, governmental policy related to the protection of the fur trade of their nationals—in the case of Russia the quasi-governmental Russian American Company, which had been granted a monopoly of the coastal trade north of fifty-five degrees with authority to extend its control southward into any territory not already occupied by any other state. The Russian company was increasingly enmeshed in bureaucracy which stifled initiative. Alexander Baranoff, its chief manager from 1799 to 1818, had envisaged an empire embracing much of the Pacific Coast, but in the 1820s the Russian company was on the defensive. The only remaining symbol of Baranoff's great dreams was Fort Ross, a fur-trading and provision depot at Bodega Bay, California. The Russian trade was beleaguered by the competition of American sea captains, and the tsar's ukase of 1821 prohibiting foreigners from trading or fishing within one hundred Italian miles of the northwest coast north of fifty-one degrees was an attempt to eliminate by governmental decree this competition which the company could not master directly.

The Hudson's Bay Company's position on the Pacific Coast derived almost entirely from the activities of the North West Company, whose traders had established control over the territory between fifty-one and fifty-five degrees. From this district, called New Caledonia, the North Westers had penetrated north into the Babine country and south into the Columbia Basin. But with the exception of Fort George (Astoria), the North Westers had confined their activities to the interior, and thus were not a direct threat to the Russians on the coast.

This was the state of affairs when Simpson became involved in the trading operations of the West Coast. During his first years as governor of the Northern Department, he had concentrated his time and energy on the trade east of the mountains and on the Red River Settlement, but he had acquired considerable information on affairs on the Pacific Coast from the London board and from his own informants. In August 1821 he directed John Lee Lewes and J. D. Cameron to visit the old North West posts and to give him their recommendations. Their report closely corresponded to the findings of James Keith, who had been given a similar mission by the Governor and Committee. They all agreed that one of the principal reasons the district had been unprofitable was the fact that there were too many employees on the rolls, many of whom were worse than useless. If these hangers-on could be eliminated and dependence on imported goods reduced, it was likely that the fur trade from the Fraser Valley north could be made profitable.[40] The future of the Columbia Valley was less promising. Keith thought it unlikely it would make a profit. The beaver of the Columbia was of lower quality than that of the north and was not much in demand in the markets of Canton, where the North West Company had been selling Pacific Coast furs under a permit from the East India Company. The Columbia, however, could not be considered strictly in terms of its own profits and losses. By treaty of 1818 the United States and Britain had agreed to leave unsettled the issue of sovereignty in the territory between California and Russian America. For the duration of the treaty the area was open to occupation by citizens of both countries, and the most likely destination for American settlers and fur traders was the Columbia Valley. It was to the interests of the Hudson's Bay Company to hold on to the fur trade of the Columbia as long as possible, as a means of keeping competitors away from the more lucrative areas to the north. Consequently, the London board decided that the district should be retained if financial losses could be reduced to relatively small proportions.[41]

The decisions necessary to carry out the board's intentions were best arrived at after Simpson's personal observation. Given his passion for travel it might have been expected that he would be eager to undertake the journey across the Rocky Mountains. But by 1823 Simpson was involved in another, personal, crisis. His sexual appetites were easily satisfied by women of the country, but marriage to a non-white woman was repugnant to both his racial feelings and his sense of status. He was now in his thirties, a veteran of many sexual encounters, but still a bachelor. He was drifting into middle age without a spouse who could contribute to the kind of social life appropriate to a governor and provide the legitimate children who would carry on his line. As always in matters affecting his career he turned to his patron Colvile. Should he return to England on leave to seek a wife or should he undertake the journey to the Columbia? The question represented both Simpson's desire for a suitable partner and his zeal to elevate himself in the esteem of Colvile and the other directors, for he was in effect saying that if business necessities required, he would forgo personal considerations. Predictably, Colvile's response was that Simpson should go to the Columbia:

> A wife I fear would be an embarrassment to you until the business gets into a more complete order & until the necessity of those distant journeys is over & if it be delayed one or two years you will be able to accumulate something before the expenses of a family come upon you.[42]

Colvile was never a man to allow sentiment to intrude into practical affairs. The decision of the board was that Simpson should defer his leave, and he acquiesced, emphasizing that he was doing so because his devotion to the Company transcended personal feelings and, with particular emphasis, that in travelling to the Columbia he would be exposing himself to great adversity and danger.[43]

The subsequent journey was one of Simpson's most memorable. His record of it is filled with the exhilaration of a great adventure. As always, he was passionate to set records for speed of transit. In this case speed was not only a source of pride but a necessity. He set out from York Factory in mid-August, stressing to his superiors that he had deferred his departure until he had made all the arrangements for the ensuing fur-trading season. Delay to so late in the season was hazardous; if the party arrived in the Rocky Mountains after winter had closed in and frozen the rivers, it faced many hardships and, possibly, death. With Simpson the risks were minimized by the fact that his two light canoes, the best available, were manned by crews who were the pick of the service, and he was accompanied by Chief Trader James McMillan, who had excellent knowledge of the Columbia district and the routes thereto. But the journey was still a prodigious one, and the journal he kept of it merits a place among the classics of travel and adventure, as well as providing much information on the fur trade, Indian life, and many other subjects.[44] And throughout it all was his emphasis on speed. "I believe there is nothing known in the annals of Rupert's Land traveling equal to our journey so far," he exulted on his arrival at Split Lake, four and a half days after leaving York.[45] This self-congratulation permeated his well-known account of his overtaking John McLoughlin's party.

McLoughlin, who had been transferred from Rainy Lake to the superintendence of the Columbia district, had left York Factory twenty days before Simpson, but Simpson's party overtook them in six weeks. McLoughlin had vowed that Simpson would not

catch him before they reached the Columbia, and he was cha-
grined that he, a veteran, would be confounded by a relative
newcomer who had never before traversed the route. Particularly
galling were the circumstances of their meeting. Simpson came
upon him at seven o'clock in the morning while McLoughlin's
men were still in their encampment. Simpson's comments in his
journal suggested a contrast between his own tireless energy and
the relative ponderousness of McLoughlin's party. Simpson admitted that McLoughlin's canoes were "much laden and weakly
manned", but the note of triumph that he expressed in his journal
undoubtedly was heard by McLoughlin.

This incident was the first harbinger of the alienation that
would make the two men bitter enemies many years later. In
almost every aspect Simpson and McLoughlin were contrasted.
Simpson was a non-practising Anglican, McLoughlin was a con-
vert to Catholicism, with all the zeal that this involved. Simpson
was a Whig, a defender of the established order; McLoughlin
hated an order of society by which power and plenty was held by a
privileged, irresponsible oligarchy. Simpson expected to rule;
McLoughlin was accustomed to independence, and his spirit
would become stronger as he became established in the remote
empire of the Columbia. These contrasts extended to their physical appearance—the cocky bantam versus the proud giant. Simpson recorded McLoughlin's appearance when he came upon him
on the Rivière la Biche:

> He was such a figure as I should not like to meet on a dark Night in
> one of the bye lanes in the neighbourhood of London dressed in
> Clothes that had once been fashionable, but now covered with a
> thousand patches of different Colors, his beard would do honor to
> the chin of a Grizzly Bear, his face and hands evidently Shewing
> that he had not lost much time at the Toilette, loaded with Arms and
> his own herculean dimensions forming a tout ensemble that would
> convey a good idea of the high way men of former days.[46]

Despite these contrasts and the momentary irritation which
Simpson must have provoked, the two proceeded amicably to-

gether toward the Columbia, Simpson noting that he had "slackened our speed in order to give the Dr. an opportunity of keeping up with us."[47]

The issue of speed had more substantial implications than mere pride. Simpson, against the advice of McLoughlin and others, had taken a different route from the usual one, and his experience convinced him that his itinerary was superior, particularly because it reduced the temptation to dawdle offered by the usual route, where parties would be detained for days at a lake waiting for the wind to subside or remain overly long in the comfort of Norway House or Cumberland.[48] This impression of laxity was strengthened by an encounter with John Clarke, who to Simpson had come to epitomize the slackness of the service. Fifteen days out of York Factory, Simpson came upon Clarke at Frog Portage. Clarke had taken thirty-four days to reach that point. The reasons for Clarke's dilatoriness were not entirely clear. After leaving York Factory with his brigade he had pushed on ahead of them in a lightly laden canoe bound for Norway House, where he had remained until the brigade arrived at that point. Simpson assumed that the initial haste and the subsequent inaction related to Clarke's concern to provide comfort for himself and for the "bit of brown" who was his wife. Clarke's absence from his men, Simpson concluded, had been responsible for an accident which resulted in the loss of a substantial quantity of trade goods, and he was determined to make an example of Clarke by charging his private account for the goods.[49]

The encounter with Clarke made Simpson more enthusiastic about the route that avoided Norway House. He later changed his mind about the superiority of this alternate route, but McLoughlin was undoubtedly ruffled by Simpson's manifestations of superiority.

McLoughlin and Simpson proceeded westward amidst scenery among the most spectacular in the world, but Simpson had not come to sightsee. He did occasionally record that some sight was particularly impressive. The view at Jasper House was "beautifully Wild & romantic''; in the heart of the Rockies the scenery was "Wild & Majestic beyond description". His primary concern, however, was with practical matters. The mountains were not only spectacular, but a barrier for travel, and he concerned himself with determining the easiest route across them. And as always he examined each post he visited with a cold eye for waste and slovenliness. When he reached the Columbia the evidence of extravagance fully confirmed reports that the district was the least efficient in the fur trade. At Spokane House he found the people depending on imported food in the midst of plentiful fish and game:

> The good people of Spokane District and I believe the interior of the Columbia generally have since its first establishment shewn an extraordinary predilection for European Provisions without once looking at or considering the enormous price it costs; if they had taken that trouble they would have had little difficulty in discovering that all this time they may be said to have been eating Gold; . . . for these three years past Five and sometimes Six Boats have been annually sent and these principally loaded with Eatables and Drinkables and other Domestic Comforts. Thompson's River and Nez Perces Districts in the same proportions as it has been considered that what was good for the one must be so for the others and to accommodate Gentlemen in this manner about 35 to 40 men (commonly called extra men) have been kept merely to transport the Superfluous property. These extra men alone (valuing the Eatables Drinkables & Luxuries they brought up at nothing) were sufficient to run away with a large share of the Columbia profits.[50]

Simpson arrived at his final destination of Fort George (Astoria) on November 8, 1824, after a journey of eighty-four days, a record twenty days less from Hudson Bay to the Pacific than any previous party. He was confident that he could do even better with the benefit of experience and without the encumbrance of McLoughlin. He had previously remarked that McLoughlin did not have the stamina to keep up the pace, and he thought that by himself he could make the trip in two months.

For the next four months Simpson in concert with McLoughlin

developed measures for the promotion of the Company's fur trade on the Pacific. He had become convinced that the Columbia should be kept not only as a defensive bastion, but as a prize which in itself was worth contesting for; indeed he thought the Pacific Coast could yield double the percentage of profits of any other area. To accomplish this, several actions had to be taken. The district must be weaned from its dependence on imported goods, the number of employees must be drastically reduced, and the competition of rival fur traders must be eliminated. The Russians were no problem; they had enough trouble defending their own territory without disturbing the Hudson's Bay Company. The principal threat came from American sea captains and, prospectively, from American trappers and traders from east of the mountains. The American maritime traders, principally from New England, had dominated the Pacific fur trade. The principal attraction had been sea otters, but intensive hunting had made the trade relatively unprofitable, and the Americans with whom Simpson had to contend were engaged in the provisions trade with California and Russian America and in trade in land furs with the Indians of the northwest coast. Simpson proposed to destroy this competition by making it unprofitable. The Company's posts would outbid the Americans, and their activity would be supplemented by a coastal vessel which would sweep up whatever other furs were available. He would further discourage the Americans by seeking an alliance with the Russians whereby the Russians could get their provisions from the Hudson's Bay Company. Against the menace of American competition from the east, a different strategy would be employed. In the "Snake Country", a vaguely defined territory south of the Columbia, inhabited by the Snakes, Piegans, and Blackfeet, the Company would try to create a "fur desert" by trapping it out. This would lessen the attraction to proceed farther, and he hoped the Indians would do the rest by annihilating any presumptuous American trapping parties. For the leadership of the Snake expedition he picked a man who had been originally denied appointment by the

Hudson's Bay Company because of his association with North West Company violence, Peter Skene Ogden. For the leadership of the rowdy, undisciplined trappers who composed the Company's Snake country expedition, Ogden was eminently qualified. Though he was of medium height, he was massive and strong, and he had the reputation of being able to outbrawl as well as outswear any of his subordinates.[51]

Since the Company depended on the Indians to provide the furs, Simpson paid considerable attention to the attributes of Indians with whom he came in contact. His observations were in the tradition of nineteenth-century whites: Indians were handsome or not in relation to the correspondence with white standards of beauty. The Flatheads, he thought, would have been attractive were it not for their habit of flattening the upper part of the back of the head. Casseno, a chief near Fort Vancouver, was "the most intelligent Indian I have seen and who endeavors to imitate the Whites in every thing." He judged Indian behavior by English standards, and showed little understanding of the trading practices that the Indians had developed in their years of association with the whites. He thought missionaries might be an asset to the Company on the Pacific Coast, provided they were cool and temperate and of a mild conciliatory disposition, since they would encourage the Indians to wear clothes and otherwise imitate Europeans and thereby force the Indians to get more furs.[52]

Some fur traders had established good relations with Indian tribes through marriage by Indian custom, and Simpson himself had an encounter with the custom. One of the most powerful chiefs was Concomely, of the Chinooks, and among the "great men" around him was Calpo. Calpo's greatness was in his status, not in his person. He was dominated by his wife, who had been of great service to the Company on several occasions, having saved its men by warning of an Indian attack. Lady Calpo suggested to Simpson that during his stay he should take her daughter, a young woman of eighteen to twenty, thus cementing good relations between the Company and the tribe, and at the same time affirming Lady Calpo's social position. Simpson indicated that he had "a difficult card to play", being desirous of maintaining good relations with the mother without being involved with the daughter. He did not record the way in which he had resolved his dilemma, but the fact that Lady Calpo was sorry to see him go and the daughter was "grieved" suggests that he put aside his scruples for the sake of good relations with the tribe.[53]

Simpson, during his months on the Columbia, displayed the qualities which made him one of the great businessmen of the nineteenth century. The grand outlines of his policies were developed by the London board, and many of the ideas he adopted were suggested by others. But Simpson had no superior in translating ideas into action, and he energized the Pacific Coast operation into an efficient enterprise which could produce the profits his superiors desired and at the same time discourage competition which might erode these profits and threaten other areas of the Company's monopoly. The achievement was not his alone; an improvement was already taking place before he arrived, and John McLoughlin deserves much of the credit. But that in no way detracts from the accomplishments of Simpson, who demonstrated his mastery as a manager and as an executive.

Simpson was pleased with his experience on the Pacific Coast. He had set out with manifest reluctance. He began his return journey with the determination to come back as soon as possible. He wrote:

> I have the satisfaction to feel that the present visit has been productive of most important advantages to the Honble Coys interests; the Work of reform is not yet however thoroughly effected and to put the whole Machine in full play I find that my presence is absolutely necessary on this side the Mountain one more Winter at least. I can scarcely account for the extraordinary interest I have taken in its affairs, the subject engrosses my attention almost to the exclusion of every other, in fact the business of this side has become my hobby and however painful, dangerous and harassing the duty may be I do not know any circumstance that would give me more real satisfaction and pleasure than the Honble Committee's authority to

take a complete survey of and personally superintend the extension and organization of their Trade on this Coast for 12 to 18 Months and if they do so I undertake to make its commerce more valuable to them than that of either of the Factories in Rupert's Land.[54]

His return to the Columbia, however, was long delayed. He had demonstrated to the London board that he was a vigorous administrator, and they had greater plans for him than the governorship of the Northern Department. He would soon become their representative for all of the fur-trade domain.

CHAPTER IV

The "Little Emperor"

Simpson set out from Fort Vancouver on his return journey to Red River on March 19, 1825. It was performed with the same hard-driving haste that characterized all his trips, made more urgent in this case by the news that a fire had destroyed the post at Norway House and that the Red River Settlement was facing famine with the failure of the corn crop. Against hazard, privation, and fatigue he asserted his invulnerability. Through the snows of the Rocky Mountains he led his exhausted men, wading through icy streams and plodding onward on frozen and lacerated feet. It said much for the discipline of the party as well as the determination of its leader that he could rouse men in this condition to resume a journey at three o'clock in the morning and keep them on the march until ten that night. Simpson's nature required that he continually demonstrate his immunity to physical weakness; his men had no such compulsion, yet there were few instances of grumbling and no evidence of rebellion. On one occasion some Iroquois who accompanied the party became drunk from sampling the contents of a keg of rum. For this he chastised the principal culprit and poured the remainder of the keg into the river, which "no doubt drew lamentations from some of them." But beyond lamentations there was no reaction from the men, and Simpson himself appeared indifferent to hardship. When the horse carrying his baggage fell, damaging his clothing and papers, he remarked that he cared little for the soaking of his own things, "they like their Master are accustomed to such refreshing dips, but I am concerned to find that my papers have got a share; this occasions the loss of a few hours in order to dry them."[1]

By the time the party had reached Edmonton it was obvious to Simpson that most of them were in no condition to continue the furious pace he had set, but he pushed on. Finally at Carlton House he determined on a daring gesture which would dramatize his endurance and his dedication to duty. He would ride, alone if necessary, the remaining distance "through plains infested by the most Warlike and hostile tribes in North America". The distance he calculated to be 800 miles—it was actually approximately 525—and the normal travelling time was twenty days. He would not require anyone to accompany him. The revelation of his plan "induced the people to believe my senses had taken leave of me." Two of his officers and most of the crew took him at his word and decided to recover their health at Carlton, but Chief Trader McMillan, though "worn down to a shadow", and four employees including his personal servant Tom Taylor "would not be denied and entreated permission" to accompany him.[2]

This was high drama indeed, well calculated to create a legend in the fur trade, and he carried it through with a flourish. Fifteen days after departing from Carlton, Simpson, having left his party behind, rode through the dead of night on his faithful charger "Jonathan" up to the gates of Fort Garry, where at midnight he pounded on the gates and "was immediately answered by a most hearty welcome" from the entire garrison. Safe at his destination, he wrote in his journal, "I purpose taking a rest of Eight Days after having performed one of most dangerous and harassing Journeys ever undertaken in the Country through which thank God I have got with no injury or inconvenience worthy of Notice."[3] He had also accomplished his trip in the record of two and a half months. Such a feat was convincing evidence to the men of the fur trade, and to Simpson himself that he was fearless and indestructible.

Simpson tarried at Red River only long enough to recover his health—he had been attacked by a severe intestinal eruption, which put him under a physician's care—and he was soon in motion again. He had to arrange the business for the ensuing year before he took the ship at York Factory for England. After a few days he pushed on to Norway House, in the process of being rebuilt after the disastrous fire, and then on to York, where he convened his council. His journey was made more pleasant by the most tangible evidence of the London board's esteem, an increase in salary to £1200 per year, £200 more than his previous compensation, and in addition a gratuity of £500. He was now certainly financially able to support a wife in the style befitting a person of substance. The economic problems which Colvile had advised him to resolve were now behind him, and he could look forward to further increases from his employers. Conclusive evidence that he had arrived as the dominant figure in the fur trade was provided by the chief factors who at the close of the council delivered to him a memorial effusive in its praise of his performance as governor. His "unremitting exertion", "painful sacrifices", and "masterly arrangements and decisive measures" entitled him, they said, to their "most unqualified approbation".[4] So laudatory were the officers that they might be suspected of sycophantish flattery. Some may have been influenced by such motives, but among the signatories were such crusty characters as Samuel Black, Simon McGillivray, and Colin Robertson, who would not have been inclined to subscribe to opinions which they did not accept.

Simpson left York Factory for England with ample grounds for self-satisfaction. His five years in North America had been characterized by unvarying success in his professional life. His only frustration had been in his desire to stabilize his personal life by marriage to a suitable British mate. He had deferred seeking such a partner for two years, and his sexual needs had continued to be supplied by mixed-blood and Indian women. What his intentions were with regard to matrimony when he finally set sail in 1825 can only be surmised. Two years before he had been anxious to return to seek a wife. Did he return at this time to seek some particular woman? Was it Eleanor Pooler, of whom he spoke so affectionately in his previous correspondence? There is no way of knowing. If he had marriage in mind on his visit to

England, he was disappointed. His relationships with the Poolers remained cordial, but his work in London consumed his attention to an extent that would have been unlikely if he had been in pursuit of his intended. A month after he arrived in England he was apologizing to Richard Pooler for not having visited the family. Business matters had been so pressing that he had not been able to take even a half holiday. He promised to visit the Poolers soon;[5] if he did, it had no lasting consequence for his life.

During the five years Simpson had been away from London the affairs of the Company had undergone a great transformation, in part as a result of his own efforts. The years of conflict had been succeeded by an era of monopoly in which the great amalgamated Company had no serious rival and was able to adjust prices to produce handsome profits for its shareholders and high returns for its officers. In 1825 the capital had been increased to £400,000 from the previous £103,950, but a dividend of ten per cent was nevertheless declared, and from then until the end of Simpson's life, and indeed thereafter, the rate of dividends did not fall below ten per cent, and was frequently much higher. These halcyon days for the proprietors were in bright contrast to the dreary years of struggle with the North West Company, when the Hudson's Bay Company had paid no more than four per cent and for five years had declared no dividends at all.[6] The great change in the Company's fortunes was highly satisfying, but there was always need for reform. One of the conditions of the coalition had been that most of the trade in Canada would be conducted by the agency of McGillivrays, Thain and Company, successors to the agents of the North West Company. The arrangement was never a successful one. One of the partners, Thain, absconded, and the firm collapsed in 1825.

The other source of concern was the Southern Department. Governor William Williams was increasingly becoming an anachronism. He had little ability in business and little understanding of managing men. The council of the Southern Department, in contrast to that of Simpson's, was wracked with dissension, made worse by Simpson's success in transferring his most unruly officers to Williams's jurisdiction. Even had Williams been more effective, a change would probably have been made because of the advantages of centralized as against divided authority. Williams's weakness made reorganization inevitable, and Simpson made certain that the London committee was made aware of his colleague's incompetence. Before he left for England his exchanges with Williams had become hostile and contemptuous, and Simpson had seen to it that all their correspondence in which he appeared to advantage reached London. Williams could not cope with Simpson either in business ability or in guile, and the directors decided that Williams must be removed. While he was in London Simpson was given charge of both the Northern and Southern Departments, as well as the Canadian agency. Though his status was not officially recognized by the board till a year later, from 1826 on he was governor of all the Hudson's Bay Company's territories.

His stay in London also involved Simpson for the first time in diplomacy, though primarily as a source of information rather than as a participant. Just before he had set out for the Columbia, the United States had suggested as a modification of the Anglo-American convention on Oregon that citizens of the United States should not settle north, or British subjects south, of fifty-one degrees. This proposal was intended as a bargaining maneuver to push Britain toward a "compromise" boundary of forty-nine degrees latitude, and was recognized as such, but it reopened active consideration of the problem at the Foreign Office. Canning's administration was prepared to back the Hudson's Bay Company in its legitimate claims, which the Company and the government agreed included control of all the territory north of the Columbia to the border of Russian North America. Simpson became a key figure in the preparation of the British case since he had greater knowledge of the Columbia area than any other man in London. Consequently he was called upon by the Company's governor, John Henry Pelly, and by the Foreign Office for information and advice.

Simpson was convinced that the Yankee settlers would soon appear in the Columbia area. The region was much too fertile and salubrious to be left only to fur traders and Indians. His opinions of Americans had not changed from the time he had fumed at those overbearing officers at the Navy Yard. He was convinced that eventually the United States would force the issue and that it was better to push immediately for a boundary treaty when the Company's bargaining position was at its strongest. This position was adopted by the board, and Simpson drafted a letter to that effect for the signature of Governor Pelly, asking the Foreign Office to press for a boundary which included some of the Snake country in British territory. Simpson was also called upon by the Foreign Office for information to bolster the British case.[7]

The Americans rejected the British proposals and the Oregon issue reverted to a stalemate not to be broken until the 1840s. But Simpson had had a stimulating experience. His first taste of high politics had been exciting, and from his new position of eminence he would be called upon for further consultations by statesmen on issues of great moment. The Simpson who left England for North America at the end of February 1826 was no mere fur-trading administrator but a man of substance who could command notice both in Britain and in Canada. It was symptomatic of this translation into a new life that he would now shift his headquarters from the wilds of Rupert's Land to Montreal, the commercial and financial capital of Lower Canada. During the six years since his first visit, Montreal had lost some of its importance as a fur-trading entrepot as a result of the coalition. The town continued to be the base from which brigades set out for posts in Canada and the Southern Department. Also "express canoes" for Red River departed from Montreal. But the amalgamated Company depended on the Hudson Bay route for most of the supplies for the Northern Department. Despite this shift, however, the prosperity of Montreal had been little affected. The export and import firms and financial houses were enjoying a period of prosperity. The opening of a canal around the Lachine Rapids in 1825 made Montreal more accessible to the western United States, and even though this development coincided with the opening of the Erie Canal which pulled much of the same commerce toward New York, the general mood was optimistic.

Simpson's selection of Montreal as his headquarters involved a variety of considerations. As governor he would be required to travel to England from time to time and Montreal provided easier access to shipping than did York Factory. There were also advantages in cementing good relations with the commercial leadership of the town. From Montreal had come the formidable competition which had beset the Hudson's Bay Company; his presence there might help to avert a future challenge. And, of course, the society of Montreal was a much more suitable environment for a person of his importance than was York Factory.

The place he selected for his headquarters was Lachine, then a village on the outskirts of Montreal. His choice was exquisitely appropriate. Lachine had derived its name from La Salle's time. When he set out on his great journey to explore the western waterways, La Salle had said that he hoped he might reach China, and when he returned after a voyage that did not quite realize this dream, the wits of French Canada called his seigneurie La Chine.[8] What La Salle did achieve was impressive enough, a monopoly of the southwestern fur trade. Perhaps it was significant that the nineteenth-century monopolist should spell Lachine in the style of La Salle's time—La Chine.

There was another, more practical consideration in the selection of Lachine. The warehouses of the Company, originally built by the North Westers, were there, situated on the Lachine Canal, from which canoes departed on their voyages westward.[9]

Residence in Montreal brought Simpson into intimate association with the commercial aristocracy of Montreal, of which he soon became a leading member. These merchants had much in common—they were English and Scottish in a province that was predominantly French, and they believed that the British government had committed a major blunder by including the progressive mercantile city of Montreal in Lower Canada where a backward majority retarded the progressive minority. They had made several efforts to escape. They had appealed to Britain to redraw the boundary so that Montreal would become part of English-speaking Upper Canada, and in 1822 they had petitioned for a union of the two Canadas and the recognition of English as the sole official language. This action eloquently expressed their opinion of the French Canadians, who, predictably, reacted with outrage. In their preoccupation with commercial interests the merchants showed little political finesse. As the North American representative of a firm which could be harmed by hostile Canadian politicians, Simpson was not inclined to follow their example. He sought to make friends and to neutralize enemies. His private opinions, however, emphatically supported the established order. French-Canadian politicians who whipped up the population against the English were treasonable and the government should deal firmly with such rabble-rousers rather than encourage them by its timidity. What Canada needed was strong leadership, not legislative licence. But before resentment erupted into rebellion, Simpson refrained from public expression of such views.

On his return to North America with wider responsibilities he had little time for social activity. Not only did he have to resume his superintendence of the Northern Department but he was now in charge of the Canadian posts and of the Southern Department. He had also to supervise the reorganization of the Company's Canadian supply system resulting from the failure of McGillivrays, Thain and Company. The bankruptcy of this company involved the settlement of claims by some of the ex-North West partners who were now officers of the Hudson's Bay Company. When they asked Simpson to act on their behalf he consented to do so. From this beginning developed a relationship which added further to Simpson's power. Other officers, hearing of his actions on behalf of their associates, asked him to act as their business agent in other matters. They had money to invest from the proceeds of fur-trade profits and many of them lacked the acumen to invest it profitably. Simpson had both the business sense and the access to information necessary for such investments, and when his willingness to act on their behalf was known they eagerly pressed him to be their agent. Until the volume of business became so great as to require a full-time staff, Simpson charged nothing for his services. But he did receive a substantial return in his beneficiaries' feelings of indebtedness. They came to rely on him not only in business matters but in such family concerns as the education of their children. He became in effect a father figure.[10] Probably his motivation was partly philanthropic; certainly it was at least partly hard-headed self-interest, a means of ensuring the loyalty of his subordinates.

Simpson did not tarry long in Montreal. He was soon in motion again. His penchant for fatigue-defying travel could now be indulged over the whole extent of British North America. During his governorship there were only three years in which he did not undertake a gruelling journey, always at a frantic pace, and in each of these three years the reason was that he was not in North America.[11] His movements in 1826 were typical of the manner in which he drove himself. After his arrival in New York, he travelled to Montreal, inspected some of the Canadian posts, and then set out for Red River, where he spent twelve days at the beginning of June. From Red River he proceeded to Norway House to preside over the council of the Northern Department, and from there travelled to York Factory to confer with John George McTavish on supply arrangements. He was back in Lachine in October, after a journey which included inspection of more of the Canadian posts. Such a regimen must have been taxing to even the strongest constitution, and the London board felt it necessary to warn him to slow down. Governor Pelly wrote him:

> Your friends in the Committee are not quite satisfied with your proceedings, as they consider that you run more risks and exert yourself more than is absolutely necessary for the service, allow me therefore to recommend you to take more care of your health and not expose yourself unnecessarily; on this subject you may shortly

expect a jobation from your sincere friend the Deputy Governor [Colvile].[12]

This gentle chastisement had no effect on Simpson. His compulsion to travel was undiminished. He justified his constant peregrinations as the only means by which he could keep information on the efficiency of the various posts and remind the men in charge that their work was subject to scrutiny at any time. These explanations were undoubtedly sincere, but the zest with which he undertook his feats of endurance nourished his physical and emotional well-being. In a moment of candor he once asserted that "it is strange that all my ailments vanish as soon as I seat myself in a canoe."[13]

During the 1820s Simpson's illnesses were minor and infrequent, occurring not when he was travelling but when he was at rest. In 1821 at York and again in 1822 at Norway House he had suffered from a sore throat, diagnosed by the amateur physicians of the fur trade as the "quinsy". The prescription for its treatment by a clerk at Norway House nearly killed him. The young man recommended hartshorn and immediately pulled down a bottle which he thought contained this medicine and applied the contents to Simpson's throat and proceeded vigorously to rub it in. Colin Robertson, who was in charge of the post and observed these ministrations, noted that during the process Simpson frequently exclaimed, "It is D . . . d hot." The clerk then poured the solution on a piece of flannel and wrapped it round Simpson's throat. Someone then chanced to note that the liquid was not hartshorn but *aqua fortis* (nitric acid). Simpson pulled the flannel from his neck and found it charred. He, however, survived a treatment which was worse than the disease. Robertson happily reported that Simpson "was completely recovered when he left". Simpson's account of his experience was a model of restraint: "I was detained at Norway House 14 days by quinsey, which nearly proved fatal, & experienced much attention from Mr. Robertson."[14] The other occasion on which he was confined to bed was brought on by sheer exhaustion after he dashed to the gates of Fort Garry at the end of his record journey to and from the Pacific in 1824–25.

This urge to be in movement, to undertake harrowing journeys, never left Simpson, but in the 1820s he manifested it with great intensity. His return to the Columbia in 1828 could be justified on a variety of bases—need for consultations with McLoughlin on business arrangements including the elimination of American competition, reconnoitering of possible new routes east to west, and others. But the way in which he drove himself and his men cannot be explained by such considerations. After concluding a council meeting at York Factory on July 11, 1828, he departed on Saturday, July 12, at one o'clock in the morning. The party proceeded in two canoes. Simpson's canoe was the finest that craftsmanship could produce. As described by one trader, its beauty of line was unmatched, its bow, "a magnificent curve of bark gaudily but tastefully painted that would have made a Roman rostrum of old hide its diminished head." The paddles were red with vermilion and were perfectly matched.[15] The two canoes, as always, were manned by the best canoemen in North America, Canadian voyageurs, who were not only virtuosos in their profession but could enliven the voyage with spirited renderings of favorite chansons. In the other canoe were Dr. Richard Hamlyn, a physician, and Chief Trader Alexander McDonald, both of whom had been assigned to the Columbia district. Simpson's schedule called for each day's journey to begin precisely at two in the morning. Breakfast was usually at eight, and dinner at one in the afternoon, involving only a few minutes' rest during which the men swallowed a mouthful of pemmican while Simpson had a glass of wine and some cold cuts, sharing his repast with either Hamlyn or McDonald. With these privileges, however, these two gentlemen also had a responsibility—they had to alternate each night in watching the time to ensure that the party would start exactly at two o'clock.[16]

One passenger unmentioned in Simpson's official correspondence was Margaret Taylor, the mixed-blood daughter of a sloop master at York, and the sister of Simpson's personal servant Tom Taylor. Precisely when Margaret became Simpson's mistress cannot be determined, but she had borne him a son in the spring of 1827, and he had assumed a responsibility for her which would warrant her being described as a wife according to the custom of the country. When he left her at York during her pregnancy he had seen to it that she had special rations, and he provided financial aid to her widowed mother.[17]

In previous journeys Simpson had left his woman at York, but he decided on this occasion to take Margaret with him. It was a testament both to his need for her companionship and to his insensitivity to the ordeal he was imposing upon her. During the first part of the trip Margaret was so fatigued that Simpson considered leaving her at a post in the Athabaska country, but she recovered sufficiently to continue, and her presence gave him not only sexual satisfaction but a relief from the company of Hamlyn and McDonald, whom he found to be bores. "The commodity has been a great consolation to me," he wrote McTavish from Stuart's Lake in September.[18]

Margaret's presence was an additional comfort for Simpson on a journey which though taxing, especially for the men who had to do the work, was not austere. Before he set out on his 1828 journey he had acquired the services of a piper, a young Scot named Colin Fraser, who had been selected for the governor by Simpson's father. His bagpipe melodies were not so well adapted to the tempo of the paddlers as the men's own boat songs, and he was sometimes so exhausted that he could not blow the pipes in any case. But he added a flair to the governor's retinue, and was an impressive addition to the ceremonial arrival at a post so dear to Simpson's heart. McDonald described the approach to Norway House:

> As we waft along under easy sail, the men with a clean change and mounting new feathers, the Highland bagpipes in the Governor's canoe, was echoed by the bugle in mine; then these were laid aside,

on nearer approach to port, to give free scope to the vocal organs of about eighteen Canadians [French Canadians] to chant one of those voyageur airs peculiar to them, and always so perfectly rendered. Our entry to Jack River House [Norway House] about seven p.m., was certainly more imposing than hitherto seen in this part of the Indian Country. Immediately on landing, His Excellency was preceded by the piper from the water to the Fort, while we were received with all welcome by Messrs. Chief Trader McLeod and Dease, Mr. Robert Clouston, and a whole host of ladies.[19]

This was the standard scenario for Simpson's arrival at a post, his form of the royal entry. McDonald thought that the ceremony was designed to impress the Indians. It almost certainly had that effect, but it also stressed the importance of the dignitary who, though not an emperor, as some of his admirers and detractors were beginning to call him, was certainly a lofty personage.

Simpson's love of status and its perquisites was becoming more apparent, but this sweet wine did not lull him from his sense of duty. After the ceremonies, when other members of his party were enjoying the social life of the fort, he was working long into the evening dictating dispatches. He would always be a man of business; and his second trip to the West most emphatically had business objectives. During his 1824—25 tour he had not been able to visit the territory of New Caledonia, which he and other officers expected to be the richest fur preserve on the Pacific Coast, protected from American competition by vigorous Company activity in the Columbia Basin and in particular in the Snake country. And he desired personally to inspect the Fraser River as a possible route from New Caledonia to the coast.

In the years before the coalition New Caledonia had been the Siberia of the fur trade, a place of exile for unwanted personnel, and in the early years of his governorship Simpson had sent officers to that district who were incompetent or obnoxious. The district's reputation was not primarily related to the severity of its climate, which was relatively mild in comparison with other areas of the fur trade. Rather, it derived from the scarcity of food which the area could provide. One post, McLeod's Lake, Simpson described as "the most wretched place in the Indian Country". Its principal staple was dried salmon, which was never available in large quantities and sometimes not at all. When Simpson visited the post, he found its occupants near starvation. They had subsisted on berries for several weeks, and "were so pale and emaciated that it was with difficulty I recognized them." Conditions at other posts were somewhat better but, as Simpson put it, "were anything but enviable."[20]

Besides the paucity of food, the New Caledonia district was plagued with tense relations between Indians and whites, which occasionally erupted in violence. Simpson's interpretations of the causes of hostility essentially expressed the stereotypes of the fur trader—Indians were thieving and treacherous—and his prescription was the standard one. The guilty must be punished, and murderers must suffer death. Unless the Company responded in this way, he was convinced, the Indians would become more insolent and the Company's position would become untenable. His view of the trading relationship was essentially one-sided. He had little understanding of the effect on Indian societies of the economic involvement with white men or of the conflicts between suppliers and middle-men which caused breaches of the peace on the Pacific slope. But despite tensions, murders were infrequent, and the Company's reactions to them were usually specific rather than retaliatory. Its officers demanded the punishment of the culprit rather than striking at the entire community. On some occasions the alleged murderer was killed by his own people, and sometimes by a Company employee. This specificity helped to avoid outbreaks of war between the Company and the Indians, in contrast to the upheavals in American territory.

Simpson was not in New Caledonia to study Indians or to view scenery. The district was significant as a source of revenue and at the time of his visit was producing a net profit of about £9,000, which he anticipated might be increased by expansion into more remote areas.[21] This was substantial enough to warrant its retention. Simpson hoped to improve the financial rewards further by finding a better route to supply the district. Transport from the lower Columbia River involved transshipments by land, and there was additionally the uncertainty as to the boundary which would replace the open occupancy agreement. If the Fraser River was navigable it would be a better route of communication on both grounds. Reports from those who had travelled on the Fraser were not encouraging, but Simpson determined to find out for himself. The experience was nearly the end of Simpson. The upper Fraser was one long succession of rapids and whirlpools. Even with the expert boatman at Simpson's disposal, his craft on several occasions was in danger of foundering. Even the Iroquois bowsman, who was "nearly amphibious", was terrified by the experience. Simpson and his party made it down the raging river but by no definition could it be described as navigable. Any thought of a Fraser River route was discarded, [22] but Simpson had been involved in another exploit which had tried his courage. The necessity to test himself was compelling. He would not avoid the challenge by assigning it to a subordinate.

The rest of the journey to Fort Vancouver was relatively uneventful, though there was some unfounded concern about being attacked by Indians. The party reached Fort Vancouver on the night of October 25, 1828, and was welcomed by Chief Factor John McLoughlin. Thus ended, wrote Simpson, "the longest Voyage ever attempted in North America in one Season, about 7000 miles".[23] He had set another record.

Simpson remained at Fort Vancouver for exactly five months, apparently without any serious conflicts with McLoughlin. This long period of amity was remarkable since the two were in almost every respect incompatible. They shared a dedication to the welfare of the Company which they served and which served them as the means to their self-realization. But Simpson expected conformity to policies as laid down by him, while McLoughlin had become accustomed to an environment in which he used his own judgment. If their approach to trading policy had been the same a clash might have been avoided, but McLoughlin's and

Simpson's perspectives were quite different. McLoughlin made decisions as a businessman; his object was maximum profits. When competition appeared he met it in ways consistent with that end. Usually he followed Company policy in undercutting the opposition in order to destroy it, but on occasion he deviated from that line. In 1829, after Simpson's departure, he bought off an American sea captain by purchasing his goods at high prices, and in the 1830s he made an agreement with Nathaniel J. Wyeth, an American fur trader, by which the Company agreed not to compete with him in a section of the Snake country and Wyeth promised not to encroach on the remainder of the territory. Such actions could be defended on the bases of expediency, but they were violations of Company policy, which Simpson was determined to enforce. To Simpson and the London board the Columbia district was a zone of battle with the Americans. Competition must be destroyed even at the price of substantial losses for the Company. If the Americans were able to make profits, their success would attract others, and the Company's campaign to hold at least the territory north of the Columbia River might be lost. Such politico-economic considerations were of no consequence to McLoughlin, and his insistence on following his own judgment was certain to bring him into conflict with Simpson.

During Simpson's sojourn with McLoughlin in 1828–29 this incompatibility was not apparent, and no negative comments about McLoughlin appeared in Simpson's correspondence. What did they talk about during the long winter evenings? Almost certainly not politics, for they were poles apart. McLoughlin's sympathies were with the downtrodden of the world, in which category he placed the French Canadians and those who had supported the lost cause of Bonnie Prince Charlie. Simpson had no patience with such notions, which were subversive not only of established authority but of the progress of mankind. Perhaps the apparent placidity of their relationship resulted from Simpson's applying the advice he had given to John George McTavish in the art of managing men: "Let me entreat that you keep your temper and do not allow yourself [to] be drawn into altercation with any of those who may be there; you can gain neither honour nor glory by quarrelling with them but can twist them round your finger by setting about it properly."[24] McLoughlin, however, was not twistable; the visit of 1828—29 would be the last in which Simpson maintained an amicable relationship with this stubborn, irascible man.

During the sojourn at Fort Vancouver, Margaret again became pregnant, but when Simpson left the Columbia area she accompanied him on another of his speedy journeys. The party departed at the end of March 1829 and two months later was back at Fort Garry. The trip was a particularly arduous one. Over the Rockies they had to plod through the deep snows on showshoes, and a note of self-doubt began to creep into Simpson's descriptions of his exploits. For the first time he experienced fatigue that hung on; he had lost the resiliency in which he took such pride. Perhaps age was taking its toll, perhaps he was beset by some ailment. He determined that he must go back to England "for the benefit of Medical advice".[25] In this preoccupation with his loss of energy Simpson expressed no concern for Margaret's condition, though he did let drop a sentimental reference to her as "my fair one", a rare departure from the demeaning references he usually used with regard to his mixed-blood sexual partners. Perhaps there was some feeling of human affection; he clearly had a sense of responsibility, for at Bas de la Rivière on Lake Winnipeg he left Margaret in the care of Chief Factor John Stuart, whose country wife was her sister Mary. There at the end of August Margaret gave birth to a son, later named John McKenzie Simpson.[26] At the time of the child's birth Simpson was in Lachine, preparing for a voyage to England which would dramatically change the course of his life and that of Margaret.

His visit to England, it soon transpired, involved affairs of the heart but not in the medical sense he had suggested to the London board. Simpson had decided that he would seek a wife appropriate to his station. When he made this decision cannot be determined, but he almost certainly had that intention when he left

Margaret at Bas de la Rivière. But also almost certainly he had no specific woman in mind as his prospective mate. During his long absence from England he had not been able, even had he been so inclined, to pursue a suit.

The Simpson who landed in Liverpool bore little resemblance to the man who had departed from there four years before. He was no older than forty-two, but he was dominated by the feeling that his best years were behind him. The fatigue of which he had complained had not lifted during his sea voyage, and he arrived in London a semi-invalid. For days on end he was confined to his room, so weak that he was unable to walk across the room. He could not concentrate. He was suffering, he thought, from a "determination of blood to the head". The debility was not constant; on occasion he felt a renewed surge of energy, but then the acute lassitude would return. His physicians could not diagnose his condition, but his vulnerability to seizures was increased by the extreme tension under which he labored and by his constant apprehension about his health. He felt that he had become old, he knew he was mortal, and these thoughts drained him emotionally. The copious bleedings and leechings which were applied as remedies were at least in part his own idea, as is indicated by the testimony of the physician who attended him at Red River in 1830:

> I have only to remind you, of your state of health when you came out in 1830, labouring under constant apprehension of Apoplexy, which had preyed on your mind to such a degree as to make you at times quite miserable, how often on these occasions when fearing an attack have you sent for me to bleed you, your arm bared up and ready for the operation a more subservient man would doubtless have met your wishes, even against his own Judgment, and probably brought you to the brink if not the grave itself, I declined bleeding being of opinion depletion had been carried too far already. I knew the struggle would be severe and the success doubtful, but depended greatly on your naturally good constitution.[27]

The physician's reservations about bleedings and leechings reflected a basic division in the medical profession as to the efficacy of the practice. However, his opinion that at least in Simpson's case this practice was dangerous was supported by another doctor who treated Simpson a little over a decade later. This practitioner in the early 1840s, noting Simpson's history of "syncope" or fainting, found his pulse unusually slow and irregular and recommended against the use of a lancet in the treatment of any disease with which Simpson might be attacked.[28]

Whether the bleeding debilitated him or not, Simpson would not allow himself to become bed-fast. He fought this mysterious ailment on this as on subsequent occasions and did not allow it to dominate him. He continued, so far as he was able, to deal with Company business and at times visited the headquarters to discuss the various problems of the fur trade. And, remarkably, he continued to think about finding a suitable wife.

While Simpson wrestled with his problems and his prospects John George McTavish arrived in England on furlough. In the nine years since they had met, the two had become close friends. With McTavish, Simpson could drop his governor's mask and all pretences and enjoy a relaxed, open relationship which he could not risk with other men.[29] Like Simpson, McTavish had decided that he must seek marriage with a proper mate rather than continuing his liaisons with mixed-blood and Indian women. McTavish's attitudes toward women of the country were similar to Simpson's. He acknowledged a degree of responsibility for their "placement" when he tired of them, but they were part of an irregular way of life and no thought of marriage to any of them could be entertained. When he had reached the stage where he would settle down to a stable, decorous existence, it would be a woman of his own class and color. McTavish had had at least two country wives. The first had borne him two children, both of whom died, reputedly smothered by their mother. Infanticide by women who were the chattels of their fur-trade mates usually occurred when the husband was on furlough in England, an indication perhaps of their fears that he would return with a white wife.[30] McTavish subsequently rejected this woman, with no provision for her security, and about 1812 took another mixed-blood mate, Nancy McKenzie, with whom he was living when he set out for his furlough in 1829. Nancy bore McTavish at least six daughters and the longevity of their association may have given her a sense of security, reinforced by the fact that he took one of their young daughters with him to England. But, like Simpson, McTavish before his departure was contemplating leaving his mate and finding a British wife.[31]

Years in the wilds of North America had not prepared these two middle-aged men for the rituals of courtship as prescribed by British society. They could not appropriate a proper English woman as they did "a woman of the country". The approach must be made with finesse. Simpson wrote McTavish:

> I see you are something like myself, shy with the fair, we should not be so much with the Browns. You have no good excuse & therefore must muster courage, "a faint heart never won a fair Lady."[32]

During his first few months in England, beset by illness, Simpson made no progress in his search for a wife. In semi-serious jest he asked McTavish early in December to "let me know if you have any fair cousin likely to suit an invalid like me."[33] McTavish's assistance proved unnecessary, for Simpson found a cousin of his own, Frances, daughter of his uncle Geddes, who had been transformed in the years since he had first known her from a small child into a beautiful young woman of almost eighteen. Simpson's announcement to McTavish of his intention to marry Frances was in the spirit of bawdy badinage that characterized their intimate correspondence:

> Would you believe it? I am in love—how I may get rid of it tis probable I may know tonight but I trust in the proper legitimate way. Do my dear Fellow muster courage and attack some fair one, if Settlements are talked of say . . . , "I shall settle my B——ks in her."[34]

This rather strange declaration was penned at the end of a letter indicating Simpson's itinerary during the next few weeks, scarcely a manifestation of a consuming ardor. The day after he asked for the hand of his intended, Simpson planned to start on a trip to Scotland, where he expected to make his headquarters at his uncle Duncan's estate, Bellevue, stopping along the way at Scarborough, England, to visit Edward Ellice, who was now not only an influential member of the Company's board but a power in the Whig party.[35] Simpson's mind rarely strayed for long from his career, and Ellice's friendship was an important asset.

The interview with Frances's parents was in the tradition of substantial families where the security of the wife was considered to be far more important than love. Simpson's description of it sounds more like a business transaction than a love match: "The preliminary arrangements are adjusted but cannot be brought to a close till my return from America in the autumn of this year."[36]

With his marital prospects substantially settled Simpson set out for a month's visit to the scenes of his boyhood. He had little opportunity to enjoy them. On his arrival at Bellevue he was again stricken with the enervating malady which required him to spend long hours in bed. His strength was gone and for several days he was so weak that he thought he was near death.[37] But then the pall lifted, and he felt sufficiently restored to return to London.[38]

During his invalidism in Scotland, Simpson had reviewed the understanding that he had reached with Frances and her family and had concluded that the marriage should not be delayed. On his return to London, he pressed the parents to accept an immediate ceremony, and they finally consented. With Frances, he noted, he had little difficulty, as she was as anxious to get married as he was.[39]

Simpson and Frances were married in Bromley St. Leonard Church, Middlesex, on February 24, 1830.[40] Two days earlier, McTavish had been wed in Edinburgh to Catherine Turner, to whom he had proposed after being rejected by another young woman approximately a month before, and he hastened south with his new bride to join the Simpsons on the voyage to Canada by way of New York.

In selecting Frances as a wife, Simpson manifested a not-uncommon middle-aged man's desire for a renewal of his youth. She was a beautiful girl, he could take pride in her being his, and her upbringing made her a suitable hostess to preside at the social functions of the governor at Lachine. But the sea-change from England to North America was beyond Frances's physical and spiritual resources. She had lived her life in the protected environment of her parents' home, and she was now married to an older man in whose experience women had been commodities for his enjoyment. He might treat his Frances as a valued possession for him to cherish and for others to admire, but he could not brook from her any departures from the role he had assigned her. She would find him a tyrant who expected absolute conformity to his ways. Even by the standards of nineteenth-century family life Simpson was an extremist in the assertion of his authority in the family. Ten years after he and Frances were married, Letitia, the wife of Chief Factor James Hargrave of York Factory, made the first of her waspish observations on Frances's subjugation. Letitia had taken a walk with Frances's mother at Gravesend, where the Hargraves were awaiting a ship for North America, and Mrs. Geddes Simpson had let flow her unhappiness at George Simpson's treatment of her daughter. He was "very fashious", said Mrs. Simpson. Frances could not spend a sixpence without his permission, and she was not allowed to express an opinion or make any decisions without his approval.[41] Frances was a deeply religious woman; her husband was guided by neither religious forms nor precepts. An incident witnessed by Letitia illustrated Frances's frustrations. Simpson refused to say grace at the family table, but on social occasions a clergyman was usually present who could be called upon. At one such dinner, however, there was no clergyman and a particularly devout couple were among the guests. Frances, not daring to confront her husband directly, asked her brother to remind Simpson to assume the responsibility, which he did in a way which added to her embarrassment. After years of indifference, he could not think of an appropriate blessing, but finally blurted out, "Lord have mercy on what is now before us." Simpson apparently felt that he had performed adequately; his wife, Letitia reported, did not recover for the rest of the night.[42]

Aside from her basic incompatibility with her husband, Frances was too fragile to withstand the life into which she now entered. On the voyage to New York she suffered from a case of seasickness so violent that Simpson would have left her in Ireland if stormy seas had not prevented it. Seasickness, as many can attest, can be experienced by people in robust health, but the frailty she evidenced on the voyage was to be her most prominent characteristic throughout her married life. For such a woman a canoe voyage from Montreal to Red River might have been considered unwise, but Simpson made the decision to take her on tour apparently without any thought of its possible ill effect on her. It can be said to his credit that he made special efforts to ensure that this trip would be as comfortable as possible for her and her companion Mrs. McTavish. But even at best the trip was an exhausting one. Crossing about forty portages between Montreal and Georgian Bay while dressed in the voluminous women's clothes of nineteenth-century England was certainly not pleasurable, even though two men were assigned to help them across, and a six-hour trip through the formidable rapids of the aptly named Maline River must have been a thrill to the point of terror—the trip today requires much longer. Also Simpson made little concession to the two women in the schedule of travel. They would be on their way at three or four in the morning, sometimes earlier, and they encamped as early as seven and as late as midnight. Yet Frances seems to have been little worse for the experience and indeed to have enjoyed it. The progress from post to post was in the nature of a royal procession, with the officers outdoing themselves in efforts to do honor to the governor and his new wife, and to show what gentility they were capable of mustering. The party (minus Mr. and Mrs. McTavish, who branched off to Moose Factory) arrived at Red River, the metropolis of the interior fur trade, on June 6, 1830, and Frances received another warm welcome. "The reception I here met with," she wrote in her diary, "convinced me that if the Inhabitants of this remote Region were plain & homely in their manners, they did not want for kindness of heart, and the desire of making every thing appear favorable, and pleasing, to the eye & mind of a Stranger."[43] The woman who appears in the diary is a generally agreeable personality, deferential to her husband "Mr. Simpson's" wishes. But she evidenced a streak of acidity like that of her husband when she referred to Colin Robertson—perhaps the opinions expressed reflected her husband's influence since her comments were particularly testy with regard to Simpson's favorite *bêtes noires,* Colin Robertson and John Clarke. Robertson, she wrote, "considers himself the Chesterfield of Rupert's Land, and therefore surpassing all others in elegant manners and polite conversation," but only succeeded in making himself "quite ridiculous and a perfect annoyance".[44] Clarke was "pompous in his manner, seems to study every word he utters, and in short affect the fine Gentleman; apparently considering himself far superior in refinement of taste & manners to his neighbours."[45]

With these exceptions, Frances's comments on the men of the fur trade were benevolent, albeit tinged with an assumption of her social superiority. With regard to Indian and mixed-blood women, however, and in particular to the institution of the "country wife", Frances Simpson's judgments were not so tolerant. She probably knew little or nothing of her husband's previous associations. She undoubtedly had no desire to inquire and Simpson was at pains to shield her from the unpleasantness of encountering his progeny. But an incident involving Mrs. McTavish at Lachine highlighted the gulf between "proper" Englishwomen and the products of interracial sex. As recounted ten years later by Letitia Hargrave, who shared Frances's prejudices, McTavish's daughter Mary arrived unexpectedly after dinner, and McTavish introduced her to his wife "who got stupid, but shook hands with the Miss who was very pretty & mighty impudent.'' Mrs. McTavish then broke into tears and rushed off to her room. Mrs. Simpson followed to commiserate with her and "found her in a violent fit of crying."[46]

Mrs. Simpson, Letitia reported, "had no idea that she had more encumbrances than Mrs. Mactavish, altho' she did say that she was always terrified to lok about her in case of seeing something disagreeable."[47] Simpson's care for the sensitivities of his wife was not matched by delicacy in his treatment of Margaret Taylor or of his mixed-blood offspring. Simpson took the responsibility of informing both McTavish's ex-mate and Peggy Taylor of their severance and for making arrangements for finding them other partners. The summary way in which McTavish had rejected his country wife of so many years had evoked a great deal of hostile comment. Donald McKenzie, Nancy's uncle, was outraged; he had expected McKenzie to formalize a marriage with his niece.[48] Simpson was shielded by his position from public expression of censure, but undoubtedly beneath the effusive expressions of delight at his new marriage and his good fortune in selecting such a beautiful and gracious bride there was an undercurrent as sour as that which surfaced with McTavish.

There was little evident sentiment in Simpson's proceedings for the disposal of his "old concern" and that of McTavish. Peggy and Nancy each continued to receive £30 per year for the support of themselves and their children. This amount was committed until they were "disposed of".[49] One concession to humaneness in this commodity transfer was Simpson's promise to Nancy McKenzie that she would not be forced against her wishes to take another mate. But in January 1831 Simpson found a man who was willing to take Nancy for a suitable dowry, Pierre le Blanc, one of the Company's employees at Red River. Simpson jubilantly wrote McTavish, "I have performed a very important operation by nailing Leblanc for your old woman." Le Blanc promised to marry Nancy within three months, if she was willing, for a dowry of £200 and pay her £200 in the event of his non-fulfillment of the contract.[50] Le Blanc was given a week off to woo the intended, and Nancy decided to accept an arrangement which gave her some degree of security. They were married by a priest at Red River, and Nancy passed out of McTavish's and Simpson's purview. Shortly thereafter Simpson made a similar arrangement for the disposal of Peggy Taylor, who was married to another Company employee, Amable Hogue, in March, with Le Blanc among the witnesses. "The Govrs little tit bit Peggy Taylor is . . . Married to Amable Hogue," wrote a Company officer, "what a downfall is here, particularly in the latter from a Governess to Sow."[51] The comment was a particularly heartless expression of a general reaction.

Simpson's treatment of his mixed-blood mates was not unusually harsh by comparison with others in the fur-trade society, though many of his contemporaries had a more elevated and humane standard. For the children of his illegitimate unions he accepted a degree of responsibility. His closest association was with his daughter Maria, born in Scotland.[52] The Scottish Maria married Donald McTavish and settled down in Ontario, where they lived on a farm near Haldimand. Her relationship with her father was not intimate, but he visited her occasionally, and she relied upon him for financial advice, particularly after her husband's death in 1849, and he provided her with some monetary assistance in her efforts as a widow to maintain herself and her five children.[53] His association with his children of the country, however, was of a different nature, perhaps because they were of mixed blood, perhaps because they did not exhibit the characteristics he valued in his offspring. He provided them with an elementary education sufficient for them to read and write, and he placed his male offspring in jobs in the fur trade but he gave them no special favors thereafter, making it clear that their success or failure depended on their own performance. His expectations for his mixed-blood sons were not high, and they justified his expectations. Of the three, most is known of George, Junior, son of Margaret Taylor. Simpson sent young George out to Oahu to work in the Company's agency, with injunctions to live a life of rectitude and to shun the temptations of vice and slothfulness, and in particular to avoid contact with such "common people" as the natives and mixed-bloods. George made a feeble effort to resist temptation. In a letter to his father in August 1842 he made brave avowals of his determination to be worthy of the paternal trust. He had kept aloof from bad company, he said, and he did not partake of spirituous liquor, except an occasional glass of wine for dinner.[54] But the young man soon fell from grace; it would have been surprising if he had not done so in the environment of Honolulu in the 1840s, particularly with the restrictions which Simpson sought to impose on the youth's associations. In a little over a year after his expression of noble purpose, George wrote that he was unhappy in Honolulu. He had few intimate acquaintances among the white population, and the mixed-bloods were "radicals" whom he feared would lead him astray to "infamous purposes". He appealed to his father to move him to San Francisco, where W. G. Rae was establishing an agency.[55] A change from Honolulu to San Francisco might be of doubtful wisdom for a young man from the wilds of North America seeking to preserve his virtue. The appeal, however, evoked no response, and Simpson received reports, presumably from the officers of the agency, that his son had fallen into dissolute ways. The nature of his waywardness can only be surmised—presumably it involved drinking and women. But the father's response was clear and emphatic. Unless George gave up his loose living, he would be cast out, with no hope of assistance from his father. Such a draconian edict was not uncommon in nineteenth-century families, but Simpson's manner of communicating it evinced little sensitivity. Instead of writing to his son directly, he incorporated his warning in an official letter to George's superior, George T. Allan, with instructions to read it to the youth. The son was understandably resentful, yet he could not express himself frankly for fear of completing the breach with his father, on whose favor he depended for his employment. Instead he avowed again to try to be good; his irritation was masked in a request that

Simpson communicate with him directly when he wished to chastise him.[56]

In 1847 George was transferred to a post in the Flat Head country, where his rectitude was not so severely taxed, and was thereafter assigned to other posts in the Columbia area. There he apparently performed competently in subordinate positions requiring little responsibility. His father had clearly never had a high opinion of George's capabilities. On one occasion he asked the son whether he had had help in the composition of his letters, since they were written in comprehensible, though undistinguished, English. George responded that he had no help, and would ask for none since "I have more pride for myself than to let any person suspect that I was in disgrace."[57] The last communication extant from George to his father, in 1850, contained a note of irony which Sir George would not have recognized. George wrote that his mother was in poor circumstances and that it was his obligation as a dutiful son to help her: "She shall not want as long as I have the means."[58]

There is no known correspondence from the other two sons. John showed no great aptitude or zeal for the fur-trade business, and James, the most reliable of the three, rose to the charge of a small post at Frog Lake, where he was stationed at the time of the Rebellion of 1885.[59]

As a properly married man, Simpson drastically altered his way of life, and the repercussions were felt throughout the fur trade. The rude accommodations at Red River which were good enough for his "bachelor" days were no longer acceptable now that he had a genteel English wife. He had a substantial stone house built for his lady and furnished it with such evidences of good taste as a pianoforte, and he bought a magnificent carriole with which to transport his wife.[60] The corollary of this new life as a cultivated, monogamous gentleman was a hardening of his views on the status of mixed-blood wives. He had never accorded such women the deference he displayed to Englishwomen, but before the arrival of Frances, the "bits of copper" had been admitted with their husbands into Simpson's society. Now he made it clear that their presence was no longer acceptable, and he expected them to be kept out of the sight of his wife and of other white women. He advised McTavish to pursue a similar line:

> I . . . understand that the other Ladies at Moose are violent and indignant at being kept at such a distance, likewise their husbands . . . . The greater distance at which they are kept the better.[61]

The only contact Frances Simpson had with Indian and mixed-blood women, therefore, was in the role of mistress to servant. This was her husband's decision, but it also accorded with her own prejudices, for she shared his opinions on the necessity of maintaining a social distance from non-white women. Her comments on Nancy McKenzie, as reported by Letitia Hargrave, exuded a sense of superiority—Nancy, she said, was "a complete savage".[62] In this judgment she reflected the prejudices—and the fears—of other white women. The availability of women of another race posed a threat to the security of the white wife and her family, which must be dealt with by strong measures of proscription.

The arrival of a white wife of the Hudson's Bay governor had considerable effect on the social and moral patterns of the "Indian country". Liaisons with women of mixed blood, which had previously been accepted as honorable, now were regarded as immoral, and men of the fur trade who sought advancement were now well advised not to enter marriages *à la façon du pays*.[63]

At Red River the social barriers which the Simpsons maintained severely restricted their circle of acquaintances. Consequently it was not surprising that both Simpsons felt a sense of dreary isolation in this frontier community. Even if she had been robust physically, Frances would have been unhappy in such an environment. As Simpson wrote McTavish, "She has no Society, no Friend, no Relative here but myself, she cannot move wt me on my different Journeys and I cannot leave her in the hands of Strangers . . . some of them very unfeeling."[64]

This judgment of Red River society reflected Simpson's view of what was best for Frances; she had the privilege only of concurrence with his views. She certainly agreed wholeheartedly with his exclusion from "polite" society of mixed-blood women; she had manifested her contempt for them in her own private diaries. But the assessment of other white women in the colony reflected George's views of what kind of people were fit to associate with a governor's wife. The wife of Donald McKenzie he described as "a silly ignorant thing, whose commonplace wise saws with which we are constantly persecuted, are worse than a blister." Mrs. Cockran, the wife of the Anglican priest, was no better—she "shines only when talking of elbow Grease & the scouring of pots and pans."[65]

The isolation of which Simpson complained was consequently self-imposed. As he had grown in power his sense of dignity had also inflated. In the North American hierarchy of the fur trade he stood alone. The officers of the fur trade—chief factors and fur traders—were entitled to the courtesies appropriate to gentlemen, but he expected from them a degree of deference, and that degree became higher as he established himself as the master of the fur trade. Thus he increasingly divorced himself from the society of the Company's officers. This withdrawal he explained in terms of the intellectual or personal limitations of the officers. His physician, Dr. Todd, he had to accept professionally since there was no alternative, but he shunned his company socially, for Todd's politics were too radical by Simpson's standards and he was over-fond of the bottle.[66] Other officers had little to offer beyond their expertise in the fur trade, a subject not appropriate for social conversation.

Toward the lower ranks in the fur trade he adopted the mien of glacial efficiency; his relationship was entirely on a business basis; and he rarely allowed manifestations of personal feeling to intrude.

Simpson, so preoccupied with his own sensitivities, had little feeling for the reactions of others. Though he became an expert manager of men and a shrewd judge of their strengths and weaknesses, he could not relate to them on an intimate, personal basis. To only one person, John George McTavish, did he open himself up to any considerable degree, and even McTavish was not privy to Simpson's most private nonsexual thoughts. Officers were treated with a surface affability; clerks and others in inferior positions saw a cold, forbidding personality. Alexander Simpson, who grew to hate his cousin George, said that " 'L'âme de glace' was the name given by the Canadians to this frozen martinet; and well did he merit it."[67] The harshness of this indictment manifests the hostility of Alexander, but it is overstatement rather than untruth.

At Red River during the early 1830s there was at least one person who shared Alexander's animus toward the governor: Thomas Simpson, younger brother of Alexander and son of George's Aunt Mary, who had contributed so much to Simpson's early life. Governor Simpson recognized a debt to his aunt, and he tried to advance the careers of her sons, yet both of them came to hate him in the conviction that he had wrecked their lives. Simpson, however, remained for many years unaware of their antagonism. These facts are revealing both of the cousins and of the governor.

Thomas Simpson, who gained renown as an Arctic explorer, was born in Dingwall in 1808. He was an intelligent boy, strongly motivated to achieve, and he did well in school. He graduated from King's College, Aberdeen, at the age of twenty, with an impressive scholarly record. Thomas was in his first year at the University when in 1825 his uncle came to visit Mary in Dingwall. The governor offered to place the young man in the Company's service, assuring him that he would have excellent prospects for advancement, but Thomas declined. After Thomas's graduation, while he was pondering his future, the offer was renewed and this time it was accepted. It is clear from Thomas's letters which have survived through his brother's book that he expected rapid advancement in the service because of his intellect and education and his blood relationship with the governor. Thomas, even adorned by the admiring prose of Alexander, appears to have been arrogant and abrasive. He considered himself superior to the officers of the fur trade, including the governor, who, after all, had not had the benefits of an advanced education and who suffered from the stigma of illegitimate birth. His expectations were that he would rise rapidly to a chief factorship, and that eventually, but not too long in the future, he would be recognized as the heir to the governorship. Thomas's hopes, in short, were divorced from reality; he was certain to suffer from disillusionment; and he was bound to find a culprit other than himself. He explained his frustrations in terms of the jealousy of the Company's officers and the governor's concern over appearing to favor a kinsman. Beyond that, Thomas condemned the governor for his coldness toward a relative who, though younger, had superior credentials and should have been treated with both affection and respect. He wrote to Alexander:

> *Entre nous,* I have often remarked that his Excellency miscalculates when he expects to get more out of people by sheer driving; it only puts every one in ill humour. . . .
>
> To myself, in particular, the difference is very great; as, with all the Governor's good will and kind intentions, he has been to me a severe and most repulsive master. I know, and he has more than once told me, that this was a matter of policy with him; but he veiled his policy very badly, so that every clerk could see through it, which would have gradually brought me into contempt; but I have this season taught them that I could command respect, and have been in consequence treated by every one, high and low, more *en bourgeois* than *en commis.* . . .
>
> I will not conceal from you that on a nearer view of his character than before had I lost much of that internal respect I entertained towards him. His firmness and decision of mind are much impaired; both in great and small matters, he has become wavering, capricious, and changeable; in household affairs (for he is his own butler and housekeeper) the very cook says openly that he is like a weathercock.
>
> He has grown painfully nervous and crabbed, and is guilty of many little meannesses at table that are quite beneath a gentleman, and, I might add, are indicative of his birth.[68]

Thomas in these expressions said at least as much about himself as the man he condemned. A paragon of sensitivity and good will could not have propitiated Thomas Simpson; George Simpson cannot be condemned for lack of support for his cousin; on the contrary, he held the young man in high regard and intended to advance him rapidly. The flaw in Simpson which Thomas revealed was not his undervaluation of talent, but his inability to sense the emanations from another human being.

Even had George Simpson been endowed with a greater sense of humanity, he might have found it difficult in the early 1830s to give his attention to the problems of others, for this was the time when he underwent the greatest crisis of his life. After the first euphoria of the canoe trip of Red River, Frances's health broke, and for the remaining twenty years of her life she was beset by illness and personal tragedy. She had become pregnant and became ill with a mysterious malady, which the physician at Red River could not diagnose. On the doctor's orders she was confined to her bed, and at the sight of her, pale and listless, Simpson was beside himself. He could not bear the thought of losing her—"I am more miserable about her than words can tell, if an evil should happen I shall be the most wretched man in existence as my whole heart and love are bound up in her."[69] He had to leave her briefly to preside over the council meeting at York Factory, but he rushed back to her side as soon as he could. She did not improve, however, and Simpson feared that she would die. In the summer she gave birth to a son. The infant was frail, but caring for him seemed to give his mother a new vitality, and she had recovered her health considerably when the child was christened George Geddes in January 1832 in a ceremony that was celebrated as a great event in the settlement.

The parents' joy was short-lived. On April 22, while Frances was on her way to church for Easter services, the child was seized with "violent retchings" and died just as she returned home from offering up her prayers for him. The tragedy was devastating to

Simpson and his wife. After a few days Simpson was able to write McTavish a letter which revealed the depth of his feeling:

> The awful transports of grief have given way to fixed & deep melancholy, & I much fear it will be long before my poor wife will recover from the shock. This poor child was the idol of our hearts. We doted on him. We lived but for him.[70]

The year after the death of George Geddes Simpson was the most miserable of Simpson's life. His wife needed care not available to her at Red River. Even before the tragedy it had become evident that they could not live happily in this frontier settlement. Now there was grave question as to whether she could live anywhere in British North America, even in Montreal. For the first time in his life Simpson was unable to devote his attention to business. In his most exhausting travels he had always been able to focus his mind on the affairs of the Company, but in this crisis of his life he could not concentrate on business. The cocky bantam of the 1820s now thought of himself as an aging man whose best days were behind him. "I am sick and tired of the country," he wrote, and he contemplated retirement.[71] When Simpson referred to "the country" he had in mind particularly the Red River Settlement. In the 1830s the turbulence which would make the colony the bane of the Company was still largely prospective, but the mixed-blood *bois brûlés* were already showing independence of spirit which portended trouble for the future. The children of the soil no longer passively accepted the Company's authority, and controlling them was difficult, particularly during the holidays when rum flowed freely. By 1835 Simpson was predicting that unless a military force was established, the Company could not assert its authority much longer.[72]

These gloomy forebodings added to Simpson's malaise. Even before the death of his son he had thought of giving up the "harassing service" and going back to England to live, but had been deterred by the news of popular disorders. The upheavals in Europe had spilled over into England, and before the passage of the Reform Bill of 1832 there were riots in the cities and in rural areas which seemed to threaten the stability of the society. Despite his wife's ill health and his own, he decided that it was wise to delay taking Frances home until order had been restored.[73] By the end of December 1832 Simpson was reassured that the threat of revolution was over, and he laid his plans to take his wife home the following summer or fall and to return alone for another two years, after which he might retire.[74]

A powerful deterrent to immediate severance from the Company was the state of his finances. During the year 1831−32 he had suffered serious financial reverses in his investments in Canada—he estimated his losses at nearly £4000.[75] These reverses necessitated that he recruit his finances before leaving the service.

There was another deterrent which Simpson at this time refused to acknowledge. Despite his repeated references to being sick of the service his involvement in it was far more intense than he recognized. Before the death of his son he had set down his judgments of key officers in the service in a "Character Book", which he carefully kept away from prying eyes. These appraisals were not written by an individual contemplating imminent retirement. They reflect judgments relating to an ongoing responsibility. His estimates in many cases were proved wrong by his own subsequent judgments, but generally he showed himself to be a shrewd judge of character whose assessments of strengths and weaknesses were usually judicious. In a few cases personal animus showed through, as in his acid comments on John Clarke, Colin Robertson, and his ex-mate's uncle Donald McKenzie.[76] And of course there was the celebrated commentary of McLoughlin, "a very bustling active man who can go through a great deal of business but is wanting in system and regularity, and has not the talent of managing the few associates & clerks under his authority." He acknowledged McLoughlin's "strict honor and integrity", but overbalanced this with a catalogue of his shortcomings.

He had an "ungovernable violent temper and turbulent disposition", and "would be a Radical in every Country under any Government and under any circumstances." He would be a source of great trouble to the Company if he had any influence with his associates. His concluding comment ended on a positive note, but was far from being an endorsement: "Altogether a disagreeable man to do business with as it is impossible to go with him in all things and a difference of opinion almost amounts to a declaration of hostilities, yet a good hearted man and a pleasant companion."[77]

After the death of his son, Simpson was for a time so distraught that he could not focus on business. This phase lasted only a few weeks, and he was again in control of himself by mid-1832. At this time he became the unwilling host to a brash young visitor who descended on him for an extended stay. Henry Hulse Berens, the son of Joseph who had been governor of the Hudson's Bay Company between 1812 and 1822, arrived with a letter from Governor John Henry Pelly asking Simpson to give him all the assistance he could in learning about the Company's operations, including access to all papers. Young Berens was being groomed for a seat on the board. Simpson soon detested him. He was "vain, egotistical, self-sufficient, boasting, and ignorant". The board could not have devised a greater annoyance at the worst possible time than to saddle Simpson with this pompous, arrogant young man who pestered him with foolish questions and made extended references to his aristocratic connections. But what was most obnoxious to Simpson was that the officious Berens was inclined to treat him, the "real governor", as a subordinate, and this he would not tolerate.[78]

Berens was still there when Simpson suffered a recurrence of the malady which had attacked him in 1829. While he was talking to Berens and a Company officer in May 1833 he was struck by an apoplectic seizure and collapsed. A physician applied the favorite remedy of leeches and cupping, a treatment which must certainly have contributed to his general debility. For days he was so weak that he could not walk without assistance. He was able to summon up enough energy to hold a meeting of the council though its venue had to be shifted from Norway House to Red River. Then he and his sick wife set out on the canoe voyage to Montreal en route to New York, from which they were to embark for England. Again, as on other occasions when he was in motion, his health markedly improved.[79] When they arrived in London he still required rest, but he was able to carry on business at Hudson's Bay House, and within a few weeks he had recovered much of his vitality.[80] No longer did he talk of imminent retirement; he was again fully involved in the affairs of his Company.

Out of his travails a new Simpson had emerged. His unrivalled knowledge of the fur trade and his superb business abilities had won him the admiration and respect of the London board. His counsel was sought not only for the information he could provide but for the breadth of vision he possessed. From this point on Simpson was much more frequently in London, involved in matters of high policy.

He returned to Red River in 1834 and was soon embroiled in a controversy which manifested the growing unrest of the Métis population and also the limitations of Thomas Simpson to deal with delicate problems. In his "Character Book" of 1832 George had described Thomas as "handy and active and will in due time if he goes on as he promises be one of the most complete men of business in the country."[81] This assessment, so in contrast to Thomas's harsh indictment of George, accorded with Thomas's own judgment. During George Simpson's absence Thomas had written to his brother:

> If the Governor does not come out again, I have no idea who will step into his shoes. Old Keith is a dried spider; good heavens! what a Governor! I wish I were five years older; in every other respect, without vanity, I feel myself perfectly competent to the situation, and, with one or two exceptions, hold the abilities of our *wigs* in utter contempt. This season I have been intimate with many of

them—have, in the Governor's absence, had much to do with the general business and see how easily these men can be led.[82]

During the governor's stay in 1834, however, Thomas demonstrated that he was temperamentally unqualified to be a leader, at least of such a population as the Métis of Red River. He became involved in an altercation with a mixed-blood Canadian employee which ended with his using physical force. Alexander noted with satisfaction that the employee "got the worst of the scuffle, coming off with a black eye and a bloody nose."[83] The incident provoked a storm of resentment among the Métis who demanded that Thomas be flogged. George Simpson temporized with the indignant settlers and indicated that Thomas would be removed from Red River. This response was probably the best under the circumstances, but Thomas regarded it as a betrayal.

Red River was an environment that George Simpson found increasingly distasteful. Not only did it evoke unhappy memories of his family life, but the rising tide of independence presented problems he did not wish to deal with at first hand. More and more he was inclined to allow such abrasive issues to be met by others on the spot, while he administered the affairs of the fur trade from his headquarters at Lachine. To the officers of the fur trade he became the "Little Emperor", an appellation that must have delighted him since he was an admirer of Napoleon and read all that he could about his hero. Though the policies he carried out were set by the board, he was increasingly involved in their formation, and the directors gave him considerable latitude in carrying them out. The councils continued to be held yearly to approve arrangements for the fur trade, but they became little more than formalities, since Simpson had made the decisions which the members were expected to approve.[84] John McLean testified that when Simpson's secretary was asked what matters were scheduled for the council's attention he replied, "Bless your heart, man! the minutes of Council were all drawn out before we arrived here; I have them in my pocket."[85] The story may be apocryphal but in substance was not far from the truth. McLean, who hated Simpson for what he considered to be bad treatment, described Simpson's power as autocratic:

> In no colony subject to the British Crown is there to be found an authority so despotic as is at this day exercised in the mercantile Colony of Rupert's Land; an authority combining the despotism of military rule with the strict surveillance and mean parsimony of the avaricious trader. From Labrador to Nootka Sound the unchecked, uncontrolled will of a single individual gives law to the land. As to the nominal Council which is yearly invoked for form's sake, the few individuals who compose it know better than to offer advice where none would be accepted; they know full well that the Governor has already determined on his own measures before one of them appears in his presence.[86]

McLean's allegation of Simpson's arbitrariness was exaggerated but, again, not entirely untrue. Secure in the confidence of the London directors, Simpson took a strong line in his management of the fur trade, and those who had the temerity to incur his ire suffered for their rashness.

Simpson recovered from his period of despondency apparently as vigorous as ever. His wife, however, was never fully restored to health. The ministrations of ill-trained people at Red River had probably contributed to her continuing bad health. But just before she left Red River she was again pregnant, and on December 30, 1833, she gave birth to a daughter, christened Frances Webster,[87] a healthy child dear to Simpson's heart. In her early years he called her "Ged", but eventually she acquired the nickname "Greyhound". The Simpsons had three other children—Augusta d'Este,[88] born in 1841; Margaret Mackenzie, nicknamed "Baby", born in 1843; and John Henry Pelly, nicknamed "Moses", born in 1850.

Simpson's gloomy prophecy that his wife would never be able to cross the Atlantic again was not fulfilled. Even at the time he uttered it he had made provision for the accommodation of his family at Lachine. In September 1833 the Company bought a house for him which was by far the largest in the village—sixty feet long and fifty feet wide and three stories high, scarcely a dwelling for a single person even if he held the exalted position of overseas governor of the Hudson's Bay Company. Frances was able to join him there in 1838 and subsequently in the 1840s, and the children spent extended periods there, although they were educated in England.

Among the inner social circle at Simpson's residence was his secretary, Edward Martin Hopkins. Hopkins first became associated with the governor in 1841. He soon demonstrated the qualities of system and regularity which Simpson held dear, and became Simpson's trusted right hand. He had accompanied Simpson on part of his journey round the world, and was in constant attendance on him at Lachine. Simpson developed a considerable affection for his model secretary. After Hopkins married Annie Ogden, daughter of Peter Skene, the young couple were guests every Sunday of the Simpson family. Simpson consulted Annie on many matters related to household management, a practice which apparently Frances treated with no evident resentment.[89] Simpson's affection for Frances was as much in evidence in the 1840s as it had been in the early years of their marriage. In Hopkins's book of canoe songs there is preserved a set of verses in Simpson's hand, which express passion for his beloved. In all probability they were directed to Frances, and were written sometime during the 1830s or 1840s:

1
My own blue Bell, my pretty blue Bell
I never will rove where Roses dwell
My Wings you view of your own bright hue
And oh! never doubt that my Heart's true blue.

2
Tho oft I own, I have foolishly flown
To peep at each Bud that was newly blown
I now have done with folly & fun
For there is nothing like constancy under the Sun.

3

Some Belles are Blues, invoking the Muse
And talking of vast intellectual views
Their Crow Quills tip in the Ink they dip
And they prate w[it]h the lore of a learned lip.

4

Blue Belles like these, may be wise as they please
But I love my Blue Bell that bends to the Breeze
Pride passes her by, but she charms my Eye
W[it]h the tint that resembles the cloudless Sky.[90]

With this tenderness, however, went autocracy. Glimpses of
the Simpsons' married life as provided by other observers suggest
that the domineering ways which he exhibited early in marriage
did not soften as the years went by, but were reinforced by an
overprotectiveness toward a woman whom he treated as a delicate piece of porcelain. Frances was his possession, and possessions do not make decisions for themselves.

Donald Smith, who later would become Governor of the
Hudson's Bay Company, experienced Simpson's jealousy when
he came to Lachine in 1838 as an apprentice clerk. Frances
Simpson, then only twenty-six, enjoyed talking with "indentured
young gentlemen", as the apprentices were called, and she took a
liking to Donald. She invited him to tea and occasionally had him
escort her on boating excursions. One day Simpson arrived at the
house from a journey to Red River and found Smith taking tea
with his wife. He flew into a towering rage and ordered the young
man out of the house. One officer who was present heard Simpson, in the high-pitched voice which excitement induced, screech
that he would not "tolerate any upstart, quill-driving apprentices
dangling about a parlour reserved to the nobility and gentry." It
was probably not coincidental that Smith's subsequent assign-
ments were to posts that had the reputation of being the least
desirable stations in Canada.[91]

Frances Simpson's need for the company of other young people like Donald Smith was in part a reflection of the age gap

between her and a husband with whom she could not communicate as an equal. But beyond that it reflected an intense loneliness, a longing for her home in England and for her family and friends in London. She could never adapt herself to life in Montreal. Her social life was restricted because of her frailty; she could not enjoy the gaiety of balls and grand dinners, though her and her husband's names were frequently on the list of patrons for social functions. She lived in a great house overlooking magnificent vistas of the St. Lawrence but she remained homesick for England. Consequently Simpson had to accept the necessity of her spending most of her time in London rather than Lachine. But life in England did not restore her to health. Beyond the strain of childbearing she was attacked by other infirmities. In 1840 during a trip to Ireland with Simpson she contracted smallpox, which threatened her life. She recovered with no apparent ill effects[92] and successfully underwent the ordeals of two pregnancies and births. Simpson was sufficiently encouraged by her condition that he decided to bring her and her youngest child back to Lachine with him in 1845.

During his absences in England the house in Lachine had been occupied by others, frequently by Duncan Finlayson and his wife, Frances's sister, whom he had married in 1838 at the same church as the Simpsons. When Simpson announced his family's imminent return to Lachine and his expectations that the Finlaysons would live with them, Finlayson was shocked. He did not dare to declare his independence, and could only vent his frustration in communications to trusted friends. He wrote James Hargrave in April 1845:

> The Gov. is coming out bag & baggage, that is wt. wife, bairn, servants &c &c & how we are going to stow them all here is more than I know.[93]

The decision to return was almost certainly not Frances's. Her years in England had not diminished her loathing for life at the big house in Lachine. Her sister's presence was a source of solace, but nothing could relieve the heartsickness of exile from London. A letter she wrote to a favorite cousin in 1846 was most revealing of her desperate unhappiness in this alien environment. She and George W. Simpson had been very close in the years before she married. George had been offered the position of private secretary to Sir George Simpson then held by Edward M. Hopkins. He was seriously considering accepting and asked Frances for her advice. She replied:

My dearest George:

. . . I think I need scarcely assure you that nothing would give me greater delight than to have you near me, but you know dear Georgy how often we have talked over LaChine, and all its disagreeables, and believe me it has not a few, and I cannot wish you to come much as I long to see you — The situation offered you is an arduous one, for the writing is incessant, and there are few comforts here to balance the many discomforts—Nevertheless, should you have nothing more inviting in prospects, I would not say decline it — but I would strongly urge you to accept it under one condition — that should you not like it after a fair trial you be at liberty to give it up. . . . While here, it would indeed be a delight to me to see you tho' the rules of this Establishment are so strict that we could not meet so often as I should wish — Still it would be a pleasure and comfort to know you were under the same roof, and we should at all events meet once a day, at Breakfast time — But I am sure you would not like it — there is nothing to recommend this place, tho' perhaps since you have been in Norway you have become in some degrees weaned from the many comforts & delights of home.

But I must not say more upon this subject — Should we meet, I shall have much to say to you, and I hope you will write to me soon, & tell me all your feelings upon this matter, and your future plans, for believe me every thing that relates to you, however trifling, is regarded by me with interest, for I can never forget dear Georgy, all yr affectionate kindness, nor the many happy hours we have passed together, in days gone by. . . .

We lead a very quiet life just now, seldom going beyond the door, & I suppose shall be so until George's return — But when he is here, he is so well known to every body that we have constant invitations to go out, or else people here — which breaks the monotony of the life we live. But I shall never like the country nor the people, & long more & more every day to return. . . .[94]

Frances's reaction to the service generally was even more pronouncedly negative. She warned her cousin:

Do not on any account bind yourself for a fixed time, and let no consideration induce you to enter the service in any other position than the one in question — I would not for Worlds dear George see you go to the Interior, for I do not hesitate to say that the young men who pass their lives in those wretched isolated Posts are utterly lost, and rendered unfit for every thing — The more I see of the service, the more I detest it, and in its present state a man may toil all his life and at the end not make sufficient to maintain himself, and all the time live far away from society, void of comfort or amusement of any sort — For you who have passed your time in so different a manner, and been accustomed to the society of your friends, & every comfort, you could not endure or submit to the life you would there have to lead — But I think I know your feelings too well to suppose for a moment you would agree to go to the Interior, unless for a month or two with George in his Summer trip.[95]

This letter revealed the gulf between Simpson and his wife. His professions of devotion to her were certainly sincere, but he could not comprehend the deep spiritual malaise which was draining away her vitality. She probably had never communicated her innermost thoughts to him; it was not in the nature of their relationship that she should do so. Had he not given her everything? They had wealth and social position and a lovely family. What more could she desire?

The advent of the Simpsons as co-residents with the Finlaysons was in no sense a happy arrangement. Finlayson found the environment oppressive. The semi-invalid Frances and her ill-disciplined children were a trial to the nerves, and enforced intimacy with the governor, who was accustomed to having his own way, was abrasive. After several years of these pressures Finlayson decided that he could not tolerate the situation much longer, and in 1852 he indicated to a friend that he would likely soon resign from the Company.[96] But within a year the community of the Finlaysons and Simpsons was broken by the tragedy of Frances Simpson's death.

Sometime after Frances's return to Lachine she contracted tuberculosis. She hung on to life for several years, but at the beginning of 1853 her condition worsened, and it was evident that death was imminent.[97] She died on March 21, at the age of forty, and was buried at the recently opened Protestant Mount Royal Cemetery.[98]

Though Frances's death had not been unexpected, the shock of severance was none the less great, and shortly afterward Simpson decided to build another house for himself away from the building that he had used as a combined office and residence for so many years. He purchased a beautiful, wooded island known as L'Isle de Dorval, not far from Lachine, on which he built a large brick house. Frances's eldest daughter was then about twenty-one years old[99] and may on occasion have acted as the mistress of his establishment before her marriage in 1856. But life on the island was not for Simpson. He retained the combined office-residence in Lachine as his principal residence, and in the last years before Simpson's death the Dorval house was rented to General Sir Fenwick Williams.[100]

Little is known about Simpson's relationship with his children by Frances during their years of growing up, but he seems to have been a doting father whose business responsibilities gave him little opportunity for family affairs. What discipline was asserted was largely left to others. In her last years Frances was unable to exercise effective supervision, and the children were frequently left to their own devices. The one time when the family was most likely to be together was at dinner-time. Angus Cameron, who had just become engaged to the Simpsons' daughter Frances, described the children's relationship with their father at dinner as follows:

> The two little ones Gussy & Maggie have always been great friends of mine. . . . They have been taught to be afraid of their own Papa—not that he is unkind, but he makes a great deal of noise with

his dogs &c & talk, in a force to frighten them. The dear Pets used to make their lunch their dinner & at our dinner time they sat at the same table & had tea—The second day I was there I asked the servant to put down plates for Gussy & Maggie—he looked at me amazed but did not dare to refuse. I asked Maggie what she would have & took a slice of the breast of chicken which I had before me—I then asked Gussy & she made signs to the dish her Papa had—I asked him to help her & he did so at once remarking ah! my girl you want Mr. Cameron to look after you—when I went into the drawing room I thought the darling Pets would have torn me to pieces.[101]

The youngest son, called by his father "Moses", remained unnamed for several years after Frances Simpson's death. A chief factor who was present at another dinner party when Moses was three reported that Simpson had been teaching his son to say "queer things". Asked to say what he had for dinner the previous evening, Moses replied, "Some beefsteak & devilish tough."[102]

There might be some question about Simpson's involvement in the training of his children. There could be no question about his devotion to them and his concern that they be well provided for in the future. In his will he bequeathed to each of the three legitimate daughters £15,000 in Halifax currency, stating that the legacy should belong to the daughter free of control by the husband,[103] but he stipulated that if any of the daughters married without the consent of his executors, she would forfeit the legacy. His greatest concern was in the perpetuation of the male line through his son, John Henry Pelly Simpson.[104] To him he bequeathed £75,000 Halifax currency and the bulk of the rest of the estate. A commentary on Simpson's urge to carry on his line was the provision that if his son had no heirs the estate would go to the male heirs of his daughters, who would be required to take the name of Simpson. By contrast, only one of his illegitimate children was mentioned—Maria, born in Scotland, the widow of Donald McTavish, was bequeathed an annuity of £100 Halifax currency.[105] For his illegitimate sons he had found jobs in the fur trade, and he accepted no further responsibility for them.

CHAPTER V

The Statesman

Simpson when he left for England in 1833 had seemed a beaten man. Oppressed with grief at the death of his son, apprehensive about the health of his wife, and despondent about his own loss of vitality, he had considered his days of power as nearly at an end. His sojourn in England produced a remarkable recovery. When he came back alone to North America he was again almost his old robust self. His endurance had returned though he was periodically plagued by an affliction in his eyes, which by the end of the decade had so affected his ability to read that he had to employ the services of an amanuensis. But, strangely, this malady did not seriously affect his vision out-of-doors,[1] and he was able to resume his strenuous regimen. More significantly, he regained his self-confidence. No longer was there any thought of early retirement; on the contrary he now became involved in the affairs of the Company on a level which he had hitherto experienced only sporadically. He was secure in the confidence of the London board, and they involved him in issues of high policy much more intimately than had previously been the case. The Company as the British presence west of Canada was involved in international problems with the United States and with Russia, and Simpson became involved in the formulation of Company policy on these issues rather than being merely a source of information.

At the same time he asserted his mastery over the trade in North America. The councils did his will and whatever grumbling occurred among the officers was expressed in private. It was easy for an outsider to develop the impression that Simpson was universally loved as well as respected by the men of the service, since none would publicly express any negative opinion. The sixth Earl of Selkirk after a tour in 1836 wrote his wife that Simpson "is worshipped here, both voyageurs and partners swear by him."[2] That judgment was far from accurate. There were many who disliked Simpson and more who feared him. But Selkirk was certainly correct when he described Simpson as "one of the most extraordinary men I ever met for activity in business".[3] Not only did Simpson demonstrate the capacity to make major decisions but he was acquainted with the details of operations at the various posts. Information gained from his prodigious correspondence, supplemented by personal observation from his periodic visits to the fur-trade posts, was stored away in a mind which seemed to forget nothing and to catalogue disparate facts into a cross-filing system which produced them instantaneously as required. Beyond the ordinary business, his investment service for officers of the fur trade had grown into a major enterprise. Most officers came to rely on him to invest their surplus funds, and his shrewd judgments repaid them handsomely. Apart from the influence such an agency gave him with the employees, there was a consideration of Company policy. The board was concerned to keep the financial status of the Company private, and they considered it dangerous to allow information on officers' incomes to be acquired by outsiders, since such intelligence could give considerable insights into the profits of the Company.[4] After 1856, because of the great amount of business this office involved, the Company charged a small percentage for this service, but Simpson continued to serve as investment adviser until his death. All of this he did with no apparent strain. He also acted as a kind of guardian general for officers' children who were being sent to Britain for education, managing the finances involved as well as acting as a general overseer of their welfare. Indeed, the virtuosity with which he carried out a wide variety of responsibilities justified Selkirk's adjective of "remarkable".

Simpson's dedication to the Company's affairs involved a corresponding lack of interest in those aspects of life unrelated to his professional career. He was in no sense an "intellectual", as the term is generally used; contemplation of great abstractions was not for him; he had no apparent interest in literature. His small library was almost exclusively composed of books devoted to exploration, Indians, and the fur trade. The major exceptions in the inventory made at his death were a family Bible and *Uncle Tom's Cabin,* the latter at least a curious aberration.

In the mid-1830s the qualities so much admired by Selkirk were manifested impressively. Simpson's resurgence was undoubtedly buoyed by the prosperity of the fur trade. The demand in England for furs provided excellent markets, and profits between 1835 and 1840 ranged from ten to twenty-five per cent per year.[5] During the next decade the increasing popularity of the silk hat would cause a depression in the Company's staple, beaver fur, but in the 1830s this change of fashion was still in the future. Furthermore, the Company's territories were subjected to little menace from within or without. The half-breeds of Red River were showing signs of fractiousness, but they were as yet not a major threat to the monopoly. The Indians, who had been angered by the lowering of prices with the end of North West competition, had now perforce acquiesced in the new era. In the east in Canada, the spread of settlement along the St. Lawrence and the Ottawa rivers had eliminated most of the fur-bearing animals, and for those which were left the Company had to compete with many petty opponents, usually part-time traders whose primary occupations were lumbering, storekeeping, or farming. This competition, however, was not a source of great concern. The Company did not expect to make profits in Canada. Its presence there was primarily to prevent the formation of powerful opposition which would penetrate into the rich fur preserves of Rupert's Land, and that purpose was effectively achieved. The petty traders remained no more than a nuisance and never became a threat.

Far to the west on the Pacific coast, conditions were never

more favorable than they were in the late 1830s. The American sea captains who had provided such strong competition in the 1820s had been ousted by the Company's spirited opposition, which had driven prices of furs to levels that made their voyages unprofitable. In 1833 there were no American vessels on the northwest coast, and though they appeared occasionally thereafter, significant competition had been ended. The diplomatic controversy between the United States and Britain over the Oregon territory was in a state of suspended animation in the 1830s. The area seemed to have been almost forgotten by the politicians of both countries, and few private citizens from the United States had made their way to the Columbia Valley. Some of these were missionaries who were regarded by the Company with justification as potentially dangerous to its interests. But the danger was still potential. In 1835 in the Willamette Valley, the only American settlement was a tiny agricultural community of twenty-eight males, including ten clergymen, and six women, wives of missionaries, hardly a significant threat without substantial reinforcements. As yet the Company's worries were not about what was but what might be.[6]

At the east of the Oregon territory expeditions under Peter Skene Ogden and others had vigorously trapped beaver in the Snake country to deter American penetration from the landward side, and again these policies had been successful. American competition, which had involved perhaps five hundred to six hundred trappers a year in the early 1830s, dropped off considerably, and by 1836 the only American party of significance was that of Nathaniel Wyeth, who co-operated with the Company, and he withdrew the next year.[7]

In the far North West, the ponderous Russian American Company had been preoccupied with defending itself rather than aggressively competing with American or British rivals. The Russian company suffered from the lassitude of political bureaucracy. It was under the control of the Ministry of Finance, which scrutinized its accounts with minute thoroughness; its chief administrative positions were occupied by naval officers; and the actions of men in the field were strictly regulated by the fur company's administration in St. Petersburg. Its organization, in short, was perfectly designed to stifle initiative. The tsar's decree of 1821, banning foreign shipping north of fifty-one degrees, had been an effort to accomplish by political means what could not be done by competition. It had not achieved the purpose, and in the 1830s the Russians had watched with increasing apprehension the advance of the Hudson's Bay Company up the coast. The two companies had nearly collided in 1834 over a fort which Ogden had built on the Stikine River. By the terms of the Anglo-Russian Treaty of 1825 the Russians had been awarded a coastal strip of ten leagues breadth south of fifty-six degrees north latitude, but the British had been granted the right of navigation of the rivers through this territory. This right, the Russians correctly judged, would result in the Hudson's Bay Company collecting many of the land furs that the Indians had previously traded with the Russians.

As a later Russian writer put it, "The Convention of 1825 which granted the English the right of free navigation of the streams flowing from the English possessions across Russian territory and out to the sea, actually made the English masters of the whole territory along the lines of the river communications."[8] The attempt to use force to prevent this produced a protest from the British government, and the Russian company at the behest of its government shifted its stance. It now looked for an accommodation with the Hudson's Bay Company.

The late 1830s consequently were as close to halcyon days as any period in the Company's history, and George Simpson luxuriated in the satisfaction of almost unvarying success. The London board expressed its high regard for him and its pleasure with the conditions of the trade when it appointed him governor-in-chief of all the Company's territories in 1839. Theretofore, he had had two commissions, as governor of the Northern and of the Southern Departments. The new title did not change his functions, but it was a mark of high regard. Then in 1841 he received another signal recognition, this time from the British government, when he was knighted. The basis for this honor was avowedly the assistance that the Company had given to the Arctic expedition of Chief Factor Peter Warren Dease and Thomas Simpson —Governor Pelly was made a baronet on the same occasion—but more fundamental was the fact that the Company was now again in the favor of the government. The peace that the monopoly had brought to the Company's territories made the government disinclined to interfere, and in 1838 the Colonial Office had endorsed a new licence of exclusive trade over the lands west of the chartered territories. For the conditions which produced that satisfaction Simpson had been to a considerable extent responsible.

Simpson's knighthood symbolized his transition from commercial man to statesman. By the late 1830s he was deeply immersed in the diplomatic negotiations affecting the Company's trade, and the experience was exhilarating. It was thrilling to be involved with men of weight and with issues of moment.

During the 1820s Simpson had been called upon for information by the Foreign Office; in the 1830s he participated in discussions affecting Britain's international relations. The first of these of major importance involved the Russian American Company.

The attempt of the Russian American Company to deny the British company access to the rivers running through Russian territory had evoked a strong response from the British government—Simpson darkly talked of the likelihood of hostilities and asked McLoughlin to ascertain the naval and military forces available to the Russians on the northwest coast.[9] But war was never in prospect; the interests of the two governments coincided; and the Stikine incident resulted in agreement rather than conflict. The Hudson's Bay Company had always regarded its fellow monopolist in a very different light from American competitors. An understanding with one American sea captain would not deter others, but an arrangement with the Russians could be mutually advantageous. One benefit could be to complete the rout of American competition, since one of the sources of profit for the Americans was in selling provisions to the Russian settlements. If the Russians would buy such supplies from the Hudson's Bay Company the Americans would probably be unable to continue, Simpson and the London board agreed. Accordingly, before he had departed from Fort Vancouver in 1829, Simpson had made an overture to the governor of the Russian company at New Archangel. He sent his relative Aemilius Simpson, who had been appointed to the command of one of the Company's ships, with a proposal for the sale to the Russians at "moderate" prices of British manufactures and of grain and beef from the Company's supplies on the Columbia.[10] By "moderate" Simpson meant whatever price was necessary to undersell the Americans. The Russians had declined the offer, but in the aftermath of the Stikine incident the proposal was revived. Chief Factor Duncan Finlayson, who at that time was in charge of the Company's coastal trade, visited the Russian governor at Sitka to try to convince him that it would be beneficial to the Russians to buy from the Hudson's Bay Company rather than from the Americans. The Russians had been impressed with the quality of goods Finlayson displayed, the prices he offered, and the prospects of a dependable supply of wheat, and the governor wrote to his superiors in St. Petersburg advocating an agreement with the British company.[11] This communication eventually produced an invitation to the Hudson's Bay Company to send representatives for discussions. The two selected to go were John Henry Pelly and George Simpson. Pelly as the governor of the Company was an obvious choice. He had held that position since 1822, during which time his influence on the board had been rivalled only by Andrew Colvile. Pelly more than any other man had been the architect of the policies which Simpson had executed.[12] The selection of Simpson might also have been obvious on the basis that Pelly needed his expertise, but as became evident during the negotiations, Simpson was now valued for his judgment as well as for his knowledge, and Pelly respected him as an associate. This was Simpson's first venture in such a role, and his sense of its importance was reflected in his keeping a diary of his experiences for the benefit of Frances. The entries therein provide insights into Simpson's personality not revealed in his business correspondence.

Simpson and the Pellys proceeded to St. Petersburg by way of Hamburg, Lubeck, Travemünde, Copenhagen, and Stockholm. The first stage of their journey began when they embarked on the steamer *Britannia* from London on July 17, 1838. The entries thereafter are replete with commentaries on what he saw and the people he encountered. At Copenhagen he went swimming in the ocean, and was impelled to compete with a Danish swimmer who considered himself first class. Simpson, by his own account, demonstrated his superiority. "Few," he noted, "can overmatch me in the water."[13]

During the journey he complained of the homeliness of the women. "Indeed," he wrote, "I have not observed what I should call a pretty looking woman in the course of my travels through these northern Regions: our Canadian and half breed women of North American are angels compared with them."[14] Frances Simpson's reaction to this observation may only be surmised.

At Christiania (Oslo) Simpson attended a "State Dinner in full puff " where to his delight he was introduced as "head of the most extended Dominions in the known world the Emperor of Russia the Queen of England and the President of the United States excepted." The entry for that day ended on a less high-flown key; "retired at 11, occupied till 12 sewing Buttons on my Shirts & mending my breeches & Waistcoat. Damned bad Needles, worse Thread & Villainous Sewing!"[15]

Simpson and Pelly arrived in St. Petersburg on August 27, 1838, with something less than the welcome which they might have expected. No one was at the quay to receive them and to help them with the vexations of passing through customs, where their baggage was "examined most Strictly every Shirt Shift Pettycoat, no soiled linen allowed to pass." His and Pelly's pistols were confiscated, presumably to be returned on departure, though the customs officer who took a fancy to Simpson's weapon refused to give him a receipt. They had to find accommodations for themselves, and finally secured lodging in a house across from the palace of the Grand Duke Michael. From that base they had ample time to tour St. Petersburg, since several days elapsed before they were afforded an opportunity to see the Board of Directors of the Russian American Company. Simpson was "astounded at the magnificence & spendour [*sic*] of the Streets Palaces Shops Houses &c." But he was not on a sight-seeing tour, and his initial impressions of the men with whom he had to deal were emphatically negative. Shortly after arrival, he and Pelly visited the British embassy to ascertain the progress of the Company's claim for damages. They were received by Milbanke, the chargé d'affaires, whom Simpson found to be the epitome of the worst in bureaucracy—"a flippant smirking smart looking man", who rationalized his disinclination to do anything by the assumption that nothing could be done.[16] Milbanke was no more helpful in providing information on the management of the Russian American Company, nor could any of the other English residents of St. Petersburg. They all found its operations mysterious, even though many of them were stockholders.[17]

When Pelly and Simpson were finally received at the Russian American Company headquarters three days had elapsed, and the reception was an occasion for still more frustration. They met with several of the directors who listened politely to the proposal for a compact but indicated that they could do nothing until the return of Baron Ferdinand Wrangell, the most powerful member of the board, who was away from the city and would not return for several days. In the meantime, the directors indicated, it would be helpful to have a written statement of the Hudson's Bay Company's proposals. Pelly and Simpson promptly composed a statement, but again were frustrated by the Russians' lackadaisical approach to business. Six days passed, three of them saints' days, before they could get the letter translated into Russian.[18]

When Wrangell finally arrived, negotiations took on a more businesslike character. Wrangell was not impressive physically. Simpson described him as "an extraordinary looking ferret Eyed, Red Whiskered & mustachioed little creature in full Regimentals not half the size of [Chief Factor Joseph] Beioley, very thin weak & delicate." But he respected his abilities as a businessman, and their relationships in St. Petersburg confirmed Wrangell's reputation as the ablest administrator in the Russian fur trade. Of course, by Simpson's judgment, there was little with which to compare him, since the other directors with whom he conferred were "Stupid to a Degree".[19]

The discussions in St. Petersburg did not result in a formal agreement, but it was evident that the two monopolies were in accord that the American petty traders must be eliminated and that there were more advantages in co-operation between the two companies than in conflict. Pelly and Simpson left St. Petersburg optimistic that the details of an alliance could be worked out, and Simpson was assigned the responsibility of negotiating with Wrangell to that end. For several months the two carried on a correspondence. By the beginning of January 1839 they had made an arrangement which was approved by the London board, and Simpson proceeded to Berlin to meet Wrangell and ratify the pact. Since Wrangell was delayed, Simpson pushed on to Hamburg where, on February 6, 1839, the two signed a contract by which the Russians leased the Alaskan panhandle to the Hudson's Bay Company and the Company agreed to supply the Russians with foodstuffs. Thus was established an alliance which continued in effect until the cession of Alaska to the United States and remained in force even at the time when the British and Russians were engaged in the Crimean War. At the suggestion of Simpson the two governments agreed to respect the neutrality of the northwest coast of America. The negotiations of 1838–39 had given the Hudson's Bay Company *de facto* control over Russian territory without the involvement of the British government. Even after the agreement was signed, the Company did not consider it necessary to communicate to the Foreign Office the terms of the arrangement. It was a remarkable example of quasi-political commercial diplomacy, and Simpson had been centrally involved in the entire proceedings.

The consummation of the Russian agreement was Simpson's first important essay in international diplomacy. He had been given the confidence of his board and he had demonstrated that their judgment of his powers was well founded.

Simpson had become in all but name a member of the board; when he was in London he participated in their deliberations, and his advice was given great weight. On occasions he virtually wrote the board's instructions to him for the forthcoming year.[20] On the rare times when the board made a decision on the trade without consulting him he reminded them that they had over-stepped their authority.[21]

In the late 1830s and in the 1840s Simpson seemed to have recovered the robust health on which he had prided himself. Aside from his defective eyesight, his constitution was strong. Lieutenant John Henry Lefroy, the explorer-scientist, described him in these terms in 1843:

> Sir George Simpson arrived on Saturday eveng and I called on him on Monday, he is the toughest looking old fellow I ever saw, built upon the Egyptian model, height two diameters, or like one of those short square massy pillars one sees in an old country church. . . . He is a fellow whom nothing will kill.[22]

Simpson was thus strong both in influence and in physical condition when he was called upon to play an active part as a Company spokesman in the active final phase of the Oregon dispute. For many years he had expected an aggressive move by the United States, but aside from a reconnoitering expedition in 1826 by William A. Slacum on the instructions of President Jackson's Secretary of State, the American government had seemed disinclined to act, even indifferent. But in 1838 Simpson heard that Congress was considering a bill authorizing the establishment of a military post at the mouth of the Willamette River. His immediate response was to order the Company's representative to occupy the land involved and to refuse to withdraw until forced to do so. If the Company's men were thus ousted, he expected that the incident could be used to produce a diplomatic crisis in which the British government would feel compelled to give strong support to the Company. By thus precipitating a crisis the Company would probably get better terms, for the longer the delay the stronger the American position was likely to become.[23] The plan was shrewdly conceived, but the United States did not co-operate by sending troops to Oregon. There was no dramatic incident; instead, the Company's position was undermined by a steadily growing migration of American farmers from 1842 onward. Oregon became important to the United States and, in Britain, the bellicose Lord Palmerston was succeeded in 1841 by the Peel government, in which the pacific Lord Aberdeen became Foreign Secretary. This combination made an American victory almost a certainty.

In 1841—42, before the Oregon dispute had reached the crisis stage, Simpson decided that the time was right to undertake a great project he had long had in view—a journey around the world. His avowed and, to an extent, his real purpose was to visit the Company's posts across North America, re-examine the Oregon scene on the spot, and review with the Russians in North America and in St. Petersburg the operation of the agreement with the Hudson's Bay Company. He had not seen the Columbia Valley and the Pacific Northwest since 1829, and a return visit was long overdue in terms of Simpson's practice of periodic firsthand inspection. But the journey served other purposes. It would be a feat on the grand scale, in which Simpson's remarkable endurance would be demonstrated to a much wider audience than his previous transcontinental trips. And he would again enjoy the experience of rapid travel, in this case to scenes and places which he had never visited. This circumnavigation would be well publicized in a book, and he was at pains to ensure that it would be written in a style which would command public attention by employing ghost writers to improve on his own notes.[24] The editorial work of his collaborators eliminated most of the acid and vinegar which tinged Simpson's private correspondence and the result was a rather bland travel book which was designed to entertain armchair explorers without offending anyone.

Simpson left London on March 3, 1841, and arrived back on October 21, 1842, after a journey of nineteen months and twenty-six days.[25] This was not a record, but nevertheless involved remarkable speed since his business responsibilities required him to spend considerable time at various places. As on previous occasions, Simpson took pride in his phenomenal pace. He reported to the London board that a party emigrating from Red River to Oregon had left Fort Garry a month before him and that he had caught them between Carlton and Edmonton after a record-breaking rush to Carlton of 580 miles in thirteen days, remarkable even for a lightly burdened party of good horses.[26] At Fort Garry, Simpson had been met by Chief Factor John Rowand, in charge of Fort Edmonton, who brought with him some "Columbia guides". It had been Simpson's intention to rely on boats, but the guides thought the Columbia River would be in full flood at the time the party proposed to descend it, and the plan was changed to arrange for a route on horseback farther to the south than he had planned to use, over a pass which the Indians thought no white man had traversed before. The pass, which was named for Simpson, was a formidable one, strewn with huge boulders which made horseback travel difficult, and the party was impeded further by dense vegetation.[27] The frustrations Simpson recorded in his book were impediments to his speed, but he nevertheless kept a remarkable pace. The party arrived at Ford Colvile on the Columbia River on August 18, 1841, "having performed a land journey of about 1900 miles, in 47 days out of which we had travelled but 41, having been detained 6 en route." To accomplish this feat, he and his men had spent about eleven hours a day in the saddle.[28]

On August 25 he reached Fort Vancouver where he again met John McLoughlin. During the thirteen years since the two had last seen each other, the gulf in their viewpoints had substantially widened. McLoughlin's natural inclination to act in accordance with his own judgments had been solidified, and these judgments did not always reflect Company policy. Indeed, in two fundamental areas his position was diametrically opposed to Simpson's. The governor and the London board considered American settlement to be a menace which must be deterred so far as the resources of the Company permitted. McLoughlin not only accepted the migration as inevitable but endeavored to establish friendly relations with the new arrivals. This "good neighbour" policy even extended to providing credit to enable them to purchase seeds and equipment, as he did in 1843. McLoughlin's actions may have been an intelligent adjustment to reality, but they were in direct contravention of his instructions. The other substantive area of conflict between Simpson and McLoughlin was in the way the trade of the Pacific Northwest should be conducted. McLoughlin believed that the trade should be carried on most profitably through a chain of trading posts up to the Russian settlements. Simpson's preference was to put primary reliance on ships, and this view was reinforced when he visited the Russian headquarters at Sitka on board the Company's steamer the *Beaver*. He took this trip a few days after he arrived at Fort Vancouver, and his conclusion was that the agreement with the Russians made trading posts unnecessary. The Americans had been driven from the coast, and the Russians were no longer competitors; consequently, fixed posts were now a needless expense. When he returned to Fort Vancouver with the decision already made, McLoughlin was irate. The *Beaver* on which Simpson placed such reliance became an object of hate to McLoughlin, the symbol of repudiation of his judgment and his authority. He was angered further by the decision of Simpson and the London board to move the Pacific Coast headquarters from Fort Vancouver to a new site on Vancouver Island. The decision was sensible, indeed necessary, from Simpson's perspective in view of what he considered to be the likelihood that the boundary would be north of the Columbia River. But McLoughlin's opposition was immutable and he did all that he could to frustrate the decision.[29]

These disputes contributed to an alienation between the two men in which neither appeared in an attractive light, and the feud became a vendetta a few months later when Simpson visited the Company's post at Stikine, where McLoughlin's mixed-blood son, John, Junior, was in charge, and found that the young man had been murdered a few days earlier.

Young McLoughlin in his earlier years had been a source of great unhappiness to his father. The senior McLoughlin had hoped he would follow a career in medicine and had sent him to Europe to study. As is so often the case when such decisions are imposed, the results were unfortunate. For a time John seemed to be making progress in his studies, but he fell from grace in 1834 when he was twenty-two years of age for committing some "unpardonable" misconduct which caused him to be sent back to Canada in disgrace. Then for over two years John floated about aimlessly, involving himself at one point in a filibustering expedition under "General" James Dickson. What precisely Dickson had in mind remains obscure, but the party which McLoughlin joined was headed for Red River. Its arrival could only be subversive to the interests of the Hudson's Bay Company, and Simpson took measures to stop it. The expedition ended on a schooner bound for Sault Ste. Marie, when an American sheriff seized the ship on the charge that it was carrying stolen cattle.[30]

Observation of young McLoughlin thus gave Simpson a highly unfavorable opinion; he was reckless and irresponsible, perhaps reflecting his Indian blood. Before McLoughlin had joined the Dickson expedition he had applied to Simpson for a position in the Company's service and had been rejected. The elder McLoughlin fully concurred in this decision. He wrote to a friend, "Gov.

Simpson writes me John applied to him for a passage to this Country which he refused that he then asked to Enter the Service, which was also refused. Is he such a fool as to suppose that people will Engage a person in this Service who had shown so Untractable a Disposition."[31]

During the Dickson scare, however, Simpson concluded it would be good policy to detach McLoughlin from the filibusterers by offering him a position as a clerk and surgeon. This decision did not indicate any change in attitude toward the young man. On other occasions the governor had removed trouble makers from Red River by giving them employment in the Company and sending them to posts remote from the settlement.[32] From 1837 to 1840 John was stationed at Fort Vancouver where he was under his father's constant surveillance. Apparently he worked conscientiously, for McLoughlin considered him to be the best man available on the coast to fill a position of responsibility at Fort Stikine. He had been sent there as assistant to William Glen Rae, his brother-in-law, but Rae was called to Fort Vancouver on another assignment, and McLoughlin was left in charge. It was a perilous position for a young man with no previous experience of managing men. He had the responsibility of controlling a rowdy staff of twenty men who had little regard for his authority. For a few months he had help from an able assistant, Roderick Finlayson, but Simpson transferred Finlayson to another post, leaving McLoughlin almost without support. The result was tragedy. McLoughlin was murdered by an employee who was probably under the influence of liquor.[33]

Simpson, dominated by his negative judgments of young McLoughlin and of the characteristics of mixed-bloods in general, immediately reached the conclusion that McLoughlin had been drunk and that his men had been provoked into revolt by his brutality. His communication to the elder McLoughlin on his son's death reflected his insensitivity at its worst. He told McLoughlin that his son's conduct and management "were exceedingly bad, and his violence when under the influence of liquor, which was very frequently the case, amounting to insanity."[34]

Even had it been true this indictment of a dead son was heartless. But the charges which Simpson thought to be true were in fact baseless. Simpson had given credence to derogatory testimony on McLoughlin because it agreed with his preconceptions. Having accepted this tainted evidence, he not only communicated it to the older McLoughlin in the most insensitive language but attempted to convince him that he should not pursue an inquiry into the murder of his son. Even when it became clear from the evidence of Chief Factor McLoughlin and others that Simpson had slandered young McLoughlin, he refused to retreat from his position. The incident was discreditable to Simpson. He was probably saved from censure by the London board by McLoughlin, who in his anger lost all sense of perspective and resorted to personal attacks on the governor. By a continual barrage of intemperate and unproved accusations, he lost any chance of support.[35] Thus, ironically, McLoughlin in the narrow sense "saved" Simpson. But Simpson had already damned himself.

McLoughlin continued on as chief officer in the Columbia Department until 1846, when he was granted three years' furlough, but his career with the Company was ruined by his collision with Simpson. His hatred of Simpson as the cause of his downfall obsessed him for the rest of his life. Years later he wrote "Sir George Simpson's Visit here in 1841 has cost me Dear."[36] The remark was partly true, but McLoughlin himself was largely responsible for his fall, and it is to Simpson's credit that he supported a more generous retirement settlement for McLoughlin than any other chief factor had received.

The feud had not yet erupted when McLoughlin accompanied Simpson on a voyage to California at the end of 1841. California had never been an area of great interest to the fur trade. Hudson's Bay trapping expeditions had visited the area since the 1820s, but the returns had not been great. California was a source of cattle and sheep. But James Douglas had come back from a mission to California in 1840 enthusiastic about the prospects for profits in sea otters, hides, and beaver, and Simpson decided to see for himself. His visit convinced him that California was not a promising area for investment, particularly under the rule of Mexico.

Simpson's judgments of Mexicans in part reflected his own commitment to efficiency, by which standard they seemed utter failures, but in large part his opinions were shaped by his belief in a divinely ordained hierarchy of races, at the summit of which was his own. The superior races he believed had an obligation to confer the blessings of civilization and commerce on the more benighted peoples of the world, and to rule those who were not able to rule themselves. His early version of the "White Man's Burden" had some novel elements, as was indicated in one passage in his published account of his journey round the world:

> It is in the view of the matter that I have in these pages, preferred the epithet *English,* as comprising both *British* and *American,* to the more sonorous form of *Anglo-Saxon*. The latter not only excludes the true objects of divine preference; but also, in excluding the Normans, it loses sight of the cooperation of Russia as the appointed auxiliary of England in permitting, perhaps by different means, the great cause of commerce and civilization, of truth and peace. Reflecting on the common origin and common destiny of Russians and Englishmen, I ought to feel that I am still to be among friends and kinsmen.[37]

The Mexicans of California were among the "races" who were incapable of developing the resources providence had given them. They were slothful—"perhaps the least promising colonists of a new country in the world."[38] Miscegenation with the Indians had degraded these descendants of the Spanish, who were interested in nothing but pleasure. They regarded work as beneath them, and manual labor was left to the "most wretched, degraded race of Indians I have ever fallen in with."[39]

The government of California was as corrupt as it was ineffec-

tive. Officials were active only in their own enrichment—
Simpson estimated that the government exacted taxes amounting to about one-third of the residents' income, and had "neither
the power nor the inclination to protect the two-thirds that are
left."[40] Governor Alvarado was "an ignorant, dissipated man",
"devoid of respectability and character".[41] "The Commander of
the Forces, General Vallejo, had no pretension to character or
respectability; he like most others with whom we have had deal-
ings in this country, betrayed a gross want of honesty and verac-
ity, and although his mode of cheating was shameless to a degree,
it was considered good policy to wink at and submit to it, rather
than risk a quarrel with this great man."[42]

This magnificent environment, Simpson concluded, was certainly not destined to be ruled for long by such backward people.
San Francisco Bay was the finest harbor on the Pacific coast of
North America, and California was capable of supporting a large
population if developed by a progressive nation. Simpson hoped
that the country which would fall heir to it would be Britain but
feared that it would be the United States. If Britain gained control, the area would be an excellent outlet for its surplus population and a market for its manufactured goods.[43] Simpson was an
expansionist; Pakenham in Washington had expressed similar
hopes with regard to California; but Whitehall had no interest in
assuming the risks and expense of adding California to the British
Empire.[44] Though he saw the beautiful coast of California as far
south as Santa Barbara, his mind was not on scenery but on
business, and the potentialities for trade under Mexican auspices
were not sufficiently attractive to justify prolonged attention. At
the end of January 1842 he departed for Honolulu, where he found
himself involved again in political issues of considerable moment.

The Hudson's Bay Company had maintained an agency in
Hawaii since 1833 when it had appointed George Pelly to represent it.[45] Pelly, who was about Simpson's age, was the first cousin
of Governor Pelly and a brother of Robert Parker Pelly, the
governor of Assiniboia from 1823 to 1825. Prior to Pelly's ap-

pointment the Company had used the services of Richard Charlton, but when Charlton became involved in competition for furs
on the Pacific Northwest Coast, he was replaced by a man whose
full commitment was to the Company and on whose loyalty it
could rely. Pelly was trustworthy but unfortunately also mediocre
in business ability.[46] Despite his deficiencies, however, the Company's Hawaiian business had prospered. Its ships visited the
Islands to trade timber, fish, and flour for Hawaiian products
and the Company's agency became the most important British
business on the Islands. At the time of Simpson's visit, British
trade with the Islands was about $150,000 per year, a large part of
which was the Company's and the volume was steadily rising.[47]

The Hawaiian Islands remained independent, but it appeared
that their days of freedom were running out. The tide of European
expansion had swept away other Pacific islands no more attractive. New Zealand had just been annexed by Britain, France
annexed the Marquesas in the same year that Simpson arrived in
Hawaii, and Tahiti was embroiled with France in a quarrel which
would result in 1843 in France's declaring a protectorate. Hawaii
was a resort of whalers on their way to their hunting grounds, and
the sugar trade was becoming an important industry. At the time
of Simpson's visit there were four American and three British
firms, including the Hudson's Bay Company.[48] And, of course,
there were the American missionaries whose influence was symbolized by the tentlike Mother Hubbards which adorned the once
naked Hawaiians.

The Kingdom of Kamehameha IV was in dire straits. Confronted with the threat of European domination the King and his
advisers twisted and turned, attempting to prevent the loss of
their independence by pitting one set of European interests
against another. The principal councillor was an ex-American
missionary, William Richards, but the Hawaiians let the British
know that they looked to them for protection. These maneuver-
ings were not always successful. In 1839 the commander of a
French frigate had threatened to bombard Honolulu in retaliation

for an alleged slight to Catholic missionaries—the same issue had resulted in the end of Tahitian independence. In this case the captain accepted $20,000, a heavy levy on the government's treasury.[49]

Among the British community there were several influential men who were anxious to promote British annexation. Most prominent of this group were Richard Charlton, who was now British consul, and Simpson's cousin Alexander. Charlton was the epitome of the arrogant Victorian, exuding a sense of moral superiority and manifesting his contempt for the backward races. As the representative of the Queen he felt it incumbent on him to maintain the dignity of the British state and he was quick to respond to any slights to his position.

Alexander Simpson over the years had risen to the rank of chief trader in the Company and now served as an assistant to George Pelly in Hawaii. But he and Pelly could not work together. Simpson had left Hawaii on hearing of the death by shooting of his brother Thomas during his Arctic explorations. When he returned he found that he had been replaced. Alexander attributed his misfortunes and, indirectly, those of his brother to the malevolence of his cousin George. The governor, he maintained, had driven Thomas from the service by a callous disregard for his welfare and sneers at his superior education and intelligence. The long hours which George had worked him had undermined his health, and his emotional stability had been wrecked by the slights to which he had been subjected. Now Alexander was also given the same ill treatment motivated by the jealousy of a man deeply sensitive about his illegitimate birth and inferior education.[50]

Alexander Simpson enthusiastically supported Charlton in his efforts to make Hawaii British. In 1841 on his way to England after the death of his brother he had drafted a letter to the Foreign Office asking that Britain bring the Hawaiian Islands under its protection as it had recently done with New Zealand. He believed that Governor Pelly supported the idea and Pelly's subsequent opposition he ascribed to the unwise counsel of the Company's agents in Hawaii and of George Simpson.[51]

George Simpson might have been expected to have the same point of view as Charlton and Alexander Simpson on the desirability of British rule. Shortly before he departed on his journey around the world, he had suggested to the Colonial Office that he would be prepared to compile a secret report for the governor on "the Commerce and Navigation of the North Pacific". Clearly implied was the assumption that it might be desirable for Britain to annex some of the islands, including Hawaii.[52] The Colonial Office so interpreted his communication and rejected it on the basis that Britain had no need to take the Hawaiian Islands, which were almost certain eventually to become American.[53] But such negativism would not in itself have been enough to deter Simpson. He had advocated that Britain take California, an equally hopeless prospect. Nor was Simpson motivated by personal animus to adopt a position contrary to that of his cousin. He could be malevolent to those who angered him but personal animosities did not enter into his judgments of Company interests. Nor did he have any sentimentality about Hawaiian independence. The only issue of substance was how the Company would fare under alternative governments, and he concluded that Hawaiian independence was preferable to the most likely alternatives. French rule would be disastrous; the Company would be subject to discriminatory treatment. American government would not be much better. Life under a benign European government, on the other hand, would be quite acceptable and remarkable—he thought of Russia as fitting these specifications. After he left Hawaii for his second visit to Sitka, he heard that the Russian government had long been interested in acquiring a naval base in the Hawaiian Islands. He believed it might be in the Company's interests to assist the Russians. Why not buy one or more islands on behalf of the Company and then resell them to the Russians at a handsome profit? The Russians, he was sure, would not hinder the

Company's trade; indeed, their occupation of the Islands might produce a greater market.[54]

This highly imaginative scheme was not pursued. The most desirable of the likely prospects was an international guarantee of Hawaiian independence, and Simpson devoted himself with energy and success to promoting that object. During his stay on the Islands, he was consulted by Kamehameha and his Queen, Kaluma, and by the Prime Minister, Kekauluohi (Auhea), and his principal adviser, the Reverend William Richards. It was a measure of his importance and of their desperation that they did so. He had political and financial weight, and they needed assistance in both areas. He also had excellent judgment, and the strategy pursued to safeguard Hawaiian independence was essentially his. At his suggestion, the government supported Richards as an emissary with full powers to negotiate with Britain, France, and the United States. Pelly, Andrew Colvile, and Simpson were named with Richards in his letters of credence as commissioners of the Hawaiian government. Furthermore, to underwrite the requisite finances for the measure Simpson provided a letter of credit for £10,000, which would be drawn upon by the commissioners.[55] He arranged that Richards should proceed immediately to London, where Simpson would meet him. But en route Richards decided to deviate from the plan and to pay a visit to Washington first, with the hope that he could get an American assurance of support for Hawaiian independence which could be used as leverage on the British and the French. Richards was partially successful in Washington. Though the United States was not willing to make a formal treaty, Secretary of State Daniel Webster gave Richards a memorandum that the United States was opposed to any power's establishing its ascendancy or achieving "any undue control over the existing Government or any exclusive privileges or preference in matters of commerce."[56]

Because of this delay Richards arrived in England later than a rival, Charlton, who was intent on subverting Simpson's and

Richards' plans, and if possible on gaining support for British annexation. There was no prospect of Charlton's achieving the latter object—the British government had no intention of further embroiling itself with the United States. But he might have frustrated Richards if it had not been for Simpson's intervention.

After he left Hawaii Simpson had revisited Sitka and then proceeded through Siberia to Russia, stopping off briefly in St. Petersburg for discussions with Baron Wrangell, and arrived back in London in November 1842. It had been a tiring journey, the exertions of which had overpowered him by the time he reached St. Petersburg. There he was so exhausted that he was confined to his room for eight days, and he was further plagued with a recurrence of the eye trouble which had periodically beset him.[57] But even in this extremity he was able to carry on his business conversations with Wrangell, and by the time he reached London his vitality had returned, though his vision remained impaired. When Richards finally arrived from the United States in February 1843, Simpson was able to give him energetic support, which was probably decisive in converting Lord Aberdeen, the Foreign Secretary, to his views. Aberdeen had considered the Hawaiian Islands to be virtually an American dependency and saw no advantage in Britain's subscribing to an empty declaration certifying to an independence which was a sham. Simpson was able to convince the Foreign Secretary that this view, partly derived from Charlton, was unjustified, and in April 1843 Aberdeen informed Simpson and Richards that Britain had decided "to recognize the independence of the Sandwich Islands under their present sovereign." This decision was made two months after Lord George Paulet, commanding the man-of-war *Carysfort,* had provisionally annexed the Hawaiian Islands, acting largely on the information and advice of Alexander Simpson. When news of this action reached Britain, Paulet was immediately disavowed. George Simpson had contributed to a temporary victory for Hawaiian independence, and he helped to solidify the achievement by accompanying Richards and his associates to Brussels and Paris, where he was involved in the Belgian and French decisions to take the same line as Britain. The joint Anglo-French convention of 1843, affirming respect for Hawaiian independence, was in large part the achievement of George Simpson, as the Hawaiian Minister of Foreign Affairs attested.[58] Simpson had been a well-informed and persuasive negotiator, and he had relished both the diplomatic interplay and the resultant success.

With the Oregon issue, which had simultaneously grown to crisis proportions, Simpson's political skills were of no avail, and he was not called upon to display them.

As events proceeded toward a denouement there was little that Simpson could do to change their direction. The Company had no resources with which to counteract the American settlers. A measure of its impotence was the attempt in 1841 to induce settlers under the leadership of James Sinclair to migrate from Red River to the Columbia. Simpson reasoned that such an emigration would serve two useful purposes—it would establish a British settlement on the Columbia and would siphon off population from a settlement which was becoming more and more a problem for the Company. Neither objective was achieved. Through Duncan Finlayson, Simpson was able to recruit twenty-three families including 121 men, women, and children of whom twenty-one families, totalling 116 people, actually arrived. The experiment was a failure. The emigrants soon moved to the Willamette Valley rather than settling on the lands north of the Columbia which the Company had assigned to them, and their departure from Red River had no discernible effect in quieting anti-Company agitation in the settlement.[59]

Simpson's efforts to influence British diplomacy were equally unsuccessful. He had no access to the Foreign Office itself except through Pelly, but in Canada he was a man of weight and he had the ear of the Governor General, Sir Charles Metcalfe. During his years at Lachine Simpson had become a prominent member of the merchant aristocracy of Montreal, esteemed not only because of his status as the Company's governor but for his conservative political views. During the rebellions of the French Canadians in 1837 and 1838, Simpson had been out of the country, but before and after these risings he had aligned himself with those British merchants who had denounced Papineau and his followers as traitors to the Crown. Among his close friends were George Moffatt, the leader of the English party in the legislature, and Peter McGill of a renowned family which had made a powerful contribution to the development of Montreal. Through his position he had entrée to the governor; through his political views he had the assurance that his reception would be a warm one. Metcalfe was particularly friendly to Simpson. Beset by "radicals", both English and French, whom he considered to be a worse menace to the British connection than the rebels of 1837–38, Metcalfe found comfort and support in men such as Simpson who assured him of the rectitude of his position. Metcalfe was receptive to Simpson for another reason—like Simpson, he was a Yankeephobe, convinced that the virus that had produced the Canadian rebellions had migrated from south of the border. Metcalfe, consequently, needed little stimulation from Simpson to recommend a strong line toward the United States, and his bellicosity was all that Simpson could have desired.[60]

But Metcalfe could not determine policy—decisions were made in Whitehall, and in November 1844 at the Governor and Committee's behest, Simpson arrived in London to participate in Company deliberations on the Oregon problem. He remained until April 1845. These months involved a critical phase in the crisis. The Peel government had privately decided that it would accept a settlement at the forty-ninth parallel, but events in the United States seemed to make such an agreement unlikely. James K. Polk had been elected President on a platform of expansionism and such militant slogans as "Fifty-four forty or fight" and "All of Oregon or none". His inaugural address was truculent, and the British government feared that war was imminent, for with all its disposition to peace it could not accept terms which were patently humiliating. Consequently plans had to be made for war, and Peel

and Aberdeen sought the advice of Simpson as a man with unrivalled knowledge of the area in dispute. At Aberdeen's request,
Simpson drew up a memorandum at the end of March 1845 on the
defence of Rupert's Land and Oregon. His plan was admirably
designed to protect the Company's interests. He proposed that a
small force of regular soldiers be stationed at Red River, which
would be the nucleus around which the mixed-bloods could
gather to defend against an American attack. Such a force, of
course, would also be useful in suppressing internal disorder in
the settlement, a consideration which Simpson chose not to men-
tion. To protect British interests on the Pacific Northwest he
recommended the dispatch of two sailing warships and two
steamers with a "large body of marines". They would take possession of Cape Disappointment at the mouth of the Columbia and
erect a battery to command the river. To supplement this force,
Simpson promised to try to raise two thousand men, mixed-
bloods and Indians, who would serve under British army officers.[61] The recruitment of such a sizeable irregular force was
probably unrealistic but Aberdeen and Peel felt the proposals
merited sufficient attention that they invited Simpson for further
talks, one at Peel's residence, and Simpson had a subsequent
meeting with Aberdeen alone at the Foreign Office. Out of these
consultations came a plan to send one or two engineer officers
with Simpson on his annual journey to the interior. Their purpose, to reconnoiter with a view to defence, would be concealed
in the guise of a hunting expedition in the wilds of North America.
The plan had the trademark of Simpson, who was delighted with
his role as a participant in highly secret measures of national
security. His self-esteem was further enhanced by his designations as a confidential agent, entitled to all the information relating to the Oregon question possessed by the British representative in Washington, Sir Richard Pakenham, and by Sir Charles
Metcalfe. Equipped with these credentials, Simpson proceeded
to Washington to confer with Pakenham. During the rail journey
from Boston, where he had disembarked, he took the opportunity

to gather what intelligence he could from "several influential members of Congress with whom I fell in the course of my journey." They informed him that Polk's language should not be taken too seriously; it was intended to please the "Loco focos", and the respectable elements of American society had no desire for war. This information he passed on to Pakenham, who indicated that he had gained the same impression.[62]

After his visit to Washington, which lasted only a few hours, Simpson hurried off to Montreal, where he saw Metcalfe and was introduced to two young officers, Lieutenants Henry J. Warre and Mervin Vavasour, who had been appointed to the reconnoitering mission. The party set out for Red River immediately, with Simpson taking every opportunity along the way to impress upon them the need for British military posts at Red River and in the vicinity of Fort William.[63] These garrisons might be some protection against American attack; they certainly would be useful in buttressing the Company's monopoly of the fur trade.

Simpson and the two officers arrived at Red River at the beginning of June 1845. After a few days of observing the area and its potentialities for defence, they departed for the Columbia with Ogden. Their subsequent experiences had little significance for the Oregon negotiations, though they provided a commentary on the problems of maintaining secrecy and on the mutual antipathies of civilians and the military. Father de Smet met the party on their way west and noted in his diary that the purpose of their journey was "neither curiosity nor pleasure", and that they had been ordered to take possession of Cape Disappointment and erect a fortress to command the entrance to the river.[64] The Company gained a considerable advantage, not in Oregon but at Red River. As a result of Simpson's representations and Warre's and Vavasour's support, the British government sent a detachment of the Sixth Royal Regiment of Foot to garrison Fort Garry, and during the two years from 1846 to 1848 that they were stationed there, the settlement was quiet.[65]

The Oregon Treaty of 1846, however, did have a continuing

relationship to Simpson's activities as a diplomatist. At the behest of the Company the agreement contained provisions guaranteeing the "possessory rights" of the Hudson's Bay Company and its subsidiary, the Puget's Sound Agricultural Company, in the lands south of the new boundary. It also conceded the right of navigation of the Columbia to the Hudson's Bay Company, "and to all British Subjects trading with the same". The latter provision was of little value to the Company in the new era, and the first was filled with ambiguities productive of future conflicts. Soon after the treaty was signed Pelly instructed Simpson to go to Washington and press Pakenham to seek a precise agreement with the United States on the boundaries of the lands belonging to the Company and its subsidiary. And, Pelly advised, if the United States offered £100,000 for these rights, Simpson should seize the opportunity and make a settlement on these terms.

Simpson went to Washington in February 1847. He found the times unpropitious. The Polk government, despite its early successes in foreign affairs, was unable to control Congress. Politicians were already looking toward the next election, and Polk's Democratic Party was fragmented into a number of factions, each supporting its own candidate rather than backing the incumbent President. Consequently, even if the administration was willing to make a settlement, there seemed little prospect that Congress would approve it. But while he was in Washington, Simpson was introduced to George N. Sanders, who confirmed Simpson's opinion of the corruption of America's politics and inspired his optimism that the Company could achieve by bribery what it could not do by honest negotiation.

George Nicholas Sanders was the son of Judge Lewis Sanders of Kentucky and Ann Sanders, the daughter of a Revolutionary War hero. He had entrée to the company of the influential. He was charming, and his entertainments were lavish and attracted the socially prominent and the socially ambitious. He could boast of his friendship with powerful people, and to some extent his claims were true. He was a close friend of Polk's Secretary of

State, James Buchanan, and had least a speaking acquaintance with other members of the cabinet. He was energetic, he was ebulliently optimistic, and he was completely unscrupulous. Simpson was much impressed. Here was a man who seemed to have the credentials to cut through all obstacles and arrange an understanding by arguments most persuasive to corrupt politicians.

Sanders first met Simpson as the representative of a joint-stock company which was headed by Captain A. C. Harris,[66] who had a contract from the Navy Department to carry mail from Panama to Oregon. Sanders proposed that this company buy out the Hudson's Bay Company's possessory rights for $500,000 (approximately the amount Pelly had authorized Simpson to accept from the United States), and then resell the property to the government at a much higher price. Sanders's fertile mind had devised a method by which this company could buy the rights with little or no immediate outlay—the Hudson's Bay Company would make a "large pecuniary advance", for the construction of the mail steamers. In making this proposal, Sanders had not bothered to secure prior approval from his associates, who later indicated that they were not interested. He then shifted his ground and offered his services as an agent of the Company to secure purchase of the rights by the government. Simpson was fascinated by this brazen self-confident entrepreneur, but also somewhat cautious.[67] Corruption with success was quite acceptable to Simpson, but with Sanders he was deluded by an influence peddler who promised more than he could deliver.

Sanders was not a charlatan. It would be closer to the truth to describe him as an inveterate optimist who in his mind converted hopes into prospects and prospects into realities. On the failure of his scheme to arrange the sale of the possessory rights to a private company, he developed another plan, involving a combination of influence and bribery, which he professed to believe would be successful. He had talked to members of Congress and concluded that they were not likely to support a proposal of more than

$300,000 for the possessory rights. Even this would not be forth-
coming unless he gave "A, B, C, D, and E" each ten per cent of
any amount over $250,000, "1, 2, 3, and 4" each five per cent,
and a few others one or two per cent, leaving himself twelve to
fifteen per cent. Simpson was to make a claim for $750,000,
including in the Company's property all conceivable assets and
the expenses involved in such projects as importing merino sheep
from England. He should also demonstrate that the investment in
land, stock, and trading assets paid a six per cent return. With
such a large claim, the United States government might make a
counter-offer the Company would accept. For his co-operation
Sanders would pay Simpson ten per cent of all the money
received.[68]

Sanders's scheme not only involved bribery of American officials but came perilously close to corruption for Simpson as well.
Here was this manipulator suggesting a secret deal by which the
overseas governor of the Hudson's Bay Company would receive
a substantial reward for co-operation in a seamy arrangement.
Simpson might have been expected to reject the proposal out of
hand on grounds of both expediency and ethics. He did not do so.
Instead he replied to Sanders that the minimum price set on the
property by the board had been $500,000, and that he did not think
they would now accept much less. He would, however, communicate Sanders's proposition, and in the meantime he could
assure Sanders that if he was able to get that price he would
receive a substantial commission—at least $10,000.[69] Simpson
did not allude to the suggestion that he receive a bonus. He would
not enter into such an arrangement without the approval of the
Governor and Committee, for however cynical his views regarding the lack of principle of other men, he was a loyal and trustworthy employee.

Simpson could hardly have expected the response to this
somewhat temporizing communication. Instead of waiting for
an answer from London, Sanders immediately set out from
Washington to Montreal. En route he was taken seriously ill with

an ailment diagnosed as erysipelas of the head. He arrived in Montreal in such pain that he sometimes seemed incoherent, and the story he told Simpson might have suggested his fantasies were unremitting. He had come, he said, at the urgent prompting of Secretary of State Buchanan who had suggested that he ask Simpson to accompany him to London to confer with the United States minister, the Company's board, and the British government to seek a tentative agreement. Simpson could not leave his business responsibilities in North America at that time, and Sanders decided to return to Washington and seek Buchanan's approval to proceed to London alone.[70]

During his conversations with Simpson, Sanders named some of the politicians he expected to help him achieve his goal —Buchanan and senators Calhoun, Cass, Crittenden, Houston, and Breese. From Simpson's summary there is no indication that these influential men were among the anonymous individuals who were to receive monetary rewards, though Senator Sidney Breese of Illinois later displayed suspicious enthusiasm for the project, as did Senator Edward Hannegan of Indiana, Chairman of the Foreign Relations Committee.[71]

Simpson did not entirely trust Sanders, but he saw the position of the Company in Oregon as increasingly desperate. The fur trade south of the international boundary had declined to insignificance, and the Company's property was not likely to be worth much as it was encroached upon by American settlers. A speedy agreement was in the Company's interests and perhaps, just perhaps, Sanders could bring it about.

Sanders sailed for London in March 1848 with introductions from Buchanan, Henry Clay, and Simpson and on April 15 met Pelly in the first of a series of interviews. Pelly had been uncomfortable about Sanders from the beginning of his involvement with Simpson. Pelly was proud of his reputation for integrity, and Sanders's proposals were highly unsavory. But perhaps that was the way business was done in Washington, as Simpson assured him. He suppressed his distaste and agreed to a contract by which

Sanders would act as the Company's agent for a year. Pelly committed the Company to accept $410,000 in United States bonds at five per cent interest. Sanders would receive a commission of two and one-half per cent of this amount and all of the payment above it. What Sanders chose to do with this money was his own concern. The price the Company was willing to accept was, of course, to be kept secret for the duration of the contract.[72]

Sanders emphasized that success depended on speedy action before opposition could become organized. Consequently it was necessary that the Company appoint a representative with full powers who could come to Washington to be available to act immediately in any American proposals. Pelly appointed Henry Hulse Berens, who was now a member of the Company's governing board. Simpson was not asked to join Berens in Washington. Instead, Duncan Finlayson was assigned the responsibility as one who was close to Simpson, and who had personal knowledge of the Company's business in Oregon.[73]

The appointment of Finlayson rather than Simpson to accompany Berens to Washington could be simply explained by the fact that the governor could not be away from headquarters for what could be considerable time. And the simple explanation was probably correct. There may, however, have been another consideration. The Berens mission came at a critical phase in Simpson's life. Since his period of deep depression in the 1830s, he had regained much of his old vitality, and apparently had put aside all thoughts of leaving the Company. But he had slowed down. In 1846 he had suggested to the board that they should appoint a resident senior governor to reside at Red River and relieve him of much of the supervision of that increasingly turbulent settlement. One factor was certainly his health. Troubles with his eyesight continued, and though his health was otherwise good, he did not have the unbounded energy of his early years. At sixty he thought of himself as an old man. He told Angus Cameron in October 1847 that he was "getting tired of knocking about" and that it was not unlikely he would retire the next year.[74] Also

Frances's precarious health was a cause of constant concern. Perhaps if they were to return to England they might enjoy some years of happiness. He had discussed his intentions with Frances's family, and like other shared secrets they soon became widely known.[75]

Beyond health and family considerations was his assessment of his past as well as his future. Even though he was deemed all-powerful by the officers of the fur trade, he was deeply conscious that he was a servant of the board. His area of autonomy was circumscribed, and when he had tried to extend it he had been reminded that the board was not prepared to surrender its powers even to a subordinate as trusted as he. In 1846, when he had sought the right to appoint clerks in the Montreal Department, Pelly had curtly rebuked him for "improper interference".[76] Thoughts of retirement soon passed, however. "Although work now becomes irksome to me at times," he wrote his friend Angus Cameron in November 1848, "I scarcely think I should be perfectly happy unless I had something to attend to in the counting house, however independent my circumstances might be."[77]

The Berens mission to Washington was another fiasco. Sanders's exuberance as usual had outrun reality. Contrary to his assertion, President Polk had taken no position on the possessory-rights issue, and though Buchanan supported purchase, he did so with the stipulations that the settlement must include relinquishment by the Company of the right of navigation of the Columbia granted it by the treaty and that the British government must accept this modification of the treaty. This the British government was not prepared to do. Heading the Foreign Office again was Lord Palmerston, the embodiment of John Bull, who denounced the Oregon Treaty as a surrender to the Americans. Consequently, though the right of navigation was virtually worthless, it was symbolically important and Palmerston had made it clear he would not be party to more surrender.[78]

Sanders's hopes for speedy action were shattered when Hannegan attempted to have the purchase considered by the Senate in secret session, only to be frustrated by another senator who moved for an evaluation of the Company's real estate before a vote. The motion was defeated, but further discussion was abandoned. This was a great blow. Now the project had to wait until the reopening of Congress in December, with all the hazards which delay would entail.

Simpson arrived in Washington the day before Congress adjourned. He had been summoned in the expectation that he would be present on an occasion of jubilation. He might have been expected to be depressed, but Sanders's magic again worked and convinced him that there was "no question that an agreement would be concluded in December."[79]

Between August and December, however, this optimism faded. Simpson, who was now invested with the power to commit the Company in place of the departed Berens, detected a note of uncertainty in the hitherto confident Sanders.[80] Pelly, on the other hand, had always doubted Sanders's ability to perform and disliked the way he operated. He expected Sanders to fail, and he gave Simpson authority to proceed on his own and make whatever terms he could.[81] Sanders, however, professed to be confident. He alerted Simpson to await a telegram announcing passage of the possessory-rights resolution by the Senate, assuring him that this action would take place not later than January 10.[82]

Simpson waited impatiently but the telegram did not come. On January 21 Sanders telegraphed that the resolution would probably pass that week, and on the thirty-first he advised him that the resolution had been introduced in secret session; on February 3 he urged Simpson to come to New York at once to be available, and on February 6 arrived the welcome news, "Special order Thursday certain pass. Come on."[83]

Simpson hastened to Washington, travelling day and night, to reach Washington on the morning of February 11, only to learn that Sanders had again misled him. A resolution had indeed been introduced, but from inquiries among knowledgeable people in Washington, he ascertained that only ten senators were favorable to it and forty were against.[84] Simpson finally had lost confidence in Sanders. The conclusion for Simpson was unusually belated.

Responsibility for the Sanders fiasco had not been Simpson's alone. Pelly, with all his concern over ethics and his distaste for Sanders, had approved an arrangement which violated his principles. But the initiative came from Simpson, and his revulsion against Sanders was on pragmatic rather than on moral grounds. After Pelly's death Simpson, with the approval of Andrew Colvile, worked with other agents who offered their influence in exchange for substantial commissions, among them George M. Dallas, Vice-President in the Polk administration. In all of these cases, however, the agents were promised only commissions. There was no longer any double pricing of the Company's property.[85] Many years later Sanders, after a long period of silence so far as the Company was concerned, appeared again with another project which was certain to succeed. In 1858 he proposed to buy up the "large floating debt" of the Oregon and Washington territories at "an enormous discount". He had information, he told Simpson that the Secretary of War would recommend payment at the next session of Congress and he and Simpson as holders of the demarcated bonds could make a profit of at least one million dollars.[86] Simpson's rejection was remarkably courteous.[87]

CHAPTER VI

The Capitalist

George Simpson's public life proceeded through four major phases, each governed by a different ruling force. During his years in the London counting-house and the first decade or so of his service in the Hudson's Bay Company he devoted himself with great energy and concentration to demonstrating to his employers that he was a paragon in the execution of the responsibilities with which they had entrusted him. In his zeal for economy, he outdid even his superiors and had to be reminded that considerations of humanity must color the Company's policy of retrenchment in the transition from competition to monopoly. The vigor he displayed in the performance of his duties exceeded any expectations that could have been entertained by any member of the London board, and indeed they felt it necessary to caution him against overly extending himself. During this facet of his career, Simpson seemed to be proving both to the board and to himself that he was indestructible. At the beginning of the 1830s, however, illness compounded by grief at the loss of his child and worry over his wife's health made him deeply aware of his vulnerability and his mortality. On his recovery he still felt the excitement of rapid canoe travel, but the frantic pace at which he had formerly driven himself was somewhat subdued. He no longer had any concern about his status in the Company; he was secure in the approval of the board; and during the remainder of the decade, his judgment on fur-trade issues carried more and more weight. He became virtually a member of the board, and the status he had achieved was underlined when he went to Russia with Pelly as a co-negotiator rather than merely as a knowledgeable subordinate. When he was knighted in 1841 he had "arrived"; he was a person of importance; there was no longer any necessity to prove his merit. During the decade of the 1840s Simpson was deeply involved in the high policy of the Company confronting such internal problems as the impact of the silk hat on the price of beaver and the rise of turbulence at Red River, as well as the international crisis on the Pacific Coast leading to the Oregon Treaty, and the subsequent issue of the Company's possessory rights. By the 1850s Simpson had moved into still another phase. His devotion to the service of the Company continued unabated, but he was increasingly involved in the business life of Canada. He saw in the railway boom an opportunity to advance his fortunes and he also directed his attention to shipping and other enterprises. These phases in Simpson's life, of course, involved no abrupt transitions. Simpson had always had an eye for any opportunities for profitable investments. But as his wealth accumulated he became increasingly involved in augmenting it further, and in so doing became intimately associated with politicians and fellow capitalists with the same preoccupations.

The shift in Simpson's attention to the development of his personal fortune coincided with a change in the nature of his responsibilities with the Hudson's Bay Company, particularly with regard to the Red River Settlement. From the beginning of his tenure he had considered the colony a potential menace to the fur trade. In 1822 he had predicted that it would ruin the trade "unless the Company could establish and enforce its monopoly rights against the inhabitants."[1] Subsequent events had confirmed his prediction. By the 1840s the private trade in furs had reached substantial proportions, and the menace to the Company's monopoly was made greater by the settlement's adjacency to the United States. During the Oregon crisis, Simpson had utilized the American military threat to induce the British government to send troops to Red River. For two years, from 1846 to 1848, four hundred men of the Sixth Royal Regiment of

Foot were garrisoned at Red River, and effectively performed the function which Simpson had really intended for them, overawing turbulent spirits in the settlement.[2]

The presence of the troops gave Simpson the physical power to carry out a tough policy against free traders. In 1844 Chief Factor Alexander Christie, who also served as governor of the colony, had issued a proclamation that any settlers importing goods on Company ships must sign a declaration that they were not engaged in illicit trade. Simpson did not initiate this decree, but he fully approved of it, and he reinforced it through the Council of the Northern Department, which imposed with certain exceptions duties of twenty per cent on goods imported from the United States and prohibited delivery of goods at York Factory to anyone not licensed by the Company. This hard line was deemed unwise by the London board, which took the position that at Red River as elsewhere the most effective means of eliminating competition was by offering better goods at lower prices, and Christie's proclamations were disallowed shortly before the arrival of the troops.[3] The reversal of Christie contained an implied rebuke to Simpson, a rare occurrence at that stage of his career, and may have influenced him to thoughts of resignation, which he expressed to Governor Pelly shortly thereafter.

Red River was the special object of Simpson's aversion for other reasons. It had been here that his young bride had suffered the complications of pregnancy and childbirth which had permanently affected her health; here their first-born child had died. The petty feuds of small-minded people were a constant irritation. This "cursed Settlement", as he called it,[4] had no redeeming features. Consequently when he discussed with Governor Pelly the conditions under which he would remain as overseas governor he was particularly anxious to rid himself of his taxing responsibility. Duncan Finlayson, who had been governor of the colony before Christie but who was now living at Lachine, expressed Simpson's sentiments as well as his own when he said in 1845 that without effective measures to stamp out the illicit trade, the settlement would become the ruination of the whole fur trade, and that he hoped to have nothing further to do with it.[5]

At Simpson's urging, the London board in January 1849 appointed Andrew Colvile's son Eden to be governor of Rupert's Land and Simpson's deputy. Simpson retained his title of governor-in-chief of all the Company's territories. Colvile was authorized to preside in the absence of Simpson at all councils of chief factors and he was appointed a member of the Council of Assiniboia, which had advisory authority on matters affecting the settlement. Colvile was assigned a remuneration of £500 for the first year and £1,000 thereafter, these amounts to be deducted from Simpson's salary.[6] Willingness to part with such a substantial amount of income was a measure both of Simpson's affluence and of his determination to relieve himself of irksome and fatiguing responsibilities.

The appointment of young Colvile—he was only thirty at the time—reflected the continuing power of his father in the councils of the Company, but he was also acceptable to Simpson, who had come to know him during his services in Canada where he had managed an estate in which his father was interested. Colvile had also been elected to the House of Assembly as a supporter of Governor Metcalfe, whose stand against "radicals" Simpson strongly approved. Colvile had accompanied Simpson to Red River and Norway House in the summer of 1848, undoubtedly in anticipation of his impending appointment, and in 1849, now as Simpson's deputy, he again attended the council with Simpson and then journeyed to the Pacific coast, where he visited Vancouver Island, which had recently been granted to the Company by the government for purposes of colonization.[7] Colvile consequently did not take up his residence at Red River until 1850, and in the meantime Simpson had to contend with a most serious outburst of defiance against the Company's monopoly. When the soldiers of the Sixth Regiment had been withdrawn, they had been replaced by a unit of fifty-six pensioners who rather than being guarantors of order became a source of problems from their lack of discipline. When Simpson arrived in the settlement in June 1849 on his way to the council meeting, he found the inhabitants in a state of great excitement. During the previous month the Company's officers had attempted to curb the free trade by prosecuting Pierre Sayer and three others for alleged illicit traffic in furs. Sayer was found guilty but, confronted by an armed crowd of Sayer's sympathizers, the authorities had prudently decided to impose no penalties. The pensioners had been conspicuous by their absence, and it was evident to all concerned that the Company was powerless to act against illicit traders.[8]

Simpson had to confront a delegation of mixed-bloods who insisted on the removal of Adam Thom, who as the recorder of Rupert's Land was the Company's principal legal adviser and who had been involved in the Sayer trial. Thom was the particular object of their ire because they believed, wrongly, that he was the prime mover in the harassment of the free traders and because they considered him hostile to the French in the colony. The latter assumption was undoubtedly correct. Just before the rebellions in Canada Thom had been the author of a series of "Anti-Gallic Letters" which appeared in the Montreal *Herald* and had infuriated the French Canadians at the same time as he had gained the esteem of the hard-shell businessmen of the town, Simpson included. Simpson had been so much impressed with Thom's courage and his legal abilities that he had recommended him for the recordership. He was thus in a very real sense "Simpson's man", though his arrogance and tactlessness made defending him particularly difficult. Simpson refused to be intimidated into recommending Thom's removal as recorder, but he sought to soften the rejection by promising to recommend that a substantial number of members of the Council of Assiniboia would be drawn from the mixed-blood population and that Thom's membership on the council would be terminated.[9] This concession did not reduce the discontent, and eventually in 1854 Thom resigned under continuing pressure from Simpson.[10]

This was Simpson's last intimate involvement with the affairs of Red River. The Governor and Committee had appointed Major William Caldwell, commander of the pensioners, as governor of Assiniboia, and in the fall of 1850 Eden Colvile arrived in the settlement to represent the Company's interests. Simpson withdrew with relief, and the abrasions of the Red River environment now were suffered by other men.

The delegation of responsibility to Colvile further emphasized Simpson's change of life-style. At the end of 1850 he wrote from Lachine to Donald Ross at Norway House that he did not intend to visit the interior during the next year and had no wish to interfere with Governor Colvile's exercise of responsibility. He added:

> The journeys to the interior & the duties I have there discharged for upwards of thirty years are becoming increasingly irksome, & unless circumstances may arise which appear to render my presence desirable I shall not in all probability recross the height of land.[11]

This determination reflected not only his declining physical resources but his desire to be close to an ailing wife. When Frances died in 1853, he was again free for long-distance travel, and he returned to Rupert's Land on several occasions. His days of record-setting journeys, however, were over, and his attention was increasingly devoted to his business affairs in Canada.

During his many years of residence at Lachine, Simpson had become one of the inner circle of the English-speaking mercantile community which dominated the city. In his position as the North American governor of a British-based monopoly he had to be somewhat circumspect with regard to public positions on partisan issues, but he could without reserve lend himself to projects designed to advance the commercial interests of Montreal, be they waterworks, railroads, shipping lines, or other progressive public works, and in the process he made investments of his own money which rewarded him handsomely.

From the day he first visited Montreal he had taken an interest in the state of the market, and after he took up residence in

Lachine he made investments for himself and for officers of the fur trade. During his early years as governor he was not always fortunate in his choice of investments for himself and for others. By his own testimony he had been compelled in 1834 to forgo thoughts of retirement because of a lack of fluid capital.[12] The vagaries of the Canadian economy made investments risky, but Simpson gained the well-merited reputation of being a shrewd balancer of risks and profits. His guiding principle, he told a friend, was to seek to place his money in enterprises which were safe and profitable. "I would prefer making 10% on a safe card to 20% by gambling."[13] By the application of this rule he built up a steadily growing fortune for himself.

In stock investments, however, "safe" is a relative term, and the vagaries of the North American and European economies in the 1830s and 1840s made safety particularly uncertain. Canada suffered sometimes in exaggerated form from depressions which struck Britain and America. The Panic of 1837 which hit the United States and Britain had an even greater effect on Canada, which was dependent on these two great markets. Prices tumbled and Montreal and other trading centers suffered a depression which lasted until 1840. Then the repeal of the British Corn Laws in 1846 eliminated Canada's tariff advantage vis-à-vis the United States in the export of grain and flour, and the timber trade was similarly dealt a severe blow by the elimination of tariff preferences. These reverses had repercussions throughout the society. Banks which came into being in boom times were wiped out in the depression, and not only depositors but promoters lost their investments.

Canada was also forced to compete with a more powerful American economy in its transportation system. The magnificent St. Lawrence waterway, on which the prosperity of Montreal depended, was closed from November to May, and above Montreal passage was blocked by rapids. The Hudson River was not blocked for so long, and the deficiency of its not reaching the Great Lakes was removed by the opening of the Erie Canal in

1825. Canada responded by building canals of its own at considerable expense to the Canadian treasury but these waterways were completed only in time to be rendered largely obsolete by the railway age which came to the United States and then to Canada.

All of these developments had an effect on the personal fortunes of Sir George Simpson, for he was involved in investments in banks, canals, and railways, and other Canadian enterprises. In Canada such transportation systems as canals and railways could not be successfully undertaken without substantial amounts of governmental subsidy, and the favor of politicians thus was much sought after by those who were promoting such enterprises. In the methods of attracting such favor Simpson had an unusual amount of expertise. From the beginning of his tenure at Lachine, Simpson had recognized the importance of courting influential politicians and some not so influential as a means of warding off attacks on the Hudson's Bay Company. His approaches took a variety of forms adapted to the individual. Mere hospitality could be of service. During the years that the celebrated Beaver Club was still continuing, invitations to its dinner meetings were much coveted. Simpson was admitted as a member in January 1827 and immediately took the opportunity to invite prominent businessmen and politicians to a greater extent than any other member.[14] After he moved into his impressive house in Lachine he entertained on a lavish scale. His wine cellar was stocked with the best wines available; he personally made the selections, and saw to it that they were properly stored, and properly decanted when the time for drinking arrived.[15] At his house the leaders of the political and commercial life of Canada dined and drank well. He could exude affability and charm, and he was able to develop close relationships with at least two of the governors who ruled Canada. Lord Sydenham was a cordial friend and used his influence on behalf of causes favored by the Company; Governor Metcalfe also was close to Simpson, in part because Simpson was his strong supporter in his fight against the "radicals", and he also gave his backing to the Company in such cases as the dispatch of troops to Red River. This rapport with the governor could be beneficial to Simpson personally and to his friends as was evidenced by the case of the Beauharnois Canal during Sydenham's administration. The canal project was one of the offshoots of the purchase of Edward Ellice's estate at Beauharnois by the North American Colonization Association of Ireland represented by Edward Gibbon Wakefield. Since the association had little ready cash, Ellice accepted a large amount of stock and consequently had a continuing interest in its affairs. He was not at all happy with Wakefield's management, and he asked Simpson and Andrew Colvile as well as Earl Fitzwilliam and Russell Ellice to serve on the board. The association sought to realize profits from the sale of land, and they hoped to make the Beauharnois property attractive to buyers by the construction of a canal between Beauharnois and Montreal as one of the links in the system which would open the route to Lake Erie for ships of medium tonnage. This canal would make the area around Beauharnois an attractive investment. Another group, however, was promoting a rival canal across the seigneuries of Soulanges and Vaudreuil. There were economic arguments for each canal, but the assumption of the Beauharnois group was that the decision would be made largely on political considerations. Lord Sydenham had expressed himself in derogatory terms both about Wakefield and the association, but he suddenly dropped his opposition and advocated that the association's projects be supported both in Canada and Britain. Until recently it was assumed that the conversion was a personal triumph for Wakefield, who had an interview with Sydenham prior to the decision. But recent research has produced a different interpretation. Sydenham had already changed his mind before Wakefield saw him. He had discussed the affairs of the association with Simpson in two long interviews and had agreed to back Simpson and Ellice. With Sydenham's support the association could hope to build either a canal or a railroad through Beauharnois under governmental auspices, as well as to establish a bank sanctioned by government. Simpson's influence and Ellice's reorganization of the board were consequently decisive.[16]

As his intervention with Sydenham indicated, Simpson understood the art of combining power and friendship to produce influence. His relationships with Canadian politicians manifested the same virtuosity. He conducted his business with politicians both directly and through an agent, Stuart Derbishire, the King's Printer, on whom he increasingly depended to secure favorable action on matters relating to the Hudson's Bay Company or to Simpson's personal interests. When Simpson first became acquainted with Derbishire is not clear. Probably it was just after Derbishire's service on the Durham mission, but in the 1840s they had become close associates. Derbishire as a lobbyist was perfectly adapted to Simpson's requirements. He was a good drinking companion, a gregarious friendly associate who could always be relied upon for the latest gossip. Derbishire came to know legislators intimately, and could assess their virtues and, more particularly, their foibles. He dispensed minor largesse to many politicians as the representative of Simpson, thus enhancing Simpson's reputation as a charming, generous man. Most of the gifts were insignificant enough to avoid any concern about bribery. One favorite present of Simpson was buffalo tongues. When one politician joked that acceptance of this delicacy might cause him to be suspected of taking bribes, Derbishire assured him that "Sir George only pleaded his cause with many tongues."[17] Other politicians might receive an Indian tent, or a canoe, or even just a box of cigars. Derbishire in 1852 wrote to Simpson:

> I would like a box of cheroots for Bouchette. You may send me one or two to spare, & if I do not place them you shall have them back. It is a delicate operation you know—if not well performed does harm & one cannot make opportunities, but only act when they make themselves. I told Bouchette you wished to shake hands with him & thank him. He said I like Sir George, everyone does—and his Agent has such an undeniable way with him.[18]

A box of cigars might seem harmless enough, scarcely a sufficient inducement to cause a legislator to change his position. But these seemingly innocuous gifts were part of a pattern of generosity and hospitality which certainly had an effect in strengthening Simpson's bonds with members of the legislature. Where large stakes were involved, more substantial contributions were necessary, as was the case in railway and shipping contracts in which Simpson was interested.[19]

In the histories of Canada and the United States there have been no more corrupt eras than those identified with railway construction. The railway age required substantial governmental involvement in the form of subsidies and guarantees; the opportunities for great wealth caused promoters to compete eagerly for the favor of powerful politicians, and that favor sometimes would be won only by substantial monetary payments. The corruption of the early years of the railway age in Canada was epitomized by Francis Hincks, the Prime Minister from 1851 to 1854. Hincks had one of the most brilliant financial minds Canada has produced; unfortunately he applied it not only to the advancement of the public interest but also to malodorous deals with special interest which violated the public trust. Donald Creighton describes him as "a clever little man—a typical sharp-eyed child of that unpleasantly public marriage between railways and responsible government".[20] The assessment is fair, though Hincks was hardly "typical". He was exceptional in his abilities, in his opportunities to influence great decisions, and in his amorality in placing personal enrichment above public responsibility. Hincks had been the author of an act in 1849 which guaranteed the bonds of railways up to five per cent interest when they had completed half their construction and authorized municipalities to provide financial assistance for railway construction. This legislation powerfully stimulated the railway boom which developed during his ministry, an administration which John A. Macdonald described as "steeped to the very lips in infamy, tainted with corruption".[21]

Before Hincks became Prime Minister, Simpson on several

occasions had utilized his services on behalf of Company interests. During the late 1840s the isolation of the region around Lake Superior and Lake Huron was broken by the discovery of iron and copper, which attracted mining companies to the area on both sides of the border. From a personal standpoint this development was beneficial to Simpson, since he invested in one of the mining companies, but the presence of a mining population threatened the Hudson's Bay Company's position with the Indians, since they could be diverted from their role as fur hunters. This counter-attraction was made stronger by the Canadian government's practice of distributing treaty payments to the Indians at Manitoulin Island on Lake Huron. Indians came from many miles to receive these payments, and they were brought into contact with influences which were subversive from the standpoint of the Company. They associated with other Indians who might be receiving better terms, and they came into contact with the miners. Simpson sought to counteract this threat by inducing the Canadian government to use the Company as its agent for the distribution of the payments, which would be made at the Company's trading posts,[22] and through Hincks's intercession he succeeded. Derbishire commented in 1850 that if Hincks did not have the power to settle a question, no one could; "He is the Government just now—so all people say, and so it is."[23] At that time, Derbishire's comment was an exaggeration, but Hincks was a useful friend, and his support became much more potent when he became Prime Minister. He was instrumental in procuring a settlement favorable to the Company of a vexatious issue involving the "King's Posts". These posts, which dated back to the French period, were located on the lower St. Lawrence and had been leased by the Company to prevent their falling into the hands of competitors who might use them as a base to attack the Company's fur trade. They were invaded, however, by settlers and lumberers, against whom the Company was powerless to act, and no protection could be expected from the Canadian government because of public antipathy toward the monopoly, particularly among the French-Canadian population. Hincks, however, carried through a settlement reducing the Company's payments from £600 per year to £60.[24] He was also responsible for a ruling by which buffalo robes were admitted into Canada as undressed furs, thus avoiding payment of duties. He told Derbishire, "You may write Sir George, veni vidi vici."[25] Such advocacy did not necessarily demonstrate corruption—Derbishire's payment as an agent in the King's Posts case was only £200,[26] and there is no evidence of money being paid to Hincks in these and other cases. But his role in shipping and railway enterprises in which Simpson was interested was clearly corrupt.

The railway boom coincided with revolutionary changes in ocean shipping. The steamship ended the era of sail, and iron replaced wood. The American Collins line instituted fast regular service between New York and Liverpool in the 1840s, and British and American companies sought to match or excel the performance of their American rival. Among the prizes for the competitors were government subsidies for the carrying of mail. These subsidies were lucrative. In 1840 the British government contracted with the Royal Mail Steam Packet Company to carry the mails to the West Indies for £240,000 per year. This shipping line had been formed the year before by James MacQueen.[27] Simpson saw this company as an excellent investment and bought stock for himself and for Company officers. He himself invested £1,000,[28] and after some vagaries in the market, the company paid off handsomely in dividends and stock prices.

This relatively small investment by Simpson was followed by a much heavier commitment of his money in a Canadian shipping enterprise which involved him with Hincks and with Sir Hugh Allan, who was well on the way to becoming the richest man in Canada. Allan was born in Scotland in 1810, the second son of a shipmaster. Like Simpson he had spent some time in a counting-house. After three years, when he was sixteen, he decided to migrate to Canada and sailed on a ship on which his father was the captain and his elder brother the second officer. He worked for a few years with a dry-goods merchant in Montreal and then joined a ship-building firm in which he became a co-partner in 1839 on the death of its head. In 1853 Allan decided that the time had come to build iron ships for the St. Lawrence—Atlantic trade, and he enlisted the support of several well-to-do Montrealers, including Simpson, in the formation of the Montreal Ocean Steamship Company.[29] The company built two ships, the *Canadian* and the *Indian,* which had a speed of eleven knots. They were intended for the Montreal—Liverpool route, but shortly after their construction they were requisitioned by the British government for the Crimean War. From the beginning Allan, Simpson, and their associates intended to bid for a mail contract with the Canadian government, which was held by a rival line, the Canadian Steam Navigation Company. The prize was a valuable one—the original contract was for £19,000 a year from Canada and £5,000 from the Portland and Montreal Railway.[30]

Simpson was assigned sole responsibility for the campaign to transfer the contract to Allan's company, and he began his suit early in 1854 through his agent Derbishire. He asked Derbishire to try to win the influence of "A" and "B" whose support was all that was required. For the identity of the individuals to whom these designations referred, Simpson told Derbishire, "you need no other clue to my meaning than that A is the *first* letter of the alphabet & B may be interpreted to mean canoe." The riddle was not a difficult one. "A" was the Prime Minister, Hincks, and "B" was his Solicitor General, John Ross, whom Simpson had recently sent a Hudson's Bay canoe. Simpson authorized Derbishire to "adduce 1000 weighty arguments" for every year of the contract, which could be paid either in one sum or from time to time, "or in such temps et lieus as might be agreeable".[31] A week later, presumably after Derbishire had communicated with Ross, since Hincks was in England, Simpson suggested that Ross write to Hincks not to encourage the owners of the rival line, the Liverpool firm of McKean and McLarty, in any hope that they might retain the contract.[32] McKean and McLarty were in a difficult position because they were caught in transition. They had depended on chartered ships which did not meet the specifications laid down by the contract for size and speed. They decided to build ships of their own, but they were not in a position to fulfil their contract to the letter without an extension of time. If the Canadian government insisted on exact fulfillment of the agreement, they would have to forfeit the contract.[33] It would thus be easy for the Hincks ministry to cancel the agreement and to award it to a Montreal-based group which was prepared to fulfil the terms of the agreement immediately.

Simpson, Allan, and their group also sought another contract, for tugboat service in the Gulf of St. Lawrence. If Hincks and Ross could deliver both contracts, he offered to produce ''10,000 golden reasons'' for their proceeding—''7000 for one, 3000 for the other'', to be paid in an interest in the company or in any other way they might desire.[34]

McKean and McLarty fought back, enlisting the support of the Montreal Board of Trade in a resolution endorsing the quality of their service.[35] Simpson, however, was not unduly concerned, and in the spring of 1854 he was confident that the Allan interests would get the contract soon after Hincks returned from England. Hincks, however, had been subjected to steadily increasing attacks centering on a transaction involving city of Toronto debentures in which he and an associate had cleared a profit of £10,000 aided by legislation which he himself had sponsored. Under fire for this and other alleged abuses and confronted by a rebellious assembly, Hincks was in no position to respond favorably to Simpson's overture, and in September he and his cabinet resigned.[36] The new government included two ''Hincksites'', one of whom was John Ross, but the immediate opportunity had been lost. The preponderance of the incoming cabinet were unfavorably disposed to Allan, and the contract with the other line was extended. In 1857, however, Allan finally won the mail contract with a subsidy of $120,000 a year,[37] and Allan who had refused to pay Derbishire for his lobbying activity finally agreed to compensate him.[38] Success probably was not the result of "10,000 golden reasons" but from the efficiency of the Allan line and the ineffectiveness of its competitor. The tugboat contract eluded Allan and Simpson; it was awarded to an influential French-Canadian politician, M. W. Baby.[39] The story probably has no moral.

Simpson was also actively involved in the formation of the Montreal Mining Company, which was founded in 1846 to exploit mineral resources on the north shore of Lake Superior. News of rich discoveries on the American side produced an interest in the Canadian shore which was further stimulated by geological reports indicating that the northern side might be even more productive than that on the south. Exploring licences were avidly sought after, and the Canadian government granted twenty-seven to "principal people", as Simpson described them. Simpson took a leading part in the formation of a group which took up twelve of these licences.[40] This enterprise, the Montreal Mining Company, acquired a monopoly of one hundred thousand acres of mineral lands, and the favoritism shown this and another company from Quebec, which received sixty thousand acres, led to charges of collusion between government officials and the promoters.[41] Simpson served as a director only between 1846 and 1848, but continued to have a financial interest in the company thereafter.[42]

Simpson also was involved in several railway projects. The earliest of these related to his place of residence. Lachine was then a small village about eight miles from Montreal, and Simpson and others thought that the inconvenience of travel by carriage for that distance would make a railroad profitable. But he and his associates had larger plans. This line also might be a link in a more extensive chain of railways. The principal promoter of the railway was James Ferrier, a Scot who had come to Montreal penniless in 1821 but who through diligence and ability rose to become an important man of business. He convinced Simpson and seventy-four other co-sponsors that the railway would be an excellent investment. Among those taking shares on Simpson's recommendation were officers of the fur trade, including Duncan

Finlayson, and Simpson and Finlayson were appointed to the board of directors.[43] In 1845 Simpson expressed to Angus Cameron his optimism about the line's future.

> We are now actively engaged in getting up a Railroad between Montreal and Lachine, the line has been surveyed & the cost is expected to be from £40000 @ £50000, but as it is likely we may hold Steamboats to Caughnawagha & Beauharnois in connection with the Railroad, the nominal Capital Stock will be £75000, of which for myself & friends, I have taken about one third. The Stock is in great demand, & it is expected will prove one of the best investments in the country.[44]

The line was opened in November 1847 with great ceremony highlighted by a sumptuous luncheon attended by people of consequence, including the governor general.[45] At first the railroad seemed to vindicate the rosy hopes of its promoters. Traffic was heavy and the shares were at a premium. But soon passengers stopped using the railway—some indicated that they preferred the safety of horse-drawn carriages to the hazards of excessive speed and reckless engine drivers—and the stock fell to about twenty-five per cent of par, with no buyers. By contrast a rival line, the Champlain and St. Lawrence, was making handsome profits, and Simpson hedged his losses by investments with this competitor.[46] Meantime Ferrier tried to save the Lachine railroad by expansion and a charter was granted to build from Caughnawaga, opposite Lachine, to the American border. The new company, formed in 1850, which absorbed the Montreal and Lachine railway, was called the Montreal and New York Railroad Company. This line became one of the competitors for traffic to and from the United States. Three years later the line made an agreement with the Champlain and St. Lawrence Railroad Company to share their rates rather than to continue to compete, and they then formally merged as the Montreal and Champlain Rail-road Company. In 1863 the great new network of railways, the Grand Trunk, leased this railroad and in 1872 bought it outright.[47] Simpson was involved in the merger with the

Montreal and Champlain and St. Lawrence which rescued the Lachine line from bankruptcy, and his shares in a foundering enterprise were converted into a profitable investment.[48]

Simpson's participation in these reorganizations and mergers does not seem to have required him to approach his political friends; the arrangements were between capitalists for mutual benefit. One other railway in which he was interested, however, had a strong political component, a line popularly called the "North Shore" which went through a variety of official designations.

Early in the railway boom the desirability of a railway between Montreal and Quebec attracted interest in both cities and rival groups were formed to seek a charter for its construction. Among those who entered the race was Joseph Cauchon, one of the most powerful politicians in French Canada. Cauchon had been elected member of the Legislative Assembly for Montmorency in 1844, when he was twenty-six, and he served in this house and in the confederation House of Commons until 1872. Cauchon had been an opponent of the Hincks administration but on its collapse he supported its successor, the MacNab–Morin government, and became Commissioner of Crown Lands. John A. Macdonald, a master of the political art, described Cauchon as follows in 1855:

> Cauchon I consider the ablest Franco-Canadian in the House, and from his energy of character & power of will, will acquire ere long a decided influence over the minds of his countrymen. The Conservative section of the Govt. were especially anxious to secure him, as he brings seven with him.[49]

Despite his differences with the Hincks government Cauchon was able to secure a franchise for the railway. How this success was achieved is not entirely clear. One Montreal paper explained it in terms of strong pressure from the French-Canadian members of the Assembly and from the support of leading citizens of Montreal. Whatever the reason, the executive council which had refused to back the road suddenly reversed its position. In the dead of winter in 1853 a committee of the council toured the route of the proposed railway and expressed its pleasure at the character of the country and its resources. The editor remarked that the fact that the country was covered with snow might have prevented other people without such perception "from making such important discoveries, or experiencing such infinite delight."[50]

Construction of the railway, however, was delayed by a serious difference of opinion among Cauchon's associates, most prominent of whom were members of the well-to-do Baby family. The basic conflict was over how extensive the project should be, whether it should involve only the line between Montreal and Quebec or whether the company should seek to undertake a great network of railways similar to that developed by the Grand Trunk a few years later. Cauchon favored the latter course. He proposed to build a railway up the Ottawa Valley which would extend to the Great Lakes and tap the markets of the American West as well as reaching out to the populous eastern United States. From his strategic position as Commissioner of Crown Lands he was confident that the company would receive four million acres from the Canadian government which would be attractive bait to English capitalists from whom he hoped to secure £4,000,000.[51]

This plan was opposed by the Babys, and both sides turned to Simpson for support—Cauchon for help in attracting English capitalists for his grand scheme and the Babys for reinforcement of their position that the risks were too great. It was a tribute to Simpson's astuteness and to the esteem in which he was held that he was able to retain the confidence of both sides.

Simpson cautioned Cauchon against being too ambitious. With some experience of his own he pointed to the numerous wrecks of railway projects, some of which were constructed through settled districts. Cauchon's gigantic scheme would involve miles of line through wilderness. The Ottawa Valley was not likely to become populous for many years to come, and without local traffic the company would probably not make a profit. But Simpson did not go so far as to reject Cauchon's ideas outright. Rather he offered his opinions as a caveat, and promised to use his good offices with influential capitalists in Britain to get Cauchon a sympathetic hearing. Among those he mentioned specifically were Eden Colvile, who had served briefly as an agent for the railroad, and Arthur Kinnaird, of the private banking firm of Ransom, Bouverie, and Company.[52]

Cauchon's plans relied upon a favorable money market, but Britain was going through a period of financial stringency, which interacted with an economic depression in the United States. Early in 1857 he broke with his associates the Babys, and M.W. Baby, a junior member of the family, introduced a bill embodying a more modest objective. It provided for the construction of the railroad from Montreal to Quebec and a spur from Three Rivers to the Grand Piles on the St. Maurice, with a subsidy of one and a half million acres. From the Piles, passengers and goods would be transported ninety miles farther inland by steamship.[53]

The contest between the Babys and Cauchon ended in victory for the Babys,[54] and Cauchon resigned from the government in disgust. Simpson agreed to serve as a director and on June 30, 1857, he was elected president by a vote of seven to two. The majority was a measure of Cauchon's defeat. "How are the mighty fallen!" exclaimed the Quebec *Chronicle*. "Mr. Cauchon and his panegyrists will perhaps soon learn how the people of Quebec estimate his much-vaunted service to the North Shore Railway and the course he has pursued in relation to that enterprise."[55]

Simpson's election was further evidence of the respect he held in the business community, particularly so since he lived in Montreal and London, and the company's headquarters were in Quebec. It was also a reflection of the hopes of the promoters that Simpson could untie the purse strings of English bankers. His efforts to do so, however, were unsuccessful. Added to the woes of the English money market were the repercussions from the rebellion in India and deepening depression in the United States. Consequently he was advised that only when the financial stringency was relieved could investors be expected to be willing to risk their money.[56] Feeling the infirmities of age and involved with many other responsibilities, Simpson resigned his presidency in August 1859.[57] He retained his position on the board, however, as well as his directorship on the Montreal and Champlain railway and on the Montreal board of the Bank of British North America.[58]

Simpson's role in the North Shore Railway had been primarily that of counsellor; he had taken no part in the political infighting between the Babys and Cauchon. He thus reconciled his private interests with his responsibilities as governor, since the Hudson's Bay Company, confronted with rising demands in Canada for an end to its monopoly, needed all the friends it could get in the legislature.

Simpson was interested in a good investment wherever it was to be made. He made a considerable profit on debentures of the Montreal waterworks.[59] He considered buying land in Scotland but decided against purchasing real estate he had not seen.[60] In 1845 he made a coup when he bought most of the estate of Sir Alexander Mackenzie, some of the choicest land in Montreal, for £9,000. This land extended from Dorchester to Sherbrooke Street. In addition it included an oblong square of fifteen acres on the mountain, a beautiful site which he bought with the idea of either using it to build a home or holding it for a rise in the market. The remainder he subdivided into small building lots. He also bought a farm of two hundred acres near Lachine for £1,300.[61] These properties and his Dorval purchase gave him a considerable investment in land. Recorded at the time of his death were various other properties in Canada, including three houses valued at $6,000 each and another farm valued at $1,540.[62]

The business abilities which made Sir George Simpson an outstanding governor of the Hudson's Bay Company also made him a wealthy man. When he died his estate contained portfolios of stocks, bonds, and real estate worth substantially in excess of £100,000. The illegitimate child through perseverance, ability, and good fortune had made himself a great success by any standard of his society. He had achieved a position of power and prestige, he had been involved in great decisions not only in business but in international relations, he consorted with leaders in politics and in commerce, and he accumulated a considerable fortune. Horatio Alger could have used George Simpson as a model.

CHAPTER VII

Last Years

During the decade of the 1850s the "Great Monopoly" that had been forged in 1820 was beleaguered by forces far more potent that its powers of resistance. The menace did not come from rival fur traders, even the free traders of Red River. Against them the techniques of the 1820s worked with undiminished effectiveness thirty years later. Opposition must be destroyed at whatever price was necessary; accommodation of opponents only encouraged others to enter the competition. This policy had preserved the fur-trade monopoly, not the charter and other legal rights which government had conferred upon the Company. At mid-century, however, the Company confronted adversaries with whom it had to come to terms or it would face certain death. The westward movement of the settler, which had swept aside the Indian-hunting society, now lapped up to the environs of the fur-trade monopoly. The railway south of the border had opened up a new west. In 1850 the white population of the territory of Minnesota, an area then larger than the present state, was only 6,077; but in ensuing years thousands of settlers arrived. Minnesota became a state in 1858, and the census of 1860 recorded a population of 172,000.[1] Red River was no longer an isolated community.

Steamer service to the United States was opened up in 1858, and the market of St. Paul drew more and more Red River carts south. The possibility that Red River might be drawn into the American economy, and perhaps be annexed to the republic, excited the apprehensions of Canadians who had ambitions for a transcontinental dominion, and contributed to agitation for the end of Company rule. What, in brief, the Hudson's Bay Company of the 1850s had to come to terms with was the coming of a new world. The old order was passing away, and with it the men who had long directed the affairs of the Company.

In the 1850s Simpson noted the deaths of those with whom he had been associated since the early days of the amalgamation. Sir John Henry Pelly, who as much as any man had been the architect of the Company's policies, succumbed in 1852 after a long illness. In 1854 Peter Skene Ogden and John Rowand, two of the giants of the fur trade, died. Simpson observed that "there are not in the Service above a dozen men who were in the country at the date of the Coalition."[2]

Simpson was more and more alone, and he was preoccupied with the thought that he soon must follow his companions. Sometime in 1851, probably in the spring, he suffered two apoplectic strokes.[3] He recovered from these seizures sufficiently to be able to journey from Lachine to Moose, but the death of his wife in 1853 left him a lonely old man. One of his acquaintances, Edward Ermatinger, described him thus:

> Our old Chief, Sir George, as you describe him, tottering under the infirmities of age, has seen his best days. His light canoe, with choice of men, and of women too! can no longer administer to his gratification.[4]

And yet there was still in Simpson a vital element which defied his physical deterioration. Despite the strokes he still seemed to be able to summon the resources to set out for the annual meeting of his council. During the almost forty years he served with the Company from 1821 until his death, there were only three years in which he did not make one of his celebrated journeys, and none of these years was in the 1850s.[5] His powers of recuperation, particularly when a canoe journey was in prospect, amazed his associates. An old man, "tottering under infirmities", as Ermatinger had seen him, was transformed into a vigorous voyageur. Indeed, some suspected he must be in league with the powers of darkness.

Simpson's resiliency of body was matched by his flexibility of mind, a more uncommon characteristic in aging people than physical vigor. He recognized that in an era of railways and settlement the Company must develop policies by which it could come to terms with changing conditions. Chartered monopolies were not only an anachronism but were attacked as a heresy to the religion of free trade. The only other survivor, the East India Company, had been stripped not only of its monopoly of the Indian trade but of its trading functions entirely. The Hudson's Bay Company had not been attacked with the same intensity, in part because its domain did not excite the same degree of cupidity as the treasure house of India, in part because of misconceptions that it presided over a land of perpetual winter hostile to human habitation. These negative protections, Simpson recognized, could not continue for long. He agreed with the opinion of Donald Ross, in charge of Norway House, who wrote him in 1848:

> We can no longer hide from ourselves the fact, that free trade notions and the course of events are making such rapid progress, that the day is certainly not far distant, when ours, the last important British monopoly, will necessarily be swept away like all others, by the force of public opinion, or by the still more undesirable but inevitable course of violence and misrule within the country itself—it would therefore in my humble belief be far better to make a merit of necessity than to await the coming storm, for come it will.[6]

Simpson considered the chartered rights to be of little value. What made the Company powerful was its inherent economic strength, its ability to overcome the competitors by offering superior goods at lower prices. Were not these practices appropriate to the new free-trade principles? Why not make a virtue of necessity by selling what was worthless before the buyer became aware of the fact? Pelly came to much the same conclusion, and he suggested to Earl Grey, the Colonial Secretary, in 1848 that the Hudson's Bay Company did not desire to stand in the way of progress and might be willing to sell its special privileges if it was guaranteed a return of ten per cent on its capital and allowed to retain the same rights of trade as other British subjects.[7] These terms were similar to those proposed by the East India Company for the relinquishment of its charter.

After Pelly's death Simpson continued to advocate that the Company try to sell the property while it still had property to sell, and his old patron Andrew Colvile, who succeeded Pelly as governor, was sufficiently impressed with the argument that he asked Simpson to draw up a valuation of the Company's assets. By Simpson's calculations, the one hundred and forty posts belonging to the Company were worth £108,000 in terms of construction and land-improvement costs. Those in the territory held under licence from the British government he valued at £66,500; the posts in Canada and Newfoundland, at £57,500; the Oregon posts at £70,500; those at Vancouver Island at £18,000; the station at Honolulu, £4,000; and the posts in Rupert's Land £161,500.[8]

Such valuations, of course, had little significance without a prospective purchaser, and the British government indicated by its silence that it had no interest. One of the cardinal principles of Imperial government was that colonies should not be a burden on the British taxpayer. Every proposed expenditure for Imperial purposes was scrutinized by the Treasury and by Parliament with a very cold eye, and governments brought requests for money before Parliament only in direst necessity. There was no such compulsion to purchase the assets of the Hudson's Bay Company.

The only problem relating to the Company which evoked any positive response from the British government was the danger of an American coup. This concern had motivated the dispatch of the Sixth Regiment in the 1840s, and had been used at least as an excuse for approving the Company's request for a company of pensioners. But sending these troops to Red River did not involve any additional expense to the government. The Company had to pay all travel expenses and provide rations and supplemental allowances to all of the officers and men. In addition, they would receive allotments of land.[9]

Since the British government had no intention of providing any funds, the only other potential buyer was Canada, and in 1850 the colony had neither the resources nor the desire to pay for the Company's property. The advocates of annexation were importunate, but they were also insistent that the transfer should be at no cost to Canada. The Company's charter, they argued, was a nullity, and if having titles were to be the basis for permission, Canada as the heir of the French had a better right to the land than did the Company.

The campaign against the Company began in the late 1840s, led by the "Clear Grit" party, which derived most of its support from farmers in what is now Ontario. The spokesman was George Brown, who in addition to this agrarian support could count on businessmen in Toronto who saw opportunities in the opening up of the lands under the Company. Two newspapers, the *Globe* and the *North American*, edited respectively by Brown and by William McDougall, gave their editorial support. Initially these newspapers focussed on the alleged iniquities of Company rule at Red River, but soon shifted their attack to the positive line that Canada's Manifest Destiny included Rupert's Land, or what they now called the North West Territories. Brown's Clear Grits represented only a portion of the electorate in the English-speaking province, but if their attacks caught fire in French Canada, Simpson recognized that the Company was in serious trouble. He was at pains to do all he could to keep his friends in the Canadian legislature and to elicit all the information he could on Brown's plans and progress. As usual, he relied on Derbishire for intelligence. In November 1850, on a day when Brown's *Globe* had devoted two columns to an attack on the Hudson's Bay Company, the ever-alert Derbishire happened to overhear an argument in Armour's bookstore between Brown and the proprietor. Armour declared that he paid no attention to anti-Company propaganda since it was spread by people with ulterior motives, and Brown angrily replied that Armour was ill informed. The Company, he said, had exploited and debauched the Indians; Derbishire understood him to say that in one year it had imported one million hogsheads of liquor for the fur trade.[10] At this early stage of agitation, the ammunition was provided by disaffected ex-servants of the Company and by Red River colonists with personal grievances. Their allegations had some effect both in Canada and in Britain. W. E. Gladstone took up the theme of the heartless monopoly extracting huge profits from the misery of the Indians and its own employees,[11] and the same charges were repeated in Charles Dickens's magazine *Household Words* in 1854.[12]

So long as the opposition directed its fire at the Company's alleged exploitative policies, it could defend itself effectively. Some charges could be proved false, others exaggerated, and the motives of the critics could be impugned. In 1848 the Governor General of Canada, Lord Elgin, dismissed the charges against the Company as malevolent and false. The Company, he found, had been a boon to the Indians, who would have been in far more miserable circumstances if their lands were opened to free trade:

> It is indeed possible that the progress of the Indians toward civilization may not correspond with the expectations of some of those who are interested in their welfare. But disappointments of this nature are experienced I fear in other quarters as well as in the Territory of the Hudson's Bay Company and persons to whom the trading privileges of the Company are obnoxious may be tempted to ascribe to their rule the existence of evils which it is altogether beyond their power to remedy. There is much reason to fear that if the Trade were thrown open and the Indians left to the mercy of the adventurers who might chance to engage in it, their condition would be greatly deteriorated.[13]

Elgin's comments could not have been more favorable to the Company if they had been drafted by Simpson, and indeed there is reason to believe that the governor was both indirectly and directly the source of Elgin's information. Elgin relied heavily on Lieutenant Colonel John F. Crofton, who had been in command of the troops at Red River, and Crofton was not an unprejudiced witness. On his arrival in Canada, Crofton went to see Simpson—whether by his own or Simpson's initiative is not evident. But what is clear is that Crofton was led to expect Company support in securing a more attractive position in the army. When Crofton went to see Elgin for an interview, Simpson accompanied him and had the opportunity to observe first-hand the value of his testimony. Simpson also helped Crofton to write his report to the War Office recommending that pensioners be sent to Red River, and repeating his testimony that the Company was not guilty of the practices charged against it. "I believe my answers have been satisfactory," he wrote Simpson.[14]

The Company's position became much more vulnerable when the emphasis shifted from the humanitarian line to that of the necessity of giving way to progress by opening the West to settlement, and the danger that this colonization would be under American rather than Canadian auspices unless action was taken soon. The Canadian government, as distinct from a mere faction in the legislature, first took this position in 1856. In September of that year the President of the Executive Council, Philip Vankougnet, declared that it was Canada's destiny to extend to the Pacific and that it was imperative that a railway be built across the Hudson's Bay territory to British Columbia. The Hudson's Bay Company must step aside:

> The charter of the Hudson's Bay Company—no charter—no power could give to a few men exclusive control over half a continent. That vast extent of territory stretching from Lake Superior and the Hudson's Bay belonged to Canada—or must belong to it.[15]

This declaration was reinforced a few months later by the full council, which asserted that it was the "general sentiment" in Canada that the country must reach out to the Pacific.[16]

This Canadian agitation brought the issue of the Hudson's Bay Company emphatically before the British government. The Company's licence of exclusive trade west of the chartered territory was about to expire, and the Canadian official declarations seemed to indicate that Canada might be willing to assume the responsibility and expense for administering the licensed territory and, perhaps, for the chartered lands as well. The result was a decision to institute a parliamentary inquiry in which Canadian and Company spokesmen would have the opportunity to present testimony.

The committee was well balanced between friends and critics of the Company. Four members were favorably disposed, including Edward Ellice, Junior, who was a member of the Company's governing board, and three including Gladstone were critics. During its deliberations another member of the Company's board, Alexander Matheson of the Jardine Matheson firm, was added to the committee, thus giving the pro-Company element a slight preponderance. One element in Simpson's strategy, with which the board agreed, was to demolish misstatements by hostile witnesses while at the same time maintaining a willingness to give up the chartered rights for suitable compensation. The other object was to try to influence the testimony of the Canadian witnesses, and here he achieved a stunning success. By a stroke of incredible good fortune, one of the two representatives was John Ross, and the other was Chief Justice William H. Draper, who had taken a moderate line with regard to the Company. The selection of these two indicated that the Canadian government had had second thoughts about immediate annexation of the West with all of the expense it would involve. John Rose, the Company's lawyer in Canada, said of Draper's appointment:

> It is a very fair way of easing off popular clamour here, as I assume the extreme limit of his mission will be to ascertain on what terms the Company will give up any territory required for settlement, and by whom,—Canada or England—the indemnity is to be made good. The danger is that Draper will be thought to be *too much* in favour of vested rights. You of course know him.[17]

Simpson indeed knew Draper well. They were close friends, and Simpson had secured the appointment of Draper's son as an apprentice clerk, though the youth died before he could enter the service.[18] Draper's testimony, which undoubtedly reflected his convictions, was generally laudatory of the Company's record, though he expressed concern that unless a strong government was soon established, the United States would swallow the Company's territories.

Ross's testimony went far beyond Draper's; much of what he had to say was in accord with Simpson's own views, and the likeness was not entirely coincidental. Before Ross went to England he and Simpson had discussed the Hudson's Bay question and Ross had indicated his desire to be of service. Ross was the anonymous source of an article in the *Toronto Leader* which he either wrote himself or provided the material for. The article maintained that the Company secured the Canadian interest by governing a huge territory until Canada was ready to assume the responsibility. At the present time, however, such annexation was greatly premature:

> If the burden were at present thrown upon Canada, its possession, involving us in constant border wars with the Indians would be a bill of costs in every way; and, for a long time, little or no profit.[19]

Simpson's greatest problem with the Select Committee came from his own testimony. One of the Company's critics on the committee pressed him about his attitude toward settlement in the Company's territories. Was his attitude really as benign as he had testified? Simpson replied that he did not feel that the fur trade should stand in the way of progress, but testified that the interior of British North America was not a promising field for agriculture. The critic then read and reread a passage from Simpson's *Journey Around the World* which described in lyrical terms the fertility of the country between Lake of the Woods and Rainy Lake. Simpson's comments on Red River were also quoted:

> The soil of Red River Settlement is a black mould of considerable depth, which, when first tilled, produced extraordinary crops . . . . even after 20 successive years of cultivation, without the relief of manure or of fallow, or of green crop it still yields from 15 to 25

bushels an acre! The wheat produced is plump and heavy; there are also large quantities of grain of all kinds, besides beef, mutton, pork, butter, cheese, and wool in abundance.[20]

Simpson could not explain that these passages reflected the excessive enthusiasm of a ghost-writer, and his assertion that he had been referring only to the banks of rivers and a few scattered plots did not convince his listeners. His testimony before hostile examiners was not impressive. He was particularly inept in his responses to the scathing cross-examination of John A. Roebuck, a persistent parliamentary critic of the Company as a barrier to progress. Simpson's performance converted at least one erstwhile admirer into an advocate of his retirement. The sixth Earl of Selkirk, who in the 1830s had been eloquent in his praise of Simpson's abilities, described his defence of the Company as a "wretched expedition". Long after Simpson's death, Selkirk wrote George Bryce:

> Simpson's mind was by that time beginning to give way. I had a high opinion at one time of his abilities but later when I was on the Committee of the Hudson's Bay Company I thought him deficient in sound judgment and latterly his nerves had quite given way.[21]

This recollection many years later by an old man of another old man should be discounted considerably. Simpson in 1857 had lost the verve of his youth, but his judgment on most matters continued to be sound. In all his years with the Company he had never encountered an environment like that of a parliamentary inquiry. Within the Company he was accustomed to deference in relations with Canadian politicians, he had effectively played the role of an affable, persuasive advocate. On this occasion, however, he had to deal with opponents who could not be influenced by the techniques he used so well in Canada, men who were accustomed to cut-and-thrust debate, who used their skills to embarrass Simpson as the Company's principal North American representative. Without a strong Canadian move to annex the territory, however, embarrassment was all that he suffered, and the move was not forthcoming. John Ross, like Draper, was a friendly witness.

Simpson congratulated his old friend Ross on his "able handling" of the issue. Ross's testimony to the committee was all that Simpson could have desired. He expressed the hope that Canada could acquire land suitable for agriculture, but recommended that the Company's monopoly be continued in other areas. "I fear very much," he told the committee, "that if the occupation of the Hudson's Bay Company, in what is called the Hudson's Bay Territory, were to cease, our fate in Canada might be just as it is with the Americans in the border settlements of their territory."[22]

In view of Ross's record of vulnerability to monetary seduction it would be tempting to try to explain his testimony in such terms. Beyond the fact that there is no evidence that he received any compensation, it would have been unnecessary for Simpson to offer such inducement. The Macdonald-Cartier administration desired that the British government assume full responsibility for ending the fur-trade monopoly and providing the necessary compensation. They had to appear to support western expansion in order to prevent Brown's activists from making too much political capital, but they had no intention of asking for a burden that Canada could not bear. Simpson's agents kept him fully informed on what was taking place in the legislature. Derbishire reported a lack of enthusiasm among ministerial supporters to take any action, and Rose, who himself became a member of the ministry in November 1857, told Simpson in March 1857 that there was little likelihood of legislation bearing on the Company's chartered rights being passed that session.[23] Simpson confirmed this impression when he saw Governor General Edmund Head in Toronto in May. The Governor told him that the cabinet took "a very reasonable and moderate view of Canadian interests" regarding the Hudson's Bay Company, and expressed satisfaction that the home government was also disinclined to take any summary measures.[24]

The languidness of the government infuriated Brown's Clear Grits, and they and their newspapers launched attacks on the ministry, thus making the issue a party question. Simpson was delighted. With the Canadians fighting among themselves, he concluded that it was best for him to remain out of the line of fire, giving discreet advice to reliable supporters but avoiding any public statements. While he was in Toronto Simpson heard from Head that at Brown's suggestion a committee of the Legislative Assembly collecting evidence on the Company's territory might summon him to give evidence, and to avoid this he cut his stay in Toronto short and made a trip to Detroit.[25]

By the end of 1857 the immediate crisis in the Company's fortunes had passed. Canada was confronted with another serious economic depression. Banks failed, unemployment soared, and the land-speculation backing which had provided fuel to the drive for the West collapsed. The Select Committee of the British House of Commons had recommended that Canada be allowed to annex agricultural lands but also that the fur-trade monopoly be continued in areas not fit for settlement. The one immediate effect of the anti-Company agitation was highly favorable to the Company interests. Not only did the Company gain a remission from governmental pressure but it also induced the British government to provide another contingent of troops for Red River. Simpson for months had been pressing the London board to seek such military assistance. In June 1856 he pointed out that the free-trade movement was radiating outward from Red River and that the Indians were becoming disaffected. At a mission station two miles from Norway House, there were between two hundred and three hundred Indians who were "acquiring a species of civilization which without improving their moral condition or rectifying the more vicious traits of the savage character has enlightened them rapidly on the subject of free trade." The missionary seemed to be a well-intentioned man, but he could not control his people. Simpson wrote:

> Here, as at Red River, it is vain to conceal from ourselves the fact that we are in a certain degree overawed & dictated to by the numerical superiority of those we are supposed to govern: we do

not admit this fact, though it really influences our proceedings, which are now framed with a view to avoiding collisions and the maintenance of our position by conciliation and gradual concession to demands which we cannot resist.[26]

Troops were not the ultimate answer—eventually the Company must come to terms with the spread of population—but their presence would check the defiance of Company authority at Red River. Canadian fear of American annexation gave him the opportunity to argue this Company interest in terms of national security. At the behest of the Company's governor, John Shepherd, he wrote a letter in August 1857 graphically describing the American menace to Red River. This little settlement of eight thousand people lay in the path of the American northward migration from Minnesota. The United States, he said, planned to establish a garrison just across the border, and there was reason to suspect this decision had a sinister purpose. Americans coveted the rich prairies of southern Rupert's Land not only for settlement but for a railroad route to Oregon and Puget Sound, which was more convenient than any south of the border. To frustrate these American intentions, he argued, Britain must show its determination to resist by sending a military contingent to Red River.[27]

This argument provided a rationalization for the Colonial Office to react. Officials did not believe that there was any serious danger of direct American aggression, and they knew that the Company's main concern was the protection of its interests against the free traders. The Colonial Secretary, Henry Labouchere, nevertheless recommended to the War Office that the troops be sent, and one hundred and twenty officers and men of the Canadian Rifles Regiment arrived at the settlement in October 1857.[28] As Simpson had expected, the presence of the troops quieted anti-Company agitation.

Simpson had contributed to forestalling a great threat to the Company's monopoly, and during the remaining three years of his life the Company prospered. In 1858 and 1859 it paid its shareholders ten per cent dividends, and in 1860 fifteen per cent.[29] Sir Edward Bulwer-Lytton, the celebrated novelist, who became Colonial Secretary in June 1858, attempted to pressure the Company into submitting the validity of its charter to legal review by threatening to refuse renewal of its licence west of the chartered territory. When the Company refused and he had to carry out his ultimatum he was confronted with the fact that Parliament would not vote any money to govern the Indian territories, and Canada showed no interest in doing so. Consequently, though the licence was terminated in 1859, the Company continued to trade in the territories without competition. Simpson knew, however, that this lull in the storm would not last. Within a few years the demand from land and railway interests would become overwhelming, and the Company must make its terms with the new era. A few years after his death his prophecy was fulfilled.

Though Simpson represented a Company which he was convinced could not prosper when its territories were opened up by the railway, he was fully alive to the revolutionary changes the railway would bring and sought to take advantage of them. This alertness was evidenced in a journey to St. Paul, Minnesota, which he took in 1858 with another old man who had retained his vitality, Edward Ellice, Senior. Ellice was a few years older than Simpson—he was born in 1783—but he had continued to be a wise and powerful member of the Company's directorate. During a visit to his estate at Beauharnois Ellice talked with Simpson about the possibility of utilizing the American rail system to bring goods to the Company's territories rather than relying entirely on the ships to Hudson Bay. Transport by rail to St. Paul and by steamboat from there to Red River would provide all-year service. During this trip west through Chicago and Milwaukee to Minnesota, the two men were much impressed with the dynamism of the American society. The Yankees might be uncouth but North America would not be developed by good manners. Ellice commented that "it would be sheer skepticism to doubt the practicability of any scheme invented by the brains, and to be executed by the energy, and ingenuity of Yankee Heads,"[30] and Simpson, despite his Yankeephobia, agreed with him.

Personal observation convinced Simpson that the St. Paul route would not only be quicker but cheaper than transport via Hudson Bay. He did not advocate depending entirely on shipments through a foreign and sometimes unfriendly country, but he thought that it would be prudent to divide exports to Rupert's Land, half continuing through the Bay, and half through the United States.[31] On Ellice's and Simpson's recommendations, the board decided to make a trial run with one hundred tons of goods, which would be transported by Canadian mail steamers to the St. Lawrence and thence by the Grand Trunk Railway and American railways to St. Paul, where they would be forwarded by steamboat to Red River.[32] The experiment was so successful that two years after Simpson's death the Company decided to make this the principal route for supplying its chartered territory.

While they were in St. Paul, Simpson and Ellice saw an opportunity to benefit themselves as well as the Company. Minnesota and the West were developing rapidly, and there seemed to be a great opportunity for profit in the banking business, and they decided to form a bank. Ellice and Simpson each would contribute $50,000 and some of their friends an additional $50,000 to provide an initial capital of $150,000.[33] They soon modified this plan to provide for an initial capitalization of $500,000 with half paid down.[34]

The success of the bank depended, they thought, on the involvement of influential Minnesota citizens. Simpson asked Governor Alexander Ramsey to become a member of the board, and he agreed to do so. After review of the immediate prospects, however, Simpson decided that the time was slightly premature to undertake the project, and it was dropped, though he believed that in a few years St. Paul "will offer a fine field in that way."[35]

The same alertness to new opportunities was evident in Simpson's response to the proposal of Perry McDonough Collins to build a transcontinental telegraph linking Europe and America via Siberia and the Bering Strait. As a first step to construction of this line Collins secured a charter for the Transmundane Telegraph Company and in September 1859 visited Simpson in Montreal to discuss the plan. Simpson agreed to allow his name to be used as one of the backers. Though he was sceptical of Collins's ability to fulfil his promises,[36] he had no doubts that such an undertaking was practicable and gave advice on how problems with the Indians and with natural barriers in North America could be overcome.[37]

Though his intellectual vigor was unimpaired, Simpson knew that he could not long continue. A succession of illnesses had ravaged his constitution, and in 1858 he wrote that he was nearly blind. In March 1859 he wrote the new governor of the Hudson's Bay Company, Henry Hulse Berens, that the time for his retirement was at hand. He had completed nearly forty years in the service of the Company, and he felt it was time for another man to replace him. He wrote:

> It will occasion me regret to sever my connection. It is high time I rested from incessant labor. Moreover, I am unwilling to hold an appointment when I cannot discharge the duties to my own entire satisfaction. I shall therefore make way for some younger man, who I trust may serve the Company as zealously and conscientiously as I have done.[38]

In February he had a severe apoplectic attack, but he was determined to dominate his infirmities and convinced himself that he had recovered. Despite the advice of his physician who warned him that he would be risking his life, he decided that he would undertake his usual journey to the interior.[39] In March he wrote a friend that he was much better and that the route by rail and steamboat was so much easier than the route by canoe that he would preside over the council in the interior again, though on this occasion he would go no farther than Red River.[40]

Simpson's assurances to his friends and to himself that his physical condition was strong enough for a long journey reflected brave resolution rather than objective analysis. He had not recovered from his succession of illnesses, as became evident soon after he set out. He left Lachine on May 14 and by the time he reached St. Paul a week later he was exhausted. After a few days' rest he returned to Lachine after designating Chief Factor William Mactavish to replace him as president of the council.

Again by some miracle the old man rallied. Somehow he stayed alive, perhaps in anticipation of the role he had been assigned in the forthcoming visit of the Prince of Wales to Canada in July and August, the high point of which would be the dedication of the Victoria Bridge across the St. Lawrence at Montreal.

Albert Edward, Prince of Wales, in 1860 bore little resemblance to the future Edward VII. He was a slim, handsome youth of eighteen, who was a perfect ambassador for his mother. He enjoyed appearances in public, and he had an instinctive ability to say and do the right thing to elicit highly positive responses from the dignitaries and the general public who had gathered to welcome him. His arrival in the Maritime provinces produced an ecstatic response from large crowds, and Montreal strove to outdo all the rest. As part of the pageantry of the Prince's visit the committee in charge had arranged that he should be entertained by Simpson at Isle Dorval. Simpson did all that he could to make the occasion a memorable one both for himself and for the Prince; the *pièce de résistance* would be a welcome by the richly decorated canoes and expert voyageurs that had transported Simpson in his voyages to the interior. Simpson spent weeks in careful preparation—every detail of the reception must be just right. The old French-Canadian voyageurs, who had provided not only skill but *joie de vivre* to these voyages, had died out, and he now had to depend on Iroquois from nearby Caughnawaga and Lake of Two Mountains. These Indians, he wrote Governor Head, were excellent men for hard labor, but they could not compare with the old Canadian canoemen when it came to dash, vivacity, and song.[41]

Despite these reservations about the new men, Simpson achieved a social triumph. On August 29 the Prince proceeded from Montreal to Lachine by carriage. The residents had made a special effort to show their loyalty by turning out en masse, and eight or nine triumphal arches had been erected spanning the road, including one at Simpson's residence. At a point across from Isle Dorval about three miles upstream from Lachine, the royal party alighted from their carriage where they boarded the barge *Valorous* for the short trip across to the island. The day was all that Simpson could have desired. Showers had bathed the landscape shortly before the Prince's arrival, and it now sparkled in brilliant sunshine. Halfway across the channel the party was met by a number of Hudson's Bay canoes—one source said nine and another a dozen—each manned by twenty Iroquois, all accoutered in the paint, scarlet cloth, and feathers which would have special appeal to a European who had heard tales of the Red Indians but had never encountered them. They formed a double line to accompany the Prince to the landing stage, where he was greeted by Simpson and escorted to Simpson's residence, which was occupied by Lieutenant General Sir Fenwick Williams, who acted as host.[42]

Simpson had arranged that the guest list was restricted to those who, as the Toronto *Globe* correspondent put it, were eligible to meet His Royal Highness's suite in terms of social equality. The only ladies invited were Simpson's niece, Mrs. McKenzie, and the wife of his personal secretary, Edward M. Hopkins, and her sister. Simpson sat on the left hand of the Prince amidst an impressive gathering of about forty, which included the Colonial Secretary, the Duke of Newcastle, the British Minister to Washington, Lord Lyons, the Marquis of Chandos, the Earl of Mulgrave, who was the new governor of Nova Scotia, and Admiral Sir Alexander Milne, commander-in-chief of the North American and West Indies station. After lunch the Prince paddled about in one of the Hudson's Bay canoes with the Duke of Newcastle and General Williams, and according to a reporter "enjoyed himself very much."[43]

The affair delighted Simpson. His pleasure was made complete by an accolade from the Duke of Newcastle, who "availed himself of the opportunity offered by personal communication to express the high opinion entertained by himself and Her Majesty's Imperial Advisers of the skillful and successful administration of one of the most extensive provinces of the British Empire.''[44]

Few individuals can end their career on a note so appropriate to their lives as did Sir George Simpson. He had striven for success, for wealth, for power, for social esteem, and his achievement had been recognized by his being selected to entertain the Prince of Wales. A few days later he was dead. During his entertainment of the Prince on Wednesday, August 29, he had seemed in excellent health. On the Prince's departure Simpson had led the canoe escort which accompanied him, directing them in the intricate maneuvers which delighted the royal party.

He was riding in his carriage from Montreal to Lachine on Saturday, September 1, when he suffered another attack of apoplexy. He was rushed to his house where a bed was made for him on the floor of the drawing room. There he lay for the next six days, alternating between delirium and apparent calm and lucidity. On one occasion he was seized by convulsions and broke out of the room; in some periods of delirium he imagined himself dead and said that the persons in the room had killed him. But in his calm intervals he appeared to his secretary Hopkins to be in full possession of his faculties. During one of these phases he expressed the feeling that he had not been sufficiently generous to some who had served him and directed Hopkins to make out substantial checks to them, which he signed. To his long-time servant James Murray he gave $1,200; Angus Cameron, his son-in-law, $5,000; Hector McKenzie, $5,000; the Reverend John Flanagan, $1,000. After his death a debate arose as to whether he had been in full possession of his senses when he had made these gifts. The attending physicians were divided, and his executors refused to honor the checks.[45]

On the morning of the seventh, Simpson was calm but obviously failing. He lapsed into a coma, and at half past ten he died.[46]

One physician theorized that the fatal apoplectic attack had been brought on by the old man's exertions in the entertainment of the Prince of Wales. The little giant of the fur trade had left life as he undoubtedly would have wished it. "The Little Emperor's light has gone out," observed Dugald Mactavish, "just after he basked in a final blaze of glory."[47]

Simpson was buried next to his wife beneath an unpretentious stone at Mount Royal Cemetery, a Protestant burial ground, which a few years before he had been involved in establishing. His monument was elsewhere.

Some of his obituaries caught the character of the man. The Montreal *Gazette* noted that after the coalition "the peculiar talents of the Governor became conspicuous; he reconciled conflicting interests, abated personal jealousies, and established a controlling influence which he retained to the last."[48]

The *Annual Register* for 1860, in an otherwise garbled report which gave an unusually doubtful date for his birth, an incorrect year for his marriage, and an imprecise number of his surviving legitimate children, gave a fair evaluation of his contributions:

> Opinions may differ as to the policy of the Hudson's Bay Company, but there is only one opinion as to the ability, energy, and uprightness of the public servant just taken from them, and whose loss they will find it difficult to replace.[49]

Indeed there could never be another Simpson. His forty years in the fur trade embraced an era that passed shortly after his death. During his governorship the Hudson's Bay Company had enjoyed an almost unchallenged monopoly and an almost unvarying prosperity. Its profits had been somewhat affected by the vogue in silk hats in the 1840s, but the price of beaver soon recovered, buoyed upward by a new demand for beaver to be used on trimmings for coats. Red River free traders had been annoying, but by 1860 they had not penetrated into the vital areas of the monopoly, and the settlement's turbulence had been quelled by a military garrison. Canadian agitation for the annexation of Rupert's Land had faded with the awareness of leading politicians that the resources of the colony on the St. Lawrence were not adequate to underwrite the costs of buying out the Company and administering these huge territories. When Simpson died, the great menaces to the fur-trade era were imminent but still prospective. The London board and Simpson's successor, Alexander Grant Dallas, had to deal with pressure for opening up Rupert's Land to railways and telegraphs, and it was evident to even the least perceptive directors that the Company must soon come to terms with a new era. Consequently in 1863 they sold their rights and assets to a group which proposed to open up southern Rupert's Land to settlement, and six years later the reorganized Company sold its chartered rights to the newly created Dominion of Canada.

Simpson's death thus marked the passing not only of a man but of a phase in North American history. The "Little Emperor of the Plains" had risen to power through a combination of his own great abilities and of the opportunities which circumstances provided him. He arrived on the scene when unrestrained competition was giving way to unchallenged monopoly. His attributes were perfectly attuned to govern the amalgamated Company. By guile and firmness he reconciled old rivals to co-operation. He ruthlessly eliminated waste and promoted efficiency. In an era of primitive communications he was given great latitude by his employers, and he soon demonstrated to them that they could rely on his judgment. He became a virtual prime minister with plenary authority. Such a man could not have appeared prior to 1820 and could not emerge after 1860. The times gave him the opportunity for greatness; he capitalized magnificently on the opportunity.

Notes

CHAPTER I

1. The range is predominantly from 1786 to 1792, but Beckles Willson in *The Life of Lord Strathcona and Mount Royal* (London, 1915), p. 40, gives the date as 1796.
2. Arthur S. Morton, *Sir George Simpson* (Toronto, 1944), pp. 3–5.
3. Alexander Simpson, *The Life and Travels of Thomas Simpson, the Arctic Discoverer* (London, 1845, reprinted Toronto, 1963), pp. 44–46.
4. *Fasti Ecclesiae Scoticanae*.
5. E. E. Rich, *The History of the Hudson's Bay Company, 1670–1870*, Vol. II (London, 1959), p. 371.
6. *Fasti Ecclesiae Scoticanae*.
7. The piper selected was Colin Fraser, who arrived at York Factory in August 1827.
8. Munro to Simpson, Nov. 20, 1851, D 5/32, Hudson's Bay Archives (hereafter HBA).
9. The register of Christ Church Cathedral, Montreal, gives his age at his death in 1860 as 73. This is not conclusive evidence. Some other scraps of information point to other dates. The register of passengers on the *Caledonia* in 1841 lists Simpson and gives his age as 50 (*Boston Daily Advertiser*, March 22, 1841), brought to my attention by Edwin G. Sanford. That would make Simpson's date of birth 1790 or 1791. But there can be no assurance that Simpson was the source for the age given; it may have been his secretary E. M. Hopkins, who was also on board. The Canadian census of 1851 gives his age as 55, but Simpson was in England at the time. I rely primarily on the fact that Aemilius Simpson treated him as an elder, and Aemilius was born in 1792. But I recognize that this is far from being adequate support for any date.
10. T. C. Smout, *A History of the Scottish People, 1560–1830* (London, 1969), pp. 347–48.

11. *Fasti Ecclesiae Scoticanae.*
12. Alexander Simpson, *Thomas Simpson*, p. 44.
13. Simpson to Angus Cameron, Nov. 25, 1848, in papers in possession of Mrs. Elaine Mitchell.
14. E. E. Rich (ed.), *Colin Robertson's Correspondence Book* (London, 1939), p. cii.
15. Rich, *Hudson's Bay Company*, II, p. 291.
16. W. L. Morton, *Manitoba* (Toronto, 1957), pp. 50–51.
17. Rosanna Seaborn, "Old-Time Company Tactics", *The Beaver*, Spring 1962, Outfit 292, pp. 52–53.
18. E. E. Rich (ed.), *Journal of Occurrences in the Athabasca Department by George Simpson, 1820 and 1821, and Report* (London, 1938), p. 467.
19. Simpson to [Richard Pooler], Oct. 5, 1815, in "Three Simpson Letters: 1815–1820", with an introduction by Muriel R. Cree, *British Columbia Historical Quarterly*, I, no. 2 (April 1937): 116. The originals are in the Archives of British Columbia.
20. Simpson, *Thomas Simpson*, p. 44.
21. W. S. Wallace (ed.), *John McLean's Notes on a Twenty-five Year's Service in the Hudson's Bay Territory* (Toronto, 1932), pp. 383–84.
22. Simpson to [Pooler], Oct. 5, 1815, in "Three Simpson Letters", pp. 115–17.
23. Rich, *Journal of Occurrences in the Athabasca Department*, p. xxxviii.
24. The territory of the charter.

CHAPTER II

1. Rich, *Journal of Occurrences in the Athabasca Department*, p. 467.
2. Rich, *Robertson's Correspondence Book,* p. civ.
3. John S. Galbraith, "Edward 'Bear' Ellice", *The Beaver,* Summer 1954, p. 28.
4. He acquired the nickname from his association with the fur trade.
5. Rich, *Journal of Occurrences in the Athabasca Department*, p. xlix.
6. Arthur S. Morton, *A History of the Canadian West to 1870–71* (London, 1939), p. 611.
7. Rich, *Hudson's Bay Company,* II, p. 373.
8. Simpson to [Pooler], Feb. 23, 1820, in *British Columbia Historical Quarterly,* I, no. 2 (April 1937): 117–18.

9. *Ibid.*
10. K. G. Davies (ed.), *Northern Quebec and Labrador Journals and Correspondence, 1819–35* (London, 1963), p. 367 n.
11. Simpson to [Pooler], April 28, 1820, in *ibid.*, pp. 118–19. Also in MG 19 A-26, Archives of British Columbia.
12. *Ibid.*
13. *Ibid.*, pp. 119–20.
14. *Ibid.*, p. 120.
15. *Ibid.*
16. Gordon C. Davidson, *The North West Company* (Berkeley, 1918), p. 245.
17. Simpson to [Pooler], April 28, 1828, *British Columbia Historical Quarterly*, I, no. 2 (April 1937): 120. Also MG 19 A-26, Archives of British Columbia.
18. *Ibid.*
19. *Ibid.*
20. For details of Robertson's capture, see Rich, *Robertson's Correspondence Book,* pp. 123 ff.
21. A *mangeur du lard*, or pork-eater, was a greenhorn, untutored in the life of the fur trade.
22. Rich, *Journal of Occurrences in the Athabasca Department,* p. 7 and 7n.
23. *Ibid.*, p. 278.
24. Journal, July 30, 1820, in *ibid.*, p. 2.
25. Journal, Aug. 22, 1820, in *ibid.*, p. 19.
26. Rich, *Robertson's Correspondence Book,* p. lxiii.
27. *Ibid.*, pp. lxx–lxxi, 40.
28. Robertson to Moffatt [August 10, 1818?], in *ibid.*, p. 61.
29. *Ibid.*
30. Journal, July 30, 1820, in Rich, *Journal of Occurrences in the Athabasca Department*, pp. 1–2.
31. Journal, Aug. 26, 1820, in *ibid.*, pp. 23–24. The italics are Simpson's.
32. Journal, Sept. 13, 1820, in *ibid.*, p. 36.
33. "Athabasca 1820: General Instructions", in *ibid.*, p. 4, Pemmican is dried meat, in this case usually buffalo, which was a staple of the fur trade.
34. Simpson to Clarke, Nov. 30, 1820, in *ibid.*, p. 170.
35. Rich, *Journal of Occurrences in the Athabasca Department*, p. xxxvi.

36. *Ibid.*, p. 426.
37. *Ibid.*, p. 42.
38. *Ibid.*, pp. 86–87.
39. Rich, *Hudson's Bay Company*, ii, p. 379.
40. Journal, March 15, 1821, in Rich, *Journal of Occurrences in the Athabasca Department*, p. 300.
41. Simpson to Greill, Sept. 30, 1820, in *ibid.*, p. 70.
42. Rich, *Hudson's Bay Company*, ii, p. 481. The man was Thomas Taylor, Simpson's personal servant, who had brought a "leud woman" into the post. Taylor was the brother of Simpson's mistress.
43. Simpson to Finlayson, Sept. 29, 1820, in Rich, *Journal of Occurrences in the Athabasca Department,* pp. 63–64.
44. Journal, March 13, 1821, in *ibid.*, pp. 297–98.
45. E. O. S. Scholefield and F. W. Howay, *British Columbia from the Earliest Times to the Present* (Vancouver, 1914), pp. 341–42.
46. E. E. Rich (ed.), *A Journal of a Voyage from Rocky Mountain Portage in Peace River to the Sources of Finlays Branch and North West Ward in Summer 1824 [by Samuel Black]* (London, HBRS XVIII, 1955), p. xxxvi.
47. Rich, *Journal of a Voyage*, p. xl.
48. *Ibid.*
49. Rich, *Journal of Occurrences in the Athabasca Department*, pp. 408–9.
50. *Ibid.*, *passim*.
51. Journal, June 18, 1821, in *ibid.*, p. 349.

CHAPTER III

1. Gov. and Comm. to Simpson, Feb. 27, 1822, D-5/1, HBA.
2. Simpson to Colvile, May 20, 1822, in Frederick Merk (ed.), *Fur Trade and Empire* (Cambridge, 1931), p. 181.
3. Account by John Tod, dated *c.* 1880, in Newton Papers, MG 19 A 38, Public Archives of Canada (hereafter PAC). Tod's memory in old age was undoubtedly somewhat faulty. Neither McGillivray, father or son, was present at York Factory in 1822. Tod may or may not have been present at the banquet. Though he probably was at York Factory in 1822, he was not yet an officer—he was made a chief trader in 1834. The story consequently may have been second-hand

and subsequently absorbed by Tod into personal experience. But it is likely that a scene much like that he described did occur.

4. Simpson to Colvile, Sept. 8, 1821, quoted in Rich, *Robertson's Correspondence Book,* pp. cxiv—cxv.

5. Simpson to Colvile, Sept. 8, 1823, in Merk, *Fur Trade and Empire,* pp. 201—2.

6. Rich, *Robertson's Correspondence Book,* p. xvi.

7. Margaret A. MacLeod, *The Letters of Letitia Hargrave* (Toronto, 1947), p. cxii.

8. This confidence was not entirely justified. He did not destroy the letters as Simpson requested.

9. Merk, *Fur Trade and Empire,* p. xx.

10. Simpson to Gov. and Comm., July 16, 1822, in Rich, *Robertson's Correspondence Book,* pp. 338—39.

11. Simpson to Colvile, May 20, 1822, in Selkirk Papers, PAC.

12. Halkett to Simpson, Sept. 3, 1822, D-4/117 HBA.

13. Rich, *Journal of Occurrences in the Athabasca Department,* p. 376.

14. *Ibid.,* p. 387.

15. *Ibid.,* p. 392.

16. Sutherland to Williams, Feb. 1, 1822; Kennedy to Simpson, March 13, 1822, both in D-4/116, HBA.

17. Simpson to Colvile, May 20, 1822, PAC.

18. Journal, April 9, 1825, in Merk, *Fur Trade and Empire,* p. 136.

19 Simpson to Gov. and Comm., July 16, 1822, D-4/85, HBA.

20. E. E. Rich and R. Harvey Fleming (eds.), *Minutes of Council, Northern Department of Rupert's Land, 1821—31* (London, 1940), pp. 60—61.

21. Merk, *Fur Trade and Empire,* pp. 181—82.

22. Rich, *Hudson's Bay Company,* II, p. 424. On West, see Arthur N. Thompson, "John West: A Study of the Conflict Between Civilization and the Fur Trade", *Journal of Canadian Church Historical Society*, XII, no.3, (Sept. 1970): 44—57.

23. Frank A. Peake, "Fur Traders and Missionaries", *Western Canadian Journal of Anthropology,* 3, no. 1 (1972): 72—92.

24. Rich, *Hudson's Bay Company,* II, p. 601.

25. The above and following general comments on this subject are derived from Sylvia Van Kirk, "Women and the Fur Trade", *The Beaver,* Winter 1972, pp. 4—21.

26. Simpson to McTavish, Nov. 12, 1822, B 239, HBA.

27. A daughter of his, name unknown, born somewhere in Great Britain, married James Cook Gordon of Jamaica. Another daughter,

named Maria, was born in Scotland. In 1833 Simpson wrote to McTavish, "I find there is a daughter of mine married or about to be married to a Don'd Mactavish." Simpson to McTavish, July 1, 1833, B 135 c/2, HBA. The man involved lived in Inverness, which raises some interesting speculations as to the date and circumstances in which the child was conceived.

28. Simpson to McTavish, June 4, 1822, in Rich and Fleming, *Minutes of Council,* p. 411.
29. Previous writers have asserted that the woman was Margaret Taylor, sister of Thomas Taylor, Simpson's personal servant, and that she bore him a daughter in October 1821. But Miss Van Kirk has established that Simpson's liaison with Margaret began much later and that the child was born in February 1822.
30. Simpson to McTavish, private, Nov. 12, 1822, in Rich and Fleming, *Minutes of Council,* p. 424.
31. Simpson to McTavish, private, June 4, 1822, in *ibid.,* p. 411.
32. Van Kirk, "Women and the Fur Trade", p. 10.
33. Simpson to McTavish, private, Nov. 12, 1822, in Rich and Fleming, *Minutes of Council,* p. 424.
34. Van Kirk, "Women and the Fur Trade", p. 12.
35. Quoted in Rich, *Robertson's Correspondence Book,* p. cxxiii.
36. These words were often used by Simpson as the motto of his administration. See Alice M. Johnson, "System and Regularity", *The Beaver,* Summer 1960, pp. 36–39.
37. John S. Galbraith, *The Hudson's Bay Company as an Imperial Factor* (Berkeley, 1957), p. 51.
38. Simpson to Colvile, Sept. 8, 1821, in Selkirk Papers, PAC.
39. Simpson to McTavish, June 4, 1822, B 239 c, HBA.
40. Keith to Gov. and Comm., Feb. 12, 1822, A-1c/2; Lewes to Simpson, April 2, 1822, D-4/116, both in HBA.
41. Rich and Fleming, *Minutes of Council,* p. 302.
42. *Ibid,* p. xxxii.
43. *Ibid.*
44. The journal and other related documents were published in Merk, *Fur Trade and Empire.*
45. Simpson to McTavish, Aug. 20, 1824, B 239 c, HBA.
46. Merk, *Fur Trade and Empire,* p. 23.
47. *Ibid.*
48. Rich, *Hudson's Bay Company,* II, p. 444.
49. Merk, *Fur Trade and Empire,* pp. 11–12.

50. *Ibid.*, pp. 47–48.
51. Galbraith, *Hudson's Bay Company*, p. 90.
52. Merk, *Fur Trade and Empire*, p. 108.
53. *Ibid.*, pp. 104–5, 112; Van Kirk, "Women and the Fur Trade", p. 12.
54. Merk, *Fur Trade and Empire*, pp. 122–23.

CHAPTER IV

1. Merk, *Fur Trade and Empire*, p. 144.
2. *Ibid.*, p. 154.
3. *Ibid.*, p. 163.
4. Council to Simpson, July 9, 1825, in Rich and Fleming, *Minutes of Council*, pp. 136–38.
5. Simpson to Pooler, Nov. 11, 1825, MG 19 A-26, Archives of British Columbia.
6. For statistics on profits, see Douglas MacKay, *The Honourable Company* (London, 1937), Appendix D.
7. Galbraith, *Hudson's Bay Company*, p. 184.
8. T. Morris Longstreth, *Quebec, Montreal and Ottawa* (London, 1933), p. 175.
9. C. P. Wilson, "Sir George Simpson at Lachine", *The Beaver*, June 1934, p. 39.
10. J. W. Chalmers, "A Family Affair", *Alberta Historical Review*, Spring 1960.
11. Grace Lee Nute, "Jehu of the Waterways", *The Beaver*, Summer 1960, pp. 15–19. For a detailed chart of his travels, see "The Journals of Sir George Simpson", *The Beaver*, June 1936, p. 33.
12. Rich, *Hudson's Bay Company*, II, pp. 457–58.
13. Galbraith, "The Little Emperor", *The Beaver*, Winter 1960, p. 25.
14. Rich, *Robertson's Correspondence Book*, pp. 183–84.
15. Malcolm McLeod (ed.), *Peace River* (Rutland, Vt., 1971), p. 41. The title gives little indication of the contents. The book contains the journal of Archibald McDonald, who accompanied Simpson on the voyage.
16. *Ibid.*, p. 2.
17. The relationship with Margaret is mentioned in Simpson's letters to McTavish. See Van Kirk, "Women and the Fur Trade", p. 13.

18. Simpson to McTavish, Sept. 22, 1828, B 239 c, HBA, quoted in Van Kirk, "Women and the Fur Trade", p. 13.
19. E. E. Rich (ed.), *Part of Dispatch from George Simpson Esqr., Governor of Rupert's Land* (London, 1947), p. xix.
20. *Ibid.*, pp. 17–19.
21. Rich, *Hudson's Bay Company*, II, p. 617.
22. Rich, *Part of Dispatch from George Simpson*, p. 34.
23. *Ibid.*, p. 47.
24. Morton, *Sir George Simpson*, p. 100.
25. Simpson to Colvile, June 4, 1829, in Selkirk Papers, PAC.
26. Van Kirk, "Women and the Fur Trade", p. 13.
27. Simpson to McTavish, Jan. 8, 1830, B 135 c/12, HBA. Todd to Simpson, 1849, quoted in Glyndwr Williams (ed.), *Hudson's Bay Miscellany* (London, 1975), p. 159.
28. "Sir George Simpson's Case, Superior Court, Montreal. The Rev. John Flanagan, Plaintiff vs. Duncan Finlayson, et al., Defendants", *American Journal of Insanity* (Utica), XIX, no. 3, Jan. 1863.
29. Simpson was undoubtedly sincere when he wrote McTavish that "I would calculate more on your friendship than that of any man in the country in any matter of serious moment." Simpson to McTavish, private, Jan 3, 1830 [1], in *ibid.*
30. Van Kirk, "Women and the Fur Trade", p. 14.
31. *Ibid.*
32. Simpson to McTavish, Dec. 5, 1829, B 135 c/2, HBA, quoted in Van Kirk, "Women and the Fur Trade", p. 14.
33. Simpson to McTavish, Dec. 5, 1829, B 135 c/2, HBA.
34. Simpson to McTavish, Dec. 26, 1829, in *ibid.*
35. *Ibid.*
36. Simpson to McTavish, Jan 8, 1830, B 135 c/2, HBA.
37. Simpson to McTavish [Jan. 15, 1830?], in *ibid.*
38. Simpson to McTavish, Jan. 26, 1830, B 135 b/2, HBA.
39. *Ibid.*
40. The wedding had originally been set for February 22, but was delayed for two days at the request of Mrs. Geddes Simpson. Simpson to McTavish, Feb. 17, 1830, B 135 c/2, HBA. The marriage was inscribed in the Bromley St. Leonard register, which has since been transferred to St. Mary Stratford-Atte-Bow.
41. Letitia Hargrave to Mrs. Dugald Mactavish, May 14–15, 1840, in MacLeod, *Letitia Hargrave*, p. 25.

42. Same to same, June 5, 1840, in *ibid.*, p. 43.
43. Frances Simpson, "Journey for Frances", *The Beaver,* Summer 1954, p. 14. The diary appears in three installments, in the issues of December 1953, March 1954, and June 1954.
44. *Ibid.*, June 1954, p. 18.
45. *Ibid.*, p. 16.
46. MacLeod, *Letitia Hargrave,* p. 36, quoted in Van Kirk, "Women and the Fur Trade", p. 16.
47. *Ibid.*
48. Simpson to McTavish, confidential July 10, 1830, B 135 c/2, HBA. McKenzie had himself rejected a country wife to marry a white woman.
49. Simpson to McTavish, Jan. 3, 1830 (1), B 135 c/2, HBA.
50. P. S. dated Jan. 10, 1831, to above.
51. W. Sinclair to Ermatinger, Aug. 15, 1831. A B 40 Er 62.3, Ermatinger Papers, Provincial Archives, British Columbia.
52. Not to be confused with Betsey Sinclair's daughter Maria, who married Robert Wallace in 1838. In the same year she and Wallace were drowned.
53. Maria Simpson Mactavish to Simpson, Jan. 26, 1850, D-5/27; same to same, April 14, 1850, April 30, 1850, both in D-5/28, all in HBA.
54. George Jr. to Simpson, Aug. 5, 1842, D-5/7, HBA.
55. George Jr. to Simpson, Dec. 21, 1843, D-5/9, HBA.
56. George Jr. to Simpson, Jan. 9, 1844, D-5/10, HBA.
57. George Jr. to Simpson, April 3, 1849, D-5/25, HBA.
58. George Jr. to Simpson, April 18, 1850, D-5/28, HBA.
59. Morton, *Simpson,* pp. 159−60.
60. G. P. De T. Glazebrook (ed.), *The Hargrave Correspondence* (Toronto, 1938), p. 59; Van Kirk, "Women and the Fur Trade", pp. 18−19.
61. Van Kirk, "Women and the Fur Trade", p. 21.
62. Letitia to Mrs. Dugald Mactavish, May 21 [1840], in MacLeod, *Letitia Hargrave,* pp. 35−36.
63. Van Kirk, "Women and the Fur Trade", p. 21.
64. *Ibid.*
65. Williams, *Hudson's Bay Miscellany*, p. 154.
66. *Ibid.*
67. Alexander Simpson, *The Life and Travels of Thomas Simpson,* p. 21.
68. *Ibid.*, pp. 31, 32.

69. Simpson to McTavish, July 7, 1831, B 135 c/2, HBA.
70. Simpson to McTavish, May 1, 1832, B 135 c/2, HBA.
71. Simpson to McTavish, private, July 19, 1832, in *ibid.*
72. Simpson to McTavish, private, Jan. 12, 1835, in *ibid.*
73. Simpson to McTavish, private, July 19, 1832, in *ibid.*
74. Simpson to McTavish, private, Dec. 2, 1832, in *ibid.*
75. Simpson to McTavish, private, July 19, 1832, in *ibid.*
76. Williams, *Hudson's Bay Miscellany,* p. 154
77. Simpson's "Character Book", 1832, A 34/2, HBA.
78. Simpson to Colvile, very private, May 15, 1833, Selkirk Papers, St. Mary's Isle, copies in HBA.
79. Simpson to McTavish, private, June 29, 1833, B 135 c/2, HBA.
80. Simpson to McTavish, private, Oct. 21, 1833, in *ibid.*
81. Preface by John Gellner to Simpson, *Thomas Simpson,* p. vii.
82. Simpson, *Thomas Simpson,* pp. 34–35.
83. *Ibid.,* p. 42.
84. Rich, *Hudson's Bay Company,* II, p. 467.
85. W. S. Wallace (ed.), *John McLean's Notes of a Twenty-Five Years' Service in the Hudson's Bay Territory* (Toronto, 1932), p. 334.
86. *Ibid.,* pp. 333–34.
87. Simpson to McTavish, private, Jan. 30, 1834, in B 135 c/2, HBA.
88. Augusta was presumably named for Sir Augustus d'Este (1794–1848), son of the Duke of Sussex who was the youngest son of George III. Sussex married Lady Augusta Murray in 1793 despite George III's disapproval, and the marriage was annulled in 1794. The union, however, had produced two children, one of whom was Augustus who was given the surname of d'Este, one of the names belonging to the house of Brunswick. The connection of George or Frances Simpson with d'Este is not clear.
89. Annie Hopkins died of cholera in 1854. See Alice M. Johnson, "Edward and Frances Hopkins of Montreal", *The Beaver,* Autumn 1971, pp. 4–17.
90. See George Simpson (?), "Blue Bell", *ibid.,* p. 58.
91. Beckles Willson, *The Life of Lord Strathcona and Mount Royal* (London, 1915), pp. 50–51.
92. Simpson to Cameron, Oct. 19, 1840, Cameron Papers.
93. Finlayson to Hargrave, April 15, 1845, in MacLeod, *Letitia Hargrave,* p. xciv.
94. Typescript, Frances to G. W. Simpson, June 26, 1846, MacLeod Collection, MG9 A75, Public Archives of Manitoba.

95. *Ibid.*
96. MacLeod, *Letitia Hargrave,* p. xciv.
97. Simpson to Cameron, March 5, 1853, Cameron Papers.
98. Record of Mount Royal Cemetery.
99. Clifford P. Wilson, "The Emperor's Last Days", *The Beaver,* December 1934, p. 49.
100. *Daily Globe* (Toronto), Aug. 30, 1860.
101. Elaine Mitchell, "Sir George Simpson: 'The Man of Feeling' ", in *Malvina Bolus* (ed.), *People and Pelts* (Winnipeg, 1972), pp. 98–99. Mrs. Mitchell depicts Sir George in warmer tones than he is described here.
102. *Ibid.,* p. 99.
103. There were three basic units of money in British North America. The relative values were £100 sterling =£120 Halifax currency = £108 Canadian sterling.
104. John Pelly Simpson died without issue.
105. Last Will and Testament, March 10, 1860, Provincial Archives, Montreal.

CHAPTER V

1. Simpson to Cameron, Jan. 16, 1840. April 25, 1840, in Angus Cameron Papers, in possession of Elaine Mitchell.
2. Selkirk to his wife, Aug. 4, 1836, Selkirk Archives, St. Mary's Isles, copies in HBA.
3. Same to same, Sept. 8, 1836, in *ibid.*
4. Simpson to Fraser, Nov. 9, 1858, D-4/84a, HBA.
5. Douglas MacKay, *The Honourable Company* (London, 1937), Appendix D, pp. 377–78.
6. Galbraith, *Hudson's Bay Company,* pp. 190–91.
7. *Ibid.,* p. 96.
8. S. B. Okun, *The Russian-American Company,* trans. Carl Ginsburg (Cambridge, Mass., 1951), p. 217.
9. Simpson to McLoughlin, June 28, 1836, D-4/22, HBA.
10. Simpson to Governor, Russian American Fur Co., Establishment of New Archangel, March 20, 1829, D-4/16, HBA.
11. Galbraith, *Hudson's Bay Company,* p. 150.
12. *Ibid.,* p. 16.
13. Introduction by Alice M. Johnson to "Simpson in Russia", *The Beaver,* Autumn 1960, p. 4.

14. *Ibid.*
15. *Ibid.*
16. *Ibid.*, p. 7.
17. Report of J. H. Pelly, 1838, F-29/2, HBA.
18. *Ibid.*
19. "Simpson in Russia", *The Beaver,* Autumn 1960, p. 11.
20. See, for example, Simpson to Pelly, Dec. 1, 1843, D-4/63, HBA.
21. Simpson to Gov. and Comm., March 27, 1844, D-4/64, HBA.
22. G. F. G. Stanley (ed.), *John Henry Lefroy in Search of the Magnetic North* (Toronto, 1955), p. 6.
23. Simpson to Douglas, March 8, 1838, D-4/23, HBA.
24. See "The Authorship of Simpson's Narrative", Appendix B, in Glyndwr Williams (ed.), *London Correspondence Inward from Sir George Simpson, 1841–42* (London, 1973), pp. 184–96.
25. See George Simpson, *Narrative of a Journey Round the World,* 2 vols. (London, 1847).
26. Williams, *London Correspondence,* p. xxvi.
27. Irene M. Spry, "Routes Through the Rockies", *The Beaver,* Autumn 1963, p. 31.
28. Simpson to Gov. and Comm., Nov. 25, 1841, in *ibid.,* p. 52.
29. These issues are discussed in detail by W. Kaye Lamb in his introduction to E. E. Rich (ed.), *The Letters of John McLoughlin From Fort Vancouver to the Governor and Committee, Second Series, 1839–44* (London, 1943), pp. xiv–xlix.
30. W. Kaye Lamb in Rich, *Letters of John McLoughlin,* pp. xxii–xxviii.
31. *Ibid.,* xxvi.
32. A notable example of this was his hiring of James Sinclair, a prominent free trader to lead a party of settlers from Red River to Oregon. See D. Geneva Lent, *West of the Mountains* (Seattle, 1963).
33. The murdered, Urbain Heroux, had the reputation of being "a wild fellow" addicted to liquor. W. Kaye Lamb in Rich, *Letters of John McLoughlin,* p. xlv.
34. Simpson to McLoughlin, April 27, 1842, in *ibid.,* p. 344.
35. W. Kaye Lamb in Rich, *Letters of John McLoughlin,* pp. xliii–xliv.
36. E. E. Rich (ed.), *The Letters of John McLoughlin from Fort Vancouver to the Governor and Committee, Third Series, 1844–46* (London, 1944), p. 171.
37. Simpson, *Narrative,* I, p. 72.
38. *Ibid.,* I, p. 293.
39. Williams, *London Correspondence,* p. 121.
40. Simpson, *Narrative,* I, p. 359.
41. Williams, *London Correspondence,* p. 118.

42. *Ibid.,* pp. 116—17.
43. *Ibid.* p. 121.
44. *Ibid.* p. xli.
45. Committee resolution, Oct. 23, 1833, A-1/58, HBA.
46. Rich, *Letters of John McLoughlin, First Series,* p. 353.
47. Harold Bradley, *The American Frontier in Hawaii* (Stanford, 1942), p. 397.
48. Williams, *London Correspondence,* pp. 126—27.
49. A. Simpson to G. Simpson, Jan. 12, 1840, D-5/5, HBA; Ralph S. Kuykendall and A. Grove Day, *Hawaii: A History* (New York, 1948), p. 61.
50. This feeling is expressed in Alexander Simpson, *Thomas Simpson, passim,* in particular, pp. 21—22.
51. Williams, *London Correspondence,* p. xlvi.
52. Pelly to Russell, Feb. 6, 1841, CO 42/485, Public Record Office (hereafter PRO).
53. Russell to Stephen, Feb. 9, 1841, in *ibid.*
54. Simpson to Pelly and A. Colvile, private, April 20, 1842, in Williams, *London Correspondence,* p. 157.
55. Williams, *London Correspondence,* p. xlix.
56. Ralph S. Kuykendall, *The Hawaiian Kingdom, 1744—1854* (Honolulu, 1947), p. 307.
57. Simpson to A. Cameron, Nov. 18, 1842, Cameron Papers, in possession of E. Mitchell.
58. Bradley, *American Frontier,* p. 428.
59. Galbraith, *Hudson's Bay Company,* pp. 211—13.
60. Stanley to Peel, Sept. 1, 1845, private, Peel Papers, Addtl. Mss. 40, 468, British Museum.
61. Memorandum, Simpson to Aberdeen, March 29, 1845, in Joseph Schafer (ed.), "Documents Relative to Warre and Vavasour's Military Reconnoissance [*sic*] in Oregon, 1845—46", *Oregon Historical Quarterly,* March 1919, pp. 13—16.
62. Simpson to Pelly, May 4, 1845, confidential, A-12/2, HBA.
63. Simpson said June 5, and the officers stated they arrived June 7. Enclosures in Metcalfe to Stanley, July 26, 1845, WO 1/552, PRO.
64. P. J. de Smet, *Oregon Missions and Travels Over the Rocky Mountains in 1845—46* (New York, 1847), p. 113.
65. Galbraith, *Hudson's Bay Company,* p. 317.
66. During the Civil War, Harris and his nephew betrayed Sanders and his son, who were working for the Confederacy. See Meriwether Stuart, "Operation Sanders", *The Virginia Magazine of History,* April 1973, pp. 157—99.

67. John S. Galbraith, "George N. Sanders, 'Influence Man' for the Hudson's Bay Company", *Oregon Historical Quarterly,* Sept. 1952, p. 162.
68. Sanders to Simpson, January 5, 1848, D-5/21, HBA.
69. Simpson to Sanders, private, Jan. 15, 1848, D-4/69, HBA.
70. Simpson to Pelly, Feb. 7, 1848, in *ibid.*
71. Polk's diary, January 20, 1849, in Milo M. Quaife, *The Diary of James K. Polk* (Chicago, 1910), IV, p. 301.
72. Memorandum of Agreement, April 28, 1848, A-37/27, Pelly to Simpson, April 15, 1848, D-5/22, both in HBA.
73. Barclay to Finlayson, July 14, 1848, HBA.
74. Simpson to Cameron, Oct. 27, 1847, Cameron Papers.
75. Pelly to Simpson, April 15, 1848, D-5/22, HBA.
76. Galbraith, "The Little Emperor", *The Beaver,* Winter 1960, p. 27.
77. Simpson to Cameron, Nov. 25, 1848, Cameron Papers.
78. Galbraith, *Hudson's Bay Company,* p. 260.
79. Simpson to Pelly, confidential, Aug. 4, 1848, D-4/70, HBA.
80. Simpson to Sanders, Nov. 24, 1848, in *ibid.*
81. Pelly to Simpson, Dec. 8, 1848, D-5/23, HBA.
82. Sanders to Simpson, Dec. 12, 1848, A-12/4, HBA.
83. Galbraith, "George N. Sanders", p. 171.
84. Simpson to Pelly, confidential, Feb. 16, 1849, same to same, confidential, February 23, 1849, D-4/70, HBA.
85. Galbraith, *Hudson's Bay Company,* p. 271.
86. Sanders to Simpson, May 31, 1848, D-5/46, HBA.
87. Simpson to Sanders, July 29, 1848, D-4/84a, HBA. The question was finally settled in 1871 when the United States paid $650,000 for the rights of the Hudson's Bay Company and the Puget's Sound Agricultural Company.

CHAPTER VI

1. Simpson to Colvile, May 20, 1822, quoted in Galbraith, *Hudson's Bay Company,* p. 311.
2. Galbraith, *Hudson's Bay Company,* p. 317.
3. Morton, *Simpson,* pp. 194–97.
4. Simpson to McTavish, Jan. 12, 1835, private, B 135 c/2, HBA.
5. Finlayson to D. Ross, April 15, 1845, private, Finlayson Papers, Ab 40, F 492, Archives of British Columbia.
6. Minutes of Governor and Committee, Jan. 3, 1849, A-1/66, HBA.

7. E. E. Rich (ed.), *London Correspondence Inward from Eden Colvile, 1849–1852* (London, 1956), pp. xcv–xcvii.
8. Galbraith, *Hudson's Bay Company,* pp. 328–29.
9. The Governor and Committee did not accept Simpson's recommendation that the council be enlarged with the addition of six men of mixed blood. Barclay to Simpson, private and confidential, April 12, 1850, D-5/28, HBA.
10. Galbraith, *Hudson's Bay Company,* p. 331.
11. Simpson to Ross, private, Dec. 17, 1850, North West Papers, MG 19, A-30, PAC.
12. Simpson to McTavish, private, Jan. 10, 1834, B 135 c/2, HBA.
13. Simpson to Derbishire, confidential, March 29, 1854, D-4/82, HBA.
14. Simpson was insulted when John Rae reported that wine he had taken from Simpson's stock for use on Rae's journey was not fit for drinking. See E. E. Rich (ed.), *John Rae's Correspondence* (London, 1953), p. 341.
15. At a dinner on February 13, 1827, he invited 7 guests, and on March 5 he invited 11, all of whom were prominent businessmen and politicians. Beaver Club, Mss. Coll. 11, McGill University.
16. Helen Taft Manning, "E. G. Wakefield and the Beauharnois Canal", *Canadian Historical Review,* March 1967, pp. 1–25. Sydenham died before his promise could be carried out, but the Beauharnois Canal was eventually authorized and was opened in 1845.
17. Galbraith, "The Little Emperor", p. 27.
18. *Ibid.*
19. *Ibid.*
20. Donald Creighton, *John A. Macdonald: The Young Politician* (Toronto, 1952), p. 198.
21. Ronald S. Longley, *Sir Francis Hincks* (Toronto, 1943), p. 235. It should be added that a select committee exonerated Hincks of "wilful dishonesty" but raised a question of the ethics of government officials using their public position to advance their private fortunes.
22. Simpson to Hincks, Dec. 24, 1849, D-4/70, HBA.
23. Derbishire to Simpson, March 13, 1850, D-5/27, HBA.
24. Simpson to Barclay, March 5, 1852, D-4/73, HBA.
25. Hincks to Derbishire, Aug. 4, 1852, D-5/34, HBA.
26. Simpson to Barclay, March 6, 1852, D-4/73, HBA.
27. C. R. Vernon Gibbs, *British Passenger Lines of the Five Oceans* (London, 1963), p. 323.

28. Simpson to Cameron, Nov. 17, 1842, Nov. 18, 1842, Cameron Papers.

29. Simpson to Cameron, Sept. 25, 1848, in *ibid*. The *Atrato* of this line, which made the first run in 1854, anticipated the first iron mail Cunarder by two years. The line attracted international attention when one of the ships, the *Trent,* was stopped by the Union navy during the Civil War and Confederate agents were removed.

30. N. R. P. Bonsor, *North Atlantic Seaway* (Prescot, Eng., 1955), pp. 77, 84.

31. Simpson to Derbishire, private, Feb. 27, 1854, D-4/82, HBA.

32. Simpson to Derbishire, confidential, March 4, 1854, in *ibid*.

33. Simpson to Derbishire, confidential, March 7, 1854, in *ibid*.

34. Simpson to Derbishire, confidential, March 4, 1854, in *ibid*.

35. *General Index of the Journals of the Legislative Assembly of the Province of Canada from 1852 to 1866, inclusive,* p. 171.

36. Creighton, *Macdonald,* p. 207.

37. Fred and W. A. Terrill, *Chronology of Montreal and of Canada* (Montreal, 1893), p. 581.

38. Derbishire to Simpson, Oct. 28, 1857, D-4/82, HBA.

39. *General Index of the Journals, Accounts and Papers,* p. 1064.

40. Simpson to Barclay, May 24, 1846, D-4/68, HBA.

41. *Montreal Gazette,* Oct. 6, 1853.

42. Campbell to Simpson, Sept. 15, 1848, D-5/22, HBA.

43. Ferrier to Simpson, Feb. 13, 1847, D-5/19, HBA.

44. Simpson to Cameron, Nov. 18, 1845, Cameron Papers.

45. *Montreal Gazette,* Nov. 19, 1847.

46. Simpson to Cameron, Nov. 25, 1848, Cameron Papers.

47. Robert G. Bales, "The Montreal & Lachine Rail Road and Its Successors", *Canadian Rail,* April 1966, pp. 95–99, 105.

48. The shareholders of the Champlain and St. Lawrence as of March 14, 1855, including Simpson and Finlayson are listed in CH 3866, S 350, McGill University Library Archives. Simpson had 43 shares and Finalyson 16.

49. Macdonald to Chamberlin, confidential, Feb. 2, 1855, in J. K. Johnson, *The Letters of Sir John A. Macdonald* (Ottawa, 1968), p. 235.

50. *Montreal Gazette,* Jan. 31, 1853, Feb. 9, 1853, Feb. 18, 1853.

51. Cauchon to Simpson, Jan. 21, 1857, D-5/43, HBA.

52. Simpson to Cauchon, private, Oct. 9, 1856; same to same, Nov. 26, 1856, both in D-4/83, HBA.

53. Baby to Simpson, May 8, 1857, D-5/43, HBA.

54. *General Index of the Journals* (1857), p. 367.

55. Quebec *Chronicle* quoted in the *Daily Globe* (Toronto), July 4, 1857.

56. Heywood and Company, London, to Simpson, Oct. 13, 1857, D-5/45, HBA.
57. Simpson to Chinie, Aug. 16, 1859, D-4/84a, HBA.
58. Simpson to Paton, May 31, 1860, in *ibid.*
59. Simpson to Hays, April 26, 1850, John A. Rose, Mss. Coll. 11, McGill University.
60. Simpson to Cameron, Jan. 16, 1850, Cameron Papers.
61. Simpson to Cameron, Nov. 18, 1845, Jan. 6, 1846, both in *ibid.*
62. Estate of Sir George Simpson, Minutes of the Proceedings of the Executors, D-6/3, HBA.

CHAPTER VII

1. Galbraith, *Hudson's Bay Company,* p. 336.
2. Simpson to Cameron, Nov. 25, 1854, Cameron Papers.
3. Letitia to James Hargrave, Aug. 10, 1851, MacLeod, *Letitia Hargrave,* pp. 258–59.
4. Edward Ermatinger to Hargrave, Nov. 8, 1853, in *ibid.,* p. cxlvi.
5. Grace Lee Nute, "Jehu of the Waterways", *The Beaver,* Summer 1960, Outfit 291, p. 15. The years he did not were 1838, 1840, and 1842.
6. Ross to Simpson, Aug. 21, 1848, private and confidential, D-5/22, HBA.
7. Pelly to Grey, March 4, 1848, A-814, HBA.
8. Galbraith, *Hudson's Bay Company,* p. 332.
9. Pelly to Simpson, March 10, 1848, private, in D-5/21; Grey to Pelly, March 11, 1848, both in HBA.
10. Derbishire to Simpson, Nov. 13, 1850, D-5/29, HBA.
11. Galbraith, *Hudson's Bay Company,* pp. 322–23.
12. Simpson analysed these charges in a letter to A. Colvile, confidential, Feb. 10, 1854, D-12/82, HBA.
13. Galbraith, *Hudson's Bay Company,* p. 320.
14. Crofton to Simpson, March 1, 1848, D-5/21, HBA.
15. *Canadian News* (London), Oct. 15, 1856.
16. Galbraith, *Hudson's Bay Company,* pp. 336–37.
17. Rose to Simpson, Feb. 9, 1857, D-5/43, HBA.
18. Simpson to Draper, March 16, April 4, July 24, 1850, all in D-4/71, HBA.
19. *The Leader* (Toronto), Dec. 8, 1856, reproduced in Chester Martin, "Sir George for the Defence", *The Beaver,* March 1948, p. 9.
20. Rich, *Hudson's Bay Company,* II, p. 774.

21. Selkirk to Bryce, Jan. 20, 1882, Bryce Papers, MG14 C15, Public Archives of Manitoba.
22. *Report of the Select Committee of the House of Commons on the Hudson's Bay Company* . . . (London, 1857), p. 2.
23. Rose to Simpson, March 9, 1857, D-5/43, HBA.
24. Simpson to Smith, May 14, 1857, D-4/76a, HBA.
25. *Ibid.*
26. Simpson to Gov. and Comm., June 26, 1856, D-4/76a, HBA.
27. Simpson to Shepherd, Jan. 6, 1857, A-7/2, HBA.
28. Galbraith, *Hudson's Bay Company,* pp. 345—46.
29. MacKay, *Hudson's Bay Company,* p. 379.
30. Ellice to Berens, Sept. 14, 1858, D-4/84a, HBA.
31. Simpson to Berens, Sept. 25, 1858, A-7/2, HBA.
32. Fraser to Simpson, Nov. 26, 1858, A-6/33, HBA.
33. Simpson to Ramsey, Nov. 3, 1858, quoted in Grace Lee Nute, "Simpson as Banker", *The Beaver,* Spring 1956, pp. 51-52.
34. Simpson to Ramsey, Nov. 26, 1858, in *ibid.*
35. Simpson to Ellice, private, July 23, 1859, D-4/84a, HBA.
36. J. S. Galbraith, "Perry McDonough Collins at the Colonial Office", *British Columbia Historical Quarterly,* XVII, nos. 3 and 4, p. 208.
37. Simpson to Drummond, April 7, 1859, D-4/78, HBA.
38. Simpson to Berens, private and confidential, March 22, 1859, D-4/84a, HBA.
39. Simpson to Mactavish, private, May 20, 1860, D-4/79, HBA.
40. Simpson to Cameron, March 29, 1860, Cameron Papers.
41. Simpson to Head, July 10, 1860, D-4/80, HBA.
42. *Daily Globe* (Toronto), Aug. 30, 1860; *Montreal Gazette,* Aug. 30, 1860, quoted in Clifford P. Wilson, "The Emperor at Lachine", *The Beaver,* September 1934, p. 50.
43. *Daily Globe,* Aug. 30, 1860.
44. *Montreal Gazette,* Aug. 30, 1860, quoted by Wilson, "Emperor at Lachine", p. 51.
45. The details can be found in "Sir George Simpson's Case, Superior Court, Montreal. The Rev. John Flanagan, Plaintiff vs. Duncan Finlayson, et al., Defendants", *American Journal of Insantiy* (Utica), XIX, no. 3 (Jan. 1863): 249—316. Flanagan sued for his money, and the court found in his favor. The editors of the journal thought the court wrong in its decision and concluded that at no time from September 1 to his death was Simpson of sound mind. The

article provides an interesting insight into medical practice in the mid nineteenth century.

46. Wilson, "Emperor at Lachine", p. 51.
47. Galbraith, "The Little Emperor", *The Beaver,* Winter 1960, p. 28.
48. *Montreal Gazette,* Sept. 8, 1860.
49. *Annual Register,* 1860, p. 488.

Index